WORLD POLITICS

MONEY, WEALTH, AND GLOBAL POWER

FIRST EDITION

EDITED BY AREF NAJI HASSAN

ST. CLOUD STATE UNIVERSITY

cognella®
academic publishing

Bassim Hamadeh, CEO and Publisher
Michael Simpson, Vice President of Acquisitions
Jamie Giganti, Senior Managing Editor
Jess Busch, Senior Graphic Designer
Mark Combes, Senior Field Acquisitions Editor
Sean Adams, Project Editor
Luiz Ferreira, Senior Licensing Specialist
Rachel Singer, Interior Designer

www.cognella.com   800-200-3908

 CONTENTS

Preface   v
BY AREF N. HASSAN

Introduction   vii
BY AREF N. HASSAN

Chapter 1: War Is a Racket   1
BY MAJOR GENERAL SMEDLEY D. BUTLER

**Chapter 2: Maps, Money,
and Monopolies**   3
BY JOSEPH P. FARRELL

**Chapter 3: The Late 1940s: World
Reconstruction and Private Banks**   19
BY NOMI PRINS

**Chapter 4: Confessions of
an Economic Hit Man**   37
BY JOHN PERKINS

**Chapter 5: Mercenaries on
the Front Lines in the New
Scramble for Africa**   53
BY ANDREW ROWELL AND JAMES MARRIOTT

**Chapter 6: The War on Drugs
in Asia: A Phony War with Real
Casualties**   73
BY PETER DALE SCOTT

Chapter 7: Banking on Dictatorship   **101**

BY JAMES S. HENRY

Chapter 8: Get Rid of This Stinker   **139**

BY STEPHEN KINZER

**Chapter 9: Considerations from
out of the Mainstream**   **157**

BY AREF N. HASSAN

Conclusion   **173**

BY AREF N. HASSAN

 PREFACE

by Aref N. Hassan

The main goal of this book is to present a new and alternative narrative to students of international relations, a narrative that views world politics and international relations from a new perspective. This book will look at international relations and world politics through the lens of economic and financial interests and the interplay of overt and covert financial and economic players.

The engine of world events has never been driven by what we are led to believe are the typical political, philosophical, or even religious motives such as loyalty to king or emperor, loyalty to empire, loyalty to god or religion, or even loyalty to the nation and country. Indeed the true motivation for what has transpired throughout history has always been money, trade routes, resources, wealth and economic power (which usually transpires into military and economic power). The true motivation for the masses who have fought and died in these wars may have been love of king, god, or nation; nonetheless the ones who planned, orchestrated, financed, and executed these wars were always driven by the true motive behind it all: MONEY, WEALTH, and GLOBAL POWER.

It appears on the face of things that the public political or religious figures (kings, emperors, popes, ayatollahs, presidents, prime ministers, et al.) have been the ones who have shaped world history (name any world leader or world religious leader here). A close examination reveals that these leaders have always worked at the behest of others and their interests, those of miners, traders, bankers, and financiers. These have been the true powers that have determined the course of world politics. As famously noted in the 1996 movie *Jerry Maguire*, starring Tom Cruise and Cuba Gooding Jr., "Show me the money" is the key to all decisions being made. At the end of the day, follow the money and it will lead you to the path of understanding world events not only in the past but in the future as well.

A good way to understand world politics and international relations is to think of a children's puppet show and to think of the citizens of the world as the children who are spectators. The kids truly believe that what they are seeing in front of them is true. They identify with the puppets and get attached to them and believe in them and what they're doing and saying. Little do these kids know that these puppets are not real and they have chosen to put their faith in a universe that exists on this stage, which is really a parallel universe to the truth: the puppeteers behind the puppets. The children (just as citizens of the world) spend their whole time at the theater watching the show and not knowing that everything they saw was not real. They will leave the theater believing the storyline and even arguing with each other about the occurrences of this play and not knowing that all along they were watching a charade that has nothing to do with reality.

We professors of politics shouldn't be teaching students about what happens in the puppet show or how to observe what the puppets are doing; rather, we should be teaching students that the puppets are not important and what they do is also not important. What we ***really*** should be teaching students is to look behind the puppet show and try to identify the puppeteers, figure out who they are, and understand that they are the ones we need to identify, study, and understand. If possible, for a deeper OR higher level of understanding, we should try to identify the producer and director of the show. As the saying goes, "Let there be light." We want our students to swallow the red pill (as Neo did in *The Matrix*) to wake up to the real world they live in.

Having a real understanding of world politics is as much about the theories and concepts and historical accounts as it is about understanding the deep powers and motives at play and the critical role of money and wealth in making the world go 'round. While students will get more than enough exposure to the theories and concepts of world politics and international relations in the multitude of courses they will attend during their career at the university or college level, we hope this book will offer a unique and complementary perspective to what they will study in these other courses.

# INTRODUCTION

by Aref N. Hassan

T he study of world politics is based on utilizing theories, concepts, and various levels of analysis to help us understand what is happening in the world of politics and international relations and why such things are happening. This understanding is also augmented by a historical account of events to know the facts of what happened and put them in a theoretical context that will help us explain and predict events.

A careful look at world politics and international relations, however, reveals that there are inner workings of covert centers of power that few know about and few see. Is power really where people think it is? Do "We the People" really know who is making decisions in this world and do we really know the real motives behind these decisions? While studying theories and concepts of international relations is necessary and helpful, it is by no means enough to uncover the true workings of the real world of politics.

There are authors and researchers who have studied and written about the inner workings of power, but they are not given the space they deserve in the discipline in general or in introductory courses in particular. In this book we present an excerpt of some of these works with the hope of introducing students to a new and untraditional way of studying and understanding world politics.

As we noted in the preface, the one common thread of secret power that seems to lay behind major events in world politics is the role of money and the pursuit of wealth. As we will see later in this book, this has taken various shapes from competition over land and sea trade routes, to control over credit, to competition over colonies and their resources and their consumer markets, to, most recently, control over information and technology. As we consider the examples provided, do we find that indeed there was a significant component of these events driven by lack of wealth or the pursuit of wealth or the disbursement of wealth?

Below are some questions to ponder (if you find these interesting, we encourage you to do further research on them):

- How much were any of the early (B.C.) imperial conquests about anything other than the pursuit of money, wealth, trade route control, and population control?

- How much of the Islamic Empire's conquests were really about religion and how much were they about adding wealth and land?

- How much were the Crusades about money and trade routes and how much were they about a safe pilgrimage route for Christians to go to Jerusalem?

- We all know that discovering America and the new world occurred in the pursuit of an alternate trade route to Asia—wasn't that about trade and building wealth?

- Weren't both the American and French revolutions ignited and partially motivated by an anti-tax sentiment?

- To what extent were the forces of poverty relevant in toppling the shah of Iran more so than the forces of conservative Shiite Islam?

- To what extent are some of the oil monarchies still in power because they give money to their citizens?

- To what extent was England's Lord Rothschild's financing of building the Suez Canal in Egypt the first step for British colonialism of Egypt?

- To what extent were French, English, and Dutch East India companies the real engines driving the colonialism of these nations?

- In addition to the racist ideology behind slavery, how much did the financial benefits of slavery present a barrier against removing slavery in the U.S. and elsewhere?

- How much of the Cold War was about freedom and democracy, and how much was it about systems of business and trade? In this context, were regimes supported or toppled because of their true democratic nature or because of their economic and financial benefits that they could extend to big capitalist business?

- How much is the war on radical Islam really about eradicating a significant threat, and how much is it about creating business for the military industrial complex? Besides, why is it that some of the very shady and questionable Islamic regimes in the world are supposedly friends or even allies of the many nations waging wars on terrorism? Is it possibly because they have their markets open to the global conglomerate corporations? Is it because they are good customers of the Western and global military industrial complex?

- How much was the regime toppling in Iraq and Libya about protecting civilians and spreading democracy, and how much was it about oil and enriching the military contracting community and the military industrial complex?

- How much of the Arab Spring was really about political freedom and expression, and how much of it was driven by poverty, lack of jobs, and dire economic prospects?

- How much of the dispute between China and the other Asian nations pertaining to sovereignty over the South China Sea related to ascertaining control over the trade routes in that sea and the supposed natural resources underneath it?

In thinking about these entire cases, one cannot but notice the role or possible role of money and the pursuit of wealth and trade. In the current world the centrality of economics and trade to world politics has become obvious. What we do see is also a world where citizens seem to be less motivated by ideology or belief systems. The question is, under what pretext can governments and leaders go to war again if they cannot convince people they are fighting for a bigger cause? Will money and natural resources become a good enough reason for people to go to war?

Few people in world history or in the current world would be willing to sacrifice their life for causes such as trade, trade routes, natural resources, precious metals, commodities, money, finance, or banking. Leaders from ancient times to the present have known that to be able to mobilize people to go to war and die, they have to present them with a cause bigger than themselves and certainly with a cause more noble than the materialist and financial/commercial motives that are driving these wars. They had to project these wars in a more noble way. They therefore pitched these wars as wars for god or religion or country or love of emperor or king.

Wars are planned by the rich and fought by the poor. Have we ever seen the children of rich people go to war? War is "Politics by other means," but what it boils down to is that rulers and the financial powers behind them have something that they want but for them to convince their people to go to war, they have to come up with a better reason than "we need you to fight and die so we can have control over wealth and natural resources and trade routes." Driven by financial incentives and the financial powers behind these incentives, the rulers had to convince their followers that they were going to war with these other people (whoever they may be) because they were a threat to them. The rulers needed to spread fear in the hearts and minds of their followers to take them to war, fear that their national identity or their religious identity were in danger. The rulers have also often appealed to their people's sense of good and justice in order to drag them to wars that had nothing to do with these noble causes and everything to do with materialist and financial causes that are important to the global elite.

Economics, trade, and finance have now become more visibly the center of what moves international relations. We are no more facing a war of isms or clear religious wars (even though some are still trying to play that record). The question is what kind of reasons will the global elite have to come up with to convince everyone to go to war?

As we know, there are various levels of analysis that can be applied to any event in world politics. There are various reasons (economic, social, political, and religious) that are also behind the movement of world history. It is not the aim of this book to argue against any of that, rather the goal is to highlight a factor that is often ignored in favor of other ones. This is not to say that world history should be reduced to a simple analysis of how money and economics are the only relevant variables, but rather to say they are among the more relevant ones that ought to be studied. In simple terms, the idea here is to keep an eye on the financial interests and monetary powers at play in the global decision-making process and in the transpiring of world events. We hope this book contributes to increasing the awareness that there is a multidirectional causal influence between politics on the one side and economics, markets, and trade on the other. Indeed, as the world grows smaller and smaller, both global politics and economics are becoming more recognizably and publicly intertwined and it is important for the students of world politics to pay closer attention to these multidirectional connections.

It is often said that cognitive roadblocks based on ideological bias prevent proper reasoning and proper processing of information. We urge students who are beginning or deepening their study of world politics to open their minds and imaginations to new perspectives that can reveal new realities, realities that many do not want them to know or discover.

chapter one

WAR IS A RACKET

by Major General Smedley D. Butler

WAR is a racket. It always has been.

It is possibly the oldest, easily the most profitable, surely the most vicious. It is the only one international in scope. It is the only one in which the profits are reckoned in dollars and the losses in lives.

A racket is best described, I believe, as something that is not what it seems to the majority of the people. Only a small "inside" group knows what it is about. It is conducted for the benefit of the very few, at the expense of the very many. Out of war a few people make huge fortunes.

In the World War [I] a mere handful garnered the profits of the conflict. At least 21,000 new millionaires and billionaires were made in the United States during the World War. That many admitted their huge blood gains in their income tax returns. How many other war millionaires falsified their tax returns no one knows.

How many of these war millionaires shouldered a rifle? How many of them dug a trench? How many of them knew what it meant to go hungry in a rat- infested dug-out? How many of them spent sleepless, frightened nights, ducking shells and shrapnel and machine

Smedley D. Butler, *War is a Racket*, pp. 4-5. Round Table Press, Inc., 1935. Copyright in the Public Domain.

gun bullets? How many of them parried a bayonet thrust of an enemy? How many of them were wounded or killed in battle?

Out of war nations acquire additional territory, if they are victorious. They just take it. This newly acquired territory promptly is exploited by the few—the selfsame few who wrung dollars out of blood in the war. The general public shoulders the bill.

And what is this bill?

This bill renders a horrible accounting. Newly placed gravestones. Mangled bodies. Shattered minds. Broken hearts and homes. Economic instability. Depression and all its attendant miseries. Back-breaking taxation for generations and generations.

For a great many years, as a soldier, I had a suspicion that war was a racket; not until I retired to civil life did I fully realize it. Now that I see the international war clouds gathering, as they are today, I must face it and speak out.

chapter two

MAPS, MONEY, AND MONOPOLIES

by Joseph P. Farrell

"The one duty we owe to history is to re-write it."

—*Oscar Wilde*[1]

We are ready to believe that conspiracies exist, at least, in modern times. Literature abounds that challenges the promoted "orthodoxies" and the "directed historical narratives" that emanate from the power centers of the world's elites. Many reading this book, for example, would question the promoted orthodoxies concerning the assassination of President John F. Kennedy, the "official story" of 9/11, and so on.

Yet, when we turn to the Middle Ages and Renaissance, we are quick to swallow the standard historical narratives, unwilling to believe that conspiracies—complete with psychological operations, cover stories, false fronts, false flag operations, and so on—could exist in those times. And at the head of this list has been the story of the voyage of Christopher Columbus in 1492. We all know the myth by heart: going before King Ferdinand and Queen Isabella of Spain, Columbus argued he would find a new direct route to the spice islands of the East, bypassing the Portuguese mastery of the route around the horn of Africa and through the Indian Ocean. That, anyway, was the story.

But as will be argued here, the story is just that: *a cover story*, and the truth may be very different. The truth may indeed be *so* different that it boggles the mind.

To see why, we need to step out of the arcane and heady world of finance, philosophy, metals, and metaphors, and into the equally arcane and heady world of navigation and ancient and medieval maps, maps that on close examination demonstrate an unusual knowledge and provenance.

A. THE STRANGE CASE OF THE PIRI REIS MAP

1. Antarctica

This bizarre story begins with the map of an Ottoman Turkish admiral named Piri Reis (ca. 1465/1470–ca. 1555). The problem of the Piri Reis map may be succinctly stated as follows: it showed something that had not been discovered yet, namely Antarctica, as the following picture shows:

Figure 2-1. Piri Reis map: Note the coast of South America, the west African bulge, and Spain, then, at the bottom of the map, that of Antarctica.

The map immediately caught the attention of science history professor Charles H. Hapgood, [1904–1982] who, with his students, went in search of precedents for this anomaly, searching ancient medieval maps called portolanos and other Renaissance world maps. It was not long before they unearthed the famous Oronteus Finaeus map of 1532, which, like many maps of the period, clearly depicted the *Terra Australis*, as the yet-to-be discovered Antarctic continent was then known.

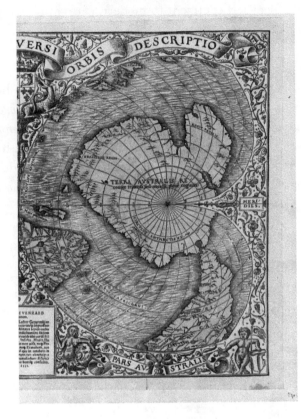

Figure 2-2. Right side of the Oronteus Finaeus Map of 1531 Showing Antarctica.[2]

The problem is obliquely admitted by the skeptical website "Bad Archaeology," which notes that "Although there are fairly obvious similarities between the general depiction of the southern continent by Oronteus Finaeus and modern maps of Antarctica, they do not stand up to close scrutiny; indeed, there are more differences than similarities, much as one would expect from a map drawn without genuine knowledge of the southern continent!"[3] In other words, the problem—for those willing simply to *look*—is that long before Captain Cook came close to the continent in 1773, and before actual contact was made in 1820, the continent, in spite of inaccuracies in the map, was being depicted *more or less* accurately, pettifogging tactics of standard academia to deny it notwithstanding.

Hapgood recounts his discovery of this anachronistically accurate map:

Then one day, I turned a page, and sat transfixed. As my eyes fell upon the southern hemisphere of a world map drawn by Oronteus Finaeus in 1531, I had the instant conviction that I had found here a truly authentic map of the real Antarctica.

The problem with the map as depicted by Oronteus was more than just the general resemblance of the depicted continent to modern cartographic representations; the problem went much deeper:

> The general shape of the continent was startlingly like the outline of the continent on our modern map … The position of the South Pole, nearly in the center of the continent, seemed about right. *The mountain ranges that skirted the coasts suggested the numerous ranges that have been discovered in Antarctica in recent years.* It was obvious, too, that this was no slapdash creation of somebody's imagination. The mountain ranges were individualized, some definitely coastal and some not … *This suggested, of course, that the coasts may have been ice-free when the original map was drawn.*[4]

A closer view will allow the reader to see what Hapgood is talking about:

Figure 2-3. Close-up of Oronteus Finaeus Map of 1532.

Oronteus Finaeus' map was not the only such map depicting the yet-to-be-encountered southern polar continent. Hapgood found others, including the Hadji Ahmed Map of 1559, once again clearly showing the southern polar continent in a Mercator-like projection:

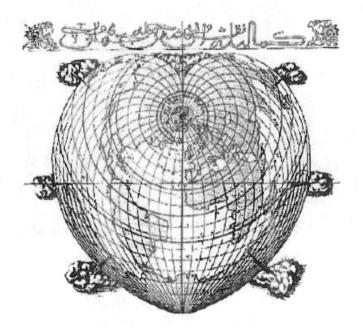

Figure 2-4. Hadji Ahmed Map of 1559[5]

All of this, as Hapgood noted, led some who had encountered such maps, especially the Piri Reis map, to speculate that portions of the coast on the Turkish admiral's map that lay under the ice and were nonetheless more or less accurately depicted must have been mapped "before the ice appeared."[6]

2. Medieval Portolans

The problem then became much more acute. Pursuing his quest for ancient maps that seemed to embody anachronistically out-of-place accuracy, Hapgood soon discovered the Dulcert Portolano of 1339, produced by Angelino Dulceti, who, interestingly enough, was probably trained in Genoa, the other great northern Italian merchant city-state with its own exclusive trading privileges with the Byzantine Empire, and the great rival of Venice.[7]

A glance at the Dulcert Portolano, though very faded, will immediately show the problem:

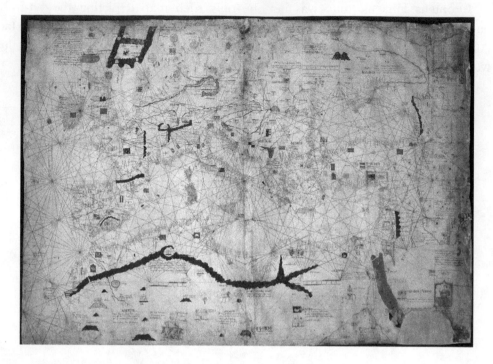

Figure 2-5. Dulcert Portolano of 133[8]

While difficult to see, the outlines of Europe, Asia Minor, and North Africa are faintly visible in the above picture, raising the questions: why is this map so *accurate*, and where did this accuracy come from? How did this knowledge come to medieval and Renaissance Europe, to spur the voyages that would confirm that another world existed, unknown to the Europeans?

3. Maps from High Antiquity

Enter Venice once again, and all that it symbolized of the great trading rivalry of Venice and Genoa for the Far Eastern trade flowing through Byzantium.

In Chapter Two, it was noted that the sudden appearance of the Hermetica in northern Italy followed the Council of Ferrara-Florence, which was, we also observed, financially sponsored in part by the Medicis of Florence. We speculated there that the presence of the Byzantine humanists Bessarion and Plethon among the Greek delegation to the council was the contact point for the Florentine merchants who may have been seeking lost knowledge that could only have come from the imperial archives of the East Roman Empire in Constantinople. We thus speculate that this contact may have been one route for the sudden appearance of apparently hidden cartographic knowledge of the Earth during this period.

But as noted also in chapter three, the contacts of Venice and its rival Genoa with the East Roman or Byzantine Empire predate those of the council of Florence by some two centuries, with the Venetian and Genoese virtual monopolies of ports and tax exemptions within Byzantium. The establishment of the Latin Empire after the Fourth Crusade by Venice would have given Venice access to the imperial archives, and thus to the charts and exemplars from which Piri Reis compiled his map. Similarly, the Genoese access to Byzantium during the period of the Venetian-Genoese rivalry would have given them a corresponding access. The question is, why did Venice not *access and utilize* this knowledge?

As we saw in chapter three, the question is easily answered by a map of the world. Venice could not easily access the Atlantic, for the route was blocked not only geographically but by the warring Moors and Castillians in Spain. Venice, in other words, if it had access to this cartographic knowledge, could not utilize it, and would have had to *suppress* the knowledge of it from being acquired by anyone else lest its favored position astride the trading routes to the Far East be jeopardized, and with it, its whole financial and mercantile empire.

The question that remains is whether or not such exemplars of the Piri Reis map actually existed. If so, then the likelihood of Venetian suppression of knowledge rises. We have already seen that medieval portolanos existed, and that these appear to have been drawn from much earlier exemplars, as Hapgood commented:

> ... (One) of the leading scholars in the field did not believe that the charts originated in the Middle Ages. A. E. Nordenskiöld, who compiled a great Atlas of these charts ... and also wrote an essay on their history ... , presented several reasons for concluding that they must have come from ancient times. In the first place, he pointed out that the Dulcert Portelano and all the others like it were a great deal too accurate to have been drawn by medieval sailors. Then there was the curious fact that the successive charts showed no signs of development. Those from the beginning of the 14th Century are as good as those from the 16th. It seemed as though somebody early in the 14th century had found an amazingly good chart which nobody was able to improve upon for two hundred years. Furthermore, Nordenskiöld saw evidence that only *one* such model chart had been found and that all the portolanos drawn in the following centuries were only copies—at one or more removes—from the original. He called this unknown original the "normal portolano" and showed that the portolanos, as a body, had rather slavishly been copied from the original. He said:

> "The measurements at all events show: (1) that, as regards the outline of the Mediterranean and the Black Sea, all the portolanos are almost unaltered copies of the same original; (2) that the same scale of distance was used on all the portolanos."[9]

Hapgood notes that Nordenskiöld believed that these measures were derived from Carthaginian and Phoenician sources.[10]

But that was not all. Nordenskiöld also compared the maps of the most famous ancient geographer, Ptolemy, whose maps were introduced to western Europe in the 1400s, with the most famous of the medieval portolanos, the Dulcert Portelano. Notably, *the medieval map was much more accurate,* as Nordenskiöld's comparison of the two clearly shows:

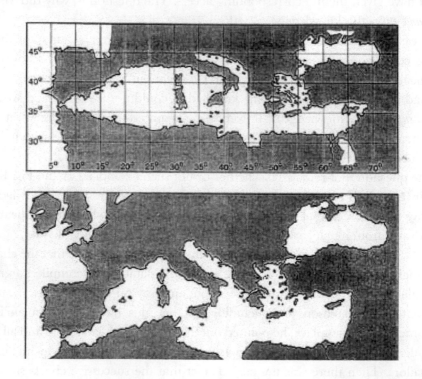

Figure 2-6. Nordenskiöld's Comparison of the Ancient Geographer Ptolemy's Map (Top), with the Medieval Dulcert Portolano (Bottom).[11]

Hapgood minces no words when stating the implications of this comparison:

> Let us stop to consider, for a moment, what this means. Ptolemy is the most famous geographer of the ancient world. He worked in Alexandria in the 2nd Century A.D., in the greatest library of the ancient world. He had at his command all the accumulated geographical information of that world. He was acquainted with mathematics. He shows, in his great work, the *Geographia* … , a modern scientific mentality. Can we lightly assume that

medieval sailors of the *fourteenth century*, without any of this knowledge, and without modern instruments except a rudimentary compass—and without mathematics—could produce a more scientific product?

Nordenskiöld felt that there had been in antiquity a geographic tradition superior to the one represented by Ptolemy. He thought that the "normal portolano" must have been in use *then* by sailors and navigators, and he answered the objection that there was no mention of such maps by the various classical writers by pointing out that in the Middle Ages, when the protolan charts were in use, they were never referred to by the Schoolmen, the academic scholars of that age. Both in ancient and in medieval times the academic mapmaker and the practical navigator were apparently poles apart.[12]

Note carefully what Hapgood is really implying here, for if medieval navigators had no more than crude mathematical techniques and even cruder navigational instruments, then the medieval portolanos, exemplified in the Dulcert portolano, must represent some hidden tradition of secret knowledge, handed down from High Antiquity and antedating even Ptolemy and the renowned library of Alexandria.

However, is there any more evidence to suggest such a notion? Indeed there is, but it is a slightly complicated matter to convey. When Hapgood and his students began to correlate the latitude and longitude positions of Piri Reis' map with actual modern calculations of positions, they discovered that Piri Reis' map was off by some 4 1/2 percent. The source of this error in Piri Reis' map appeared to have stemmed from Eratosthenes' computation of the circumference of the Earth.[13] When Piri Reis' map was redrawn with this correction, an astounding thing resulted, one with profound implications:

> We found that this resulted in reducing all the longitude errors until they nearly vanished.
>
> This was a startling development. It could only mean that the Greek geographers of Alexandria, when they prepared their world map using the circumference of Eratosthenes, had in front of them source maps that had been drawn *without the Eratosthenian error*, that is, apparently without any discernible error at all … suggesting that the people who had originated the maps possessed a more advanced science than that of the Greeks.[14]

In other words, there was a more ancient, and hidden, tradition of knowledge behind the medieval portolanos, and indeed, behind the map of Admiral Piri Reis.

Hapgood summarizes these implications in no uncertain terms:

To sum up, then, this part of the Piri Re'is [*sic, et passim*] Map suggests that Piri Re'is had a source map of Africa, Europe, and the Atlantic islands, based on maps probably drawn originally on some sort of trigonometric projection adjusted to the curvature of the earth. By default of any alternative, we seem forced to ascribe the origin of this part of the map to a pre-Hellenic people—not to Renaissance or Medieval cartographers, and not to the Arabs, who were just as badly off as everybody else with respect to longitude, and not to the Greeks either. The trigonometry of the projection (or rather its information on the size of the earth) suggests the work of Alexandrian geographers, but the evident knowledge of longitude implies a people unknown to us, a nation of seafarers, with instruments for finding longitude undreamed of by the Greeks, and, so far as we know, not possessed by the Phoenicians, either.[15]

Elsewhere, Hapgood is even more deliberate in pointing out the obvious implications of a lost culture and knowledge from High Antiquity:

The picture that seems to emerge, therefore, is one of a scientific achievement far beyond the capacities of the navigators and mapmakers of the Renaissance, of any period of the Middle Ages, of the Arab geographers, or of the known geographers of ancient times. It appears to demonstrate the survival of a cartographic tradition that could hardly have come to us except through some such people as the Phoenicians or the Minoans, the great sea peoples who long preceded the Greeks but passed down to them their maritime lore.[16]

This method of dividing the circle is not modern; it is the oldest way of dividing the circle known to man. Furthermore, since it involves counting by tens, it alone can explain how the ancient source map of the Antarctic, probably drawn ages before either Phoenicians or Babylonians existed, had on it the circle that Oronteus Finaeus took for the Antarctic Circle, but which we have shown may have been the 80th parallel. *The implication from this is that the 360-degree circle and the twelve-wind system were ancient before the rise of Babylonia and long before Tyre and Sidon were built by the Phoenicians. Babylonian science was thus, perhaps, a heritage from a much older culture.*[17]

That is, Piri Reis' map represents the survival of a hidden, ancient tradition, one stemming—as Hapgood notes—from Alexandria, Egypt. This now brings us at last to a consideration of the famous voyage that broke the back of the monopoly of the northern Italian city-states on the trading routes to the East, and particularly the Venetian monopoly. It brings us to …

B. CHRISTOPHER COLUMBUS' VOYAGES AND THE HIDDEN CARTOGRAPHIC TRADITION

It brings us to the implied *hidden* reasons for it, reasons carefully disguised behind the story—most likely a cover story—that Columbus was merely trying to find a direct oceanic route to trade with the Orient.

1. Piri Reis' Statements on Columbus

Significantly, it is the Turkish admiral Piri Reis who, once again, pries open the door to a significant mystery regarding Columbus and the possible *real*—though very definitely *secret*—purposes of his initial voyage for Ferdinand and Isabella of Spain. On his now famous map there are marginal notes by the admiral himself, and in one of these, Piri Reis states:

> This section explains the way the map was prepared. Such a map is not owned by anybody at this time. I, personally, drawn (sic) and prepared this map. In preparing this map, I made use of about twenty old charts and eight Mappa Mundis, i.e., of the charts called "Jaferiye" by the Arabs and prepared at the time of Alexander the Great and in which the whole inhabited world was shown; of the chart of (the) West Indies; and of the new maps made by four Portugueses (sic) containing the Indian and Chinese countries geometrically represented on them. *I also studied the chart that Christopher Columbus drew for the West.* Putting all these material (sic) together in a common scale I produced the present map. My map is as correct and dependable for the seven seas as are the charts that represent the seas of our countries.[18]

Note that Piri Reis states that he is relying upon a chart drawn by Columbus "for the West." But the questions are, when did Columbus draw this chart, before, or after, his first voyage? And more importantly, what did it show?

The standard answer is of course that Columbus drew his chart "for the West" after his return to Europe from his first voyage. However, in yet another marginal note the Turkish admiral states something truly astounding. Ponder these words closely:

> But it is reported thus, that a Genoese infidel, his name was Colombo, he it was who discovered these places. For instance, *a book fell into the hands of the said Colombo, and he found it said in this book that at the end of the Western Sea (Atlantic) that is, on its western side, there were coasts and islands and all kinds of metals and also precious stones.* The above-mentioned, having studied this book

thoroughly, explained these matters one by one to the great of Genoa and said: "Come, give me two ships, let me go and find these places." They said: "O unprofitable man, can an end of a limit be found to the Western Sea? Its vapour is full of darkness." The above-mentioned Colombo saw that no help was forthcoming from the Genoese, he sped forth, went to the Bey of Spain (king), and told his tale in detail. They too answered the Genoese. In brief Colombo petitioned these people for a long time, finally *the Bey of Spain gave him two ships, saw that they were well equipped, and said:*

"O Colombo, if it happens as you say, let us make you kapudan (admiral) to that country." Having said which he sent the said Colombo to the Western Sea.[19]

Note carefully what we have here, for according to Piri Reis:

1. Columbus possessed a book relating the knowledge of the New World, in other words, Columbus had access to knowledge not generally available, to secret knowledge, and therefore possibly had access to a secret cartographic tradition as well;

2. That knowledge stated that there was an abundance of bullion and gems, in other words, a source of bullion *not* in the hands of the Orient, nor the Venetians, and thus, a means of breaking the bullion and banking monopolies of Italy; and finally and most importantly;

3. The publicly-stated purpose for Columbus' voyage—the version taught to this day in standard academic histories— namely, that the Genoese navigator was seeking a direct trade route to the Far East, was *not* the real purpose of the voyage; the real purpose *from the outset was to find "Atlantis,"* the lands of the Western Sea, to find the New World, and its riches.

We can see why King Ferdinand and Queen Isabella would back such a venture, for if Columbus' effort to find the New World failed, a direct trade route to the Far East might nonetheless be opened, bypassing the rival Portuguese monopoly routes around the horn of Africa and through the Indian Ocean. If, on the other hand, Columbus *did* discover the New World and thus the potential for vast new sources of spices, bullion, and gems, then again, Ferdinand and Isabella would gain. It was, for them, a win-win proposition, but one whose true purpose—*the testing of a tradition of hidden knowledge*—had to be maintained in deepest secrecy lest Spain lose its jump-started position in the race for those riches. Indeed, it was the historian Las Casas who stated that *prior* to his first voyage, Columbus "had a world map, which he showed to King Ferdinand and Queen Isabella, and which, apparently, convinced them that they should back Columbus."[20]

One can reconstruct a possible sequence of events. Columbus originally approached the Spanish monarchs, and shared with them the details from his book. After several attempts to persuade them had failed, he finally produced what he was holding back in order to convince them: a world map depicting portions of the New World. Such a map would have had to be detailed in other particulars *known* to the Spanish in order to convince them. Is there any evidence of such a map?

Indeed there is.

And it exists independently of any speculative reconstructions surrounding Columbus.

The map, made by Martin Behaim in 1492 *prior* to Columbus' voyage, clearly shows early depictions of the mouth of the St. Lawrence seaway and portions of Newfoundland:

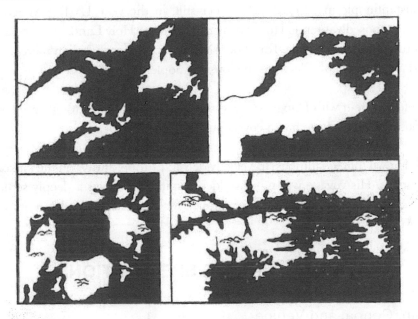

Figure 2-7. Hapgood's Reproduction of the Modern Cartographic depiction of the St. Lawrence Channel (Upper Left), the map of Sebastion Cabot (1544) in the upper right, the Lescarbot Map of 1606 in the Lower Right, and Martin Behaims Map of 1492, prior to Columbus' Return, in the lower left.[21]

In other words, Behaim clearly had access to some cartographic tradition depicting the New World before Columbus had even returned, raising the possibility that Columbus had access to such a tradition as well.

But if so, where does it come from?

At the beginning of this section, we noted that Venice is the most likely possibility, since it had sacked Constantinople in 1204 during the Fourth Crusade, and made off with a number of important treasures, some, no doubt, from the imperial archives, which would have likely included *some* remnants from the ancient library of

Alexandria. We have also, in other chapters of this book, pointed out that the arrival of the Byzantine humanists at the Council of Ferrara-Florence in the early fifteenth century represents another possible source of hidden, Hermetic, and esoteric tradition and lore. Hapgood himself is alive to all this possibility:

> We have seen that Piri Re'is, in all probability, had ancient maps at his disposal in Constantinople. It is quite possible that copies of these had reached the West long before his day. Greek scholars fleeing from the Turks brought thousands of Greek manuscripts to Italy before the fall of Constantinople in 1453. Much earlier still, in the year 1204, a Venetian fleet, supposedly intended to carry a crusade to the Holy Land, attacked and captured Constantinople. For about sixty years afterward Italian merchants had access to map collections in Constantinople.[22]

We therefore concur with Hapgood's assessment, an assessment strongly implying that Columbus' original voyage had a covert purpose:

> It is known that (Columbus) traveled widely in Europe, always on the lookout for maps. His voyage was not a sudden inspiration; it was a deeply settled objective, one followed with perseverance for many years, and it required, above all, maps.[23]

C. SOME FURTHER SPECULATIONS

1. Spain, Genoa, and Venice

With this, we are now in a position to begin to reassemble some pieces, and to construct a speculative scenario of what might have really been going on behind the scenes of Columbus' voyage, and its sponsorship by Ferdinand and Isabella.

1. We assume that at some point, the Italian city-states, and in particular Venice, gained knowledge of the existence of the New World via Greek manuscripts and maps taken when that city sacked Constantinople in 1204;

2. Thus, Venice, at least, had knowledge of the New World, and actively *suppressed* this knowledge for nearly three centuries. The reason for such suppression is abundantly clear, for the New World would represent possible *new* sources of bullion, ending the virtual Venetian monopoly on international bullion trade, and it would also represent an end to the Venetian near-monopoly on trade with the Far East, since Venice, isolated as it was, had no easy access to the Atlantic Ocean and the trading possibilities it represented.

3. *Consequently, one sees two familiar patterns—first appearing in ancient times, and continuing into modern times—of a financial elite that is*

    a) *actively seeking ancient sources of information, and*

    b) *seeking to monopolize and suppress it, lest that knowledge break out of the closed system of finance that made their power, position, and prestige, possible.*

Columbus' discovery of the New World was the game changer for the closed system of bullion trade and finance that Venice dominated, *and it was meant to be.* Unlike with Giordano Bruno, however, Genoa could not simply arrange for all of Spain to be burnt at the stake for opening the system.

It is worth pointing out yet another speculative possibility as to how this monopoly of hidden knowledge was *broken.* In chapter two, and again earlier in this chapter, I pointed out that *one* likely source for the sudden explosion of Hermeticism in northern Italy was the Greek humanists who accompanied the imperial delegation to the Council of Ferrara-Florence (1438–1439) a mere four decades prior to Columbus' fateful voyage. It is likely *here* that the Venetian monopoly over hidden cartographic tradition—if indeed there was one—was broken, and it is significant that a seaman from Genoa, the great rival of Venice, should be the one to break it.[24]

Indeed, Genoa could not burn all of Spain at the stake for daring to open up the system again, but it is suggestive, and perhaps also significant, that for a brief moment in history, Genoese bankers became the financiers to the Spanish crown, as if in repayment of a "hidden secret protocol" in the negotiations between Ferdinand, Isabella, and Christopher Columbus. After all, it was the Genoan adventurer that they named Admiral of the Atlantic upon his return to Spain, and it was the bankers of Genoa who for that brief moment in history made profit from Spain's new sources of bullion.

Nor can we assume for a moment that the revisionist explanation that Columbus was after a new source of slaves somehow evades the implications of the speculations entertained in this chapter, for slavery, as we know by now all too well, was an integral component of the bullion-coinage-military-slavery complex.

ENDNOTES

1. Oscar Wilde, "The Critic as Artist."

2. Charles H. Hapgood, *Maps of the Ancient Sea Kings* (Kempton, Illinois: Adventures Unlimited Press, 1996), pp. 81–82.

3. "The Oronteus Finneus Map," http://www.badarchaeology.com/?page_id=979

4. Hapgood, *Maps of the Ancient Sea Kings,* pp. 79–83, emphasis added.

5. Ibid., p. 100.

6. Ibid., p. 2.

7. For Dulcert, see "Angelino Dulcert," http://en.wikipedia.org/wiki/Angelino_Dulcert. For Genoa's rivalry with Venice and its trading privileges in the Byzantine Empire, see Robert Crowley's excellent popular treatment, *City of Fortune*, pp. 143, 154–171.

8. Hapgood, *Maps of the Ancient Sea Kings*, p. 8.

9. Ibid., p. 9, citing A.E. Nordenskiöld, *Periplus: An Essay in the Early History of Charts and Sailing Directions*. Trans, from the Swedish by F.A. Bathev. (Stockholm: Norstedt, 1897), p. 24.

10. Ibid., pp. 9–10.

11. Hapgood, *Maps of the Ancient Sea Kings*, p. 10.

12. Ibid., p. 11.

13. Ibid., p. 33.

14. Ibid., p. 33, emphasis in the original.

15. Ibid., p. 49.

16. Ibid., p. 40.

17. Ibid., p. 185, emphasis added.

18. Ibid., p, 217, emphasis added.

19. Ibid., p, 220, emphasis added.

20. Ibid., p. 59.

21. Ibid., p. 58.

22. Ibid., pp. 58–59.

23. Ibid., p. 59.

24. Another possibility is mentioned by Crowley, namely, that another objective of Columbus "was to find a fresh stock of human beings to enslave," (Crowley, *City of Fortune*, p. 136). Crowley notes that Genoa at the time held more slaves than any other city within medieval Europe. Venice, it will be recalled, also engaged in slaving activity.

IMAGE CREDITS

chapter three

THE LATE 1940S: WORLD RECONSTRUCTION AND PRIVATE BANKS

by Nomi Prins

> **"We must unite to win the peace with the same assurance and in the same businesslike manner as we organized to win the war."[1]**
> —*Chase chairman Winthrop Aldrich, September 30, 1947*

World War II had not just revitalized the American economy; it had resuscitated the reputation of the banker as a public servant, a partner of the president, a defender of America. The bankers, through more unifying speeches and less ostentatious styles, had demonstrated their desire to support the war—and the peace—effort beyond simple financing. The result of this shift was their ability to influence global finance in a much broader way than their predecessors had, with less scrutiny.

On July 2, 1946, Truman told Chase chairman Winthrop Aldrich that he looked to him as chairman of the Committee for Financing Foreign Trade to organize the work of its members.[2] It was a critical component of the White House agenda. Truman had written each member personally to say that "the conduct and financing of foreign trade should be handled by private industry with the cooperation and such assistance as is necessary from the proper Government agencies."

Truman had positioned himself as playing backup to private industry and the bankers as far as foreign economic policy was concerned. This was exactly what Aldrich had wanted; a supportive government that gave private bankers latitude. But Truman didn't leave matters fully up to Aldrich. Instead, he asked each committee member to draft a report on problems concerning foreign trade and to provide recommendations for handling them to the National Advisory Council, which would prepare a definite plan of procedure.[3]

Two and a half months later, the twelve-man committee (which included Bank of America head A. P. Giannini and National City Bank chairman Gordon Rentschler) gathered in Washington for their first official meeting with the president.[4] These would become frequent occurrences as America's global role was mapped out.

Truman grew to trust Aldrich, much as Wilson had grown to trust Morgan's Thomas Lamont after World War I. For his part, Aldrich became a leading figure in organizing financial relief to Europe during and after World War II, with great influence over the direction of the IMF. As Lamont had been extremely vocal about the need for Wilson's League of Nations, Aldrich was the banker most publicly supportive of the Marshall Plan, which spelled out how the United States would aid foreign nations. As it would turn out, he added ideas of his own to benefit private industry and banking.

During the postwar phase of the late 1940s, Aldrich traveled the world in a triple capacity: as chairman of the Chase bank, president of the International Chamber of Commerce, and chairman of the Committee for Financing Foreign Trade. The impact on the bank's bottom line was substantial. In 1946, Chase reported, "The volume of business handled in all divisions of the foreign department increased enormously."[5] Chase commercial loans in London doubled that year. Aldrich's dual work as public servant and private banker was reaping rewards for his firm, and for his status as a diplomat. His partnership with Truman assured him of both.

TRUMAN'S TREASURY SECRETARY AND POSTWAR SAVINGS BONDS

Another aspect of the banking-government alliance was the makeup of public debt, which had quintupled during the war and totaled $270 billion on June 30, 1946. Between war defense and finance programs, government obligations represented 60 percent of all outstanding debts, public and private, compared to less than 25 percent in 1939. Commercial banks held $84.5 billion, or about one-third of the US debt securities, representing 71 percent of their total assets.[6] War financing replenished the banking systems assets and offered it a foundation of securities upon which to expand.

Though he was not of the eastern bankers' ilk, Trumans Treasury secretary, John Snyder, was still quite familiar with the world of banking. He had served as vice president at First National Bank of St. Louis, Missouri, for a couple of years before joining the Truman administration.[7] Snyder would take a lead role as the communication point between Truman and the bankers through the late 1940s.

As "one of Truman's closest advisors on not only financial matters, but also general domestic and foreign policy issues," according to the Treasury Department and Federal Reserve, Snyder was "often the last person to whom Truman spoke before he made final decisions."[8]

Snyder was a banker's perfect Treasury secretary, comfortable on both sides of the political aisle. As he later said, "I like many of the Democratic aims and objectives. I was brought up a Democrat. Of course, my private business associations have been largely with Republicans. The officers in the banks that I've associated with have been largely Republicans."[9]

Bankers eagerly advised Snyder on issues of postwar debt management, "selecting the right kind of securities to offer to the public," and various tax matters. But Snyder tended to rely more on bankers hailing from outside the New York area. Among his most trusted confidants in the banking industry were A. P. Giannini and his son, Mario.[10]

When it came time to reconsider the postwar savings bond program, Snyder enlisted the Gianninis' advice. He needed a new way to entice the population to buy bonds and realized that an appeal based on a patriotic act would no longer do. This was potentially a big problem: the government still had its own debt to pay down, and turning to citizens for financing needs had proven quite useful during the war. Snyder now needed the bankers to collaborate with him to "sell the idea that savings was good for the individual to prepare him to buy the things that he might otherwise miss buying: an education for his children, a new house, maybe an automobile in the future … an economic purpose, a standard of living purpose."[11] The more people saved, went his reasoning, the more they would consider investing in things like bonds.

Thus, Snyder played a key role in fashioning the acceptability of debt to fund the pent-up needs and desires of postwar America. The bankers did their share to provide the credit to support that way of life, appealing to the public to both save and borrow. The Federal Reserve played its part, too. The Fed had accommodated the war by maintaining the low interest rates that fueled private banks' ability to lend to manufacturing companies.[12] From 1937 to 1947, the Fed kept its "rediscount rate," enjoyed by commercial banks borrowing cash against Treasuries, at 1 percent.

During the war, there was widespread bipartisan support for rising deficits and taking on additional debt to fund the war. But afterward, the Truman administration continued to favor lower interest rates as a means of economic stimulus, while the Fed wanted to raise them to fight inflation.

ALDRICH SUPPORTS THE MARSHALL PLAN

For Truman, navigating postwar peace less than a decade after the Great Depression without economic fallout would prove challenging.

The World Bank and the IMF had been shaped at Bretton Woods and then refined by Congress with input from the private banking community. Another pillar of global reconstructive and foreign policy efforts, the Marshall Plan, would provide further aide to "friendly" countries in the early years of the Cold War. The plan would also establish the bedrock upon which the nations premier bankers would propel their international lending and other foreign businesses.

Truman carefully unveiled the Marshall Plan in the spring of 1947. To foster public support, he played it up as a way to counter the threat of Communism. He warned the nation that Europe was disintegrating economically, and said he feared that Greece and Turkey would come under Communist control. In addition, the Communist Party had become the biggest left-wing party in France and Italy. America's new perceived enemy was not Germany or the Nazis but the doctrine of Communism, which was manifesting itself more broadly in the postwar era. Recall Aldrich's speech associating capitalism with democracy, linking bankers' goals with American foreign policy ones. Communism was opposed to capitalism, and as such it stood in the way of American prosperity.

Trumans concerns directly led to the Truman Doctrine, a foreign policy initiative by which the United States agreed to support Greece and Turkey economically and militarily to keep them from falling prey to Soviet expansion. The Truman Doctrine became the cornerstone of the more expansive Marshall Plan, which divided the non-Communist and Communist allies for the purposes of apportioning economic aid.

In a speech at Harvard on June 5, 1947, Secretary of State George Marshall, a retired general, announced the US-led economic assistance program that the Europeans would administer on the western side of the Iron Curtain. Congress approved $13 billion to reconstruct Western Europe for two reasons: first, to aid Europe's fight against Communism; and second, to bolster trading partners for American industry and banks.

Additionally, as more currencies became readily available to be converted to the dollar, it would become easier to solve the problem of dollar scarcity without new restrictions, which would be "disastrous both for the United States and for the people of Europe." The more dollars in the world, the fewer barriers to foreign trade. The Marshall Plan wasn't just about helping allies; it was also about ensuring the domination of the dollar, a plan supported by President Truman and the bankers.[13] The theme of Communism vs. American democracy would be the selling point to the broader population.

Even before the Marshall Plan was approved, banks had begun negotiating private postwar loans to allied countries. In 1945, Chase became the first big bank to start the process with a loan to the Netherlands. The firm continued lending money to France alongside the Morgan Bank. Giannini flew to the country of his forebears, Italy, to extend credit to Italian banks. These divisions enabled banks to profit in postwar reconstruction efforts along nationalist lines. The White House took note. "The President [Truman] and I are pleased," John Snyder, then head of the Office of War Mobilization and Reconversion, wrote Giannini. "I regard this type of action as a positive contribution to worldwide recovery."[14]

Aldrich's support for the Marshall Plan was solid from the start. Arriving in New York from England on July 1, 1947, he declared that it provided "new hope for the people of Europe."[15] To further establish the supremacy of private business in global affairs, Aldrich also sought to establish "a [nonpartisan] Government Corporation ... as the United States Corporation for European Reconstitution ... to encourage direct investment by American firms and corporations in the plants and industrial equipment of Western Europe."

Hence, Aldrich would combine the notions of political stability (lending to developing nations and fighting Communism, which often amounted to the same thing) and private direct investment. Big banks would be engaged in both efforts.

The Marshall Plan wouldn't just help distribute financial aid; it would give each major US bank its own European country to play in. Chase would beat them. From 1948 to 1952, the bank amassed the biggest commitments to Europe, at nearly $1 billion, followed closely by National City Bank. The Bank of America, with its focus on Italy, stood in sixth place, with $389 million.[16]

The Marshall Plan delivered a bevy of new opportunities for US banks in Europe. But it also enabled major European banks to spring back to life through incoming funds and associated US political relationships, though at first in the shadows of their American counterparts. Again, it was Aldrich who put the situation into perspective. President Coolidge had said that "the business of America is business," but to Aldrich the business of the world was business, and it was there for the American banker to take.

The mass-circulation *Life* magazine put its weight behind the Marshall Plan by underscoring the need to fight Communists:

> Last week in Paris, the 16 nations that responded to Secretary of State George C. Marshall's plea for a concrete European recovery plan put their reports in a green manila folder, bounded up with a ribbon of shocking pink and sent it to Washington. The Europeans said they needed $22.4 billion worth of goods and dollars in the next four years.... Whether the US Congress and the American people were prepared for the sacrifices such a

program would entail was far from clear.... [But] Paris, LIFE correspondent Charles Wertenbaker cabled, "if no new credits are allowed, France will be virtually bankrupt in 3 weeks. No American aid would mean big communist gains."[17]

In late 1947, Chase extended its German and Japanese branches, becoming the first US bank invited to expand in postwar Germany. (National City and Bank of America made it to Japan first, mostly to service US military bases.)

THE NATIONAL ADVISORY COUNCIL AND THE RISE OF JOHN MCCLOY

As important as his Treasury secretary post was in shaping economic policy, Snyder held an even more critical position in foreign financial policy as the first chairman of the less-known but powerful National Advisory Council, the entity that called the shots for the World Bank and IMF.

Congress had established the council to be the "coordinating agency for United States international financial policy" and as a mechanism to direct that policy through the international financial organizations. In particular, the council dealt with the settlement of lend-lease and other wartime arrangements, including the terms of foreign loans, details of assistance programs, and the evolving policies of the IMF and World Bank.[18] Snyder carried a vast amount of influence over those entities, as many major decisions were discussed privately at the council meetings and decided upon there.

There was one ambitious lawyer who understood the significance of Snyder's role. That was John McCloy, an outspoken Republican whose career would traverse many public service and private roles (including the chairmanship of Chase in the 1950s), and who had just served as assistant secretary of war under FDR's war secretary, Henry Stimson. McCloy and Snyder would form an alliance that would alter the way the World Bank operated, and the influence that private bankers would have over it.

It was Snyder who made the final decision to appoint McCloy as head of the World Bank. McCloy, a stocky Irishman with steely eyes, had been raised by his mother in Philadelphia. He went on to become the most influential banker of the mid-twentieth century. He had been a partner at Cravath, Henderson, and de Gersdorff, a powerful Wall Street law firm, for a decade before he was tapped to enter FDR's advisory circle.

After the war, McCloy returned to his old law firm, but his public service didn't translate into the career trajectory that he had hoped for. Letting his impatience be known, he received many offers elsewhere, including an ambassadorship to Moscow; the presidency of his alma mater, Amherst College; and the presidency of Standard Oil. At that point, none other than Nelson Rockefeller swooped in with an enticing proposition that would allow McCloy to stay in New York and get paid well—as a partner at the family's law firm, Milbank, Tweed, Hope, and Hadley.[19]

The job brought McCloy the status he sought. He began a new stage of his private career at Milbank, Tweed on January 1, 1946. The firm's most important client was Chase, the Rockefeller's family bank. But McCloy would soon return to Washington.

Truman had appointed Eugene Meyer, the seventy-year-old veteran banker and publisher of the *Washington Post*, to be the first head of the World Bank. But after just six months, Meyer abruptly announced his resignation on December 4, 1946.[20] Officially, he explained he had only intended to be there for the kick-off. But privately, he admitted that his disagreements with the other directors' more liberal views about lending had made things untenable for him. His position remained vacant for three months.

When Snyder first approached McCloy for the role in January 1947, he rejected it. But Snyder was adamant. After inviting McCloy to Washington for several meetings and traveling to New York to discuss how to accommodate his stipulations about the job—conditions that included more control over the direction of the World Bank and the right to appoint two of his friends—Snyder agreed to his terms.

Not only did Snyder approve of McCloy's colleagues, but he also approved McCloy's condition that World Bank bonds would be sold through Wall Street banks. This seemingly minor acquiescence would forever transform the World Bank into a securities vending machine for private banks that would profit from distributing these bonds globally and augment World Bank loans with their private ones. McCloy had effectively privatized the World Bank. The bankers would decide which bonds they could sell, which meant they would have control over which countries the World Bank would support, and for what amounts.

With that deal made, McCloy officially became president of the World Bank on March 17, 1947.[21] His Wall Street supporters, who wanted the World Bank to lean away from the liberal views of the New Dealers, were a powerful lot. They included Harold Stanley of Morgan Stanley; Baxter Johnson of Chemical Bank; W. Randolph Burgess, vice chairman of National City Bank; and George Whitney, president of J. P. Morgan.[22] McCloy delivered for all of them.

A compelling but overlooked aspect of McCloy's appointment reflected the post-war elitism of the body itself. The bank's lending program was based on a supply of funds from the countries enjoying surpluses, particularly those holding dollars. It so happened that "the only countries [with] dollars to spare [were] the United States and

Canada." As a result, all loans made would largely stem from money raised by selling the World Bank's securities in the United States.[23]

This gave the United States the ultimate power by providing the most initial capital, and thus obtaining control over the future direction of World Bank financial initiatives—all directives for which would, in turn, be predicated on how bankers could distribute the bonds backing those loans to investors. The World Bank would do more to expand US banking globally than any other treaty, agreement, or entity that came before it.

To solidify private banking control, McCloy continued to emphasize that "a large part of the Bank capital be raised by the sale of securities to the investment public." McCloy's like-minded colleagues at the World Bank—vice president Robert Garner, vice president of General Foods and former treasurer of Guaranty Trust; and Chase vice president Eugene Black, who replaced the "liberal" US director Emilio Collado—concurred with the plan that would make the World Bank an extension of Wall Street. McCloy stressed Garner and Black's wide experience in the "distribution of securities."[24] In other words, they were skilled in the art of the sale, which meant getting private investors to back the whole enterprise.

The World Bank triumvirate was supported by other powerful men as well. After expressing his delight over their appointments to Snyder on March 1, 1947,[25] Nelson Rockefeller offered the three American directors his Georgetown mansion, plus drinks, food, and servants, for a three-month period while they hammered out strategies. No wives were allowed.[26] Neither were the other directors.[27] This was to be an exclusive rendezvous.

It is important to note here that the original plan as agreed upon at Bretton Woods did not include handing the management and organization of the World Bank over to Wall Street. But the new World Bankers seemed almost contemptuous of the more idealistic aspects of the original intent behind Bretton Woods, that quaint old notion of balancing economic benefits across nations for the betterment of the world. Armed with a flourish of media fanfare from the main newspapers, they set about constructing a bond-manufacturing machine.

With the Cold War hanging heavily in the political atmosphere, the World Bank also became a political mechanism to thwart Communism, with funding provided only to non-Communist countries. Politics drove loan decisions: Western allies got the most money and on the best terms.

MCCLOY'S RETURN TO WALL STREET VIA GERMANY

By early 1948, World Bank loans had spread to Asia, Latin America, and various African countries. Within ten months, the media were declaring McCloy's World Bank initiative and its bonds an utter success. It was McCloy's particular view that Latin America should be more open to private investment. This view was widely shared by the banking community, the 1929 Crash of the regions bonds notwithstanding.

In a letter to Snyder on January 7, 1949, McCloy pressed the opening of Latin America in this manner: "I believe that both of our institutions should be more and more devoted to the flow of private capital into that area." Snyder approved of the progress that McCloy's Latin American loaning program was making.[28] With Snyder and McCloy's coordinated efforts, the doors of Latin America were pried open to allow a rush of private investment, which reduced the ability of the region to control its own economic destiny. These developments significantly extended Americas political control over the region, propping up the dictators that toed the US line and punishing the ones who didn't by means of might and money.

In the background, the man who had penned the initial plan for the IMF, Harry White, was forced to resign from the IMF and dragged before the House Un-American Activities Committee in August 1948. Congressman Richard Nixon and others pelted him with questions about his alleged Communist loyalties. Three days after testifying, he died. He was fifty-five. The extent of his involvement with Soviet spy rings and his motivations have been a subject of debate in the history profession since his death, overshadowing the means by which his plans were augmented by the banker contingent.

THE ECONOMIC COOPERATION ADMINISTRATION

The Marshall Plan easily passed through Congress on April 3, 1948. Also called the Foreign Assistance Act of 1948 and the Economic Cooperation Act of 1948, it was approved by the Senate by a vote of 69 to 17 and passed the House by a vote of 329 to 74.[29]

Truman set up the Economic Cooperation Administration to oversee the Marshall Plan. In practice, it controlled many foreign economic activities, including trading patterns and international finance initiatives. Aldrich made it a point to throw his backing behind the entity. As a result, the correspondent banks came to Chase to service a large chunk of their international financing needs. He had again successfully steered the fortunes of Chase and public foreign policy concurrently.

As he expanded the Chase empire to support the foreign policy goals of the US government, Aldrich thought it only fair to obtain federal assurances of safety for Chase's private endeavors in return. So he requested that the Treasury Department back the risk Chase was taking in setting up private offices in war-torn countries.

On July 27, 1948, Snyder obtained support for Aldrich's request from Secretary of the Army Kenneth Royall, to whom he wrote, "The American Express Company, Inc., and the Chase National Bank have requested that the agreements executed by them be amended to exclude any liability for the loss under certain specified circumstances of … foreign funds lost, stolen, captured or destroyed by or because of enemy action …. The Treasury Department feels that the requests … are not unreasonable and is willing to enter into agreement with these two banks, and other banks similarly."[30]

The United States ultimately approved approximately $13 billion in aid during the four years that the Marshall Plan was active. At first, Europe's economy slowly improved, though it was unclear if that was related to the US monies. As far as the American people were concerned, though, the Marshall Plan was an anti-Communism device as marketed by Truman, the bankers, and the popular press. It was fear rather than altruism at work.

TRUMAN'S FOUR POINTS PLAN

Though Truman employed antibanker rhetoric in his 1948 presidential election campaign, as most Democratic presidential candidates tended to do for political reasons, he maintained a balance between appearing prolabor and hard on Communism. With the exception of throwing some political capital at the Wall Street Seventeen—a case involving investment bank price rigging, which went on for years and was dismissed under the Eisenhower administration—Truman didn't get much in the way of the New York bankers. In fact, he brought those he deemed trustworthy into his cabinet or appointed them to committees.

Truman unveiled his "Four Points" plan during his 1949 inaugural address. The first point was support for the United Nations. The second was reiterating US determination to work for world recovery by giving full measure to the Marshall Plan in promoting trade for all the world's markets. The third point centered on the North Atlantic Security plan. He said, "We will strengthen freedom-loving nations against the dangers of aggression … within the recognized framework of the United Nations charter and in the pattern of the Western Hemisphere arrangement." In his fourth point, Truman proposed a program for sharing American scientific and industrial progress with the rest of the world.

McCloy, still smarting because he believed Marshall Plan financing might upend financing for the World Bank, expressed his frustration with Point Four to the *New York Times*, where he pouted that the World Bank "would simply have to take a back seat to Point Four aid in the developing world."[31]

For Aldrich, however, the Point Four program to begin technical assistance to underdeveloped countries was a gold mine. As a result of increased federal support, 1949 would become the most active year Chase's foreign department had ever experienced.[32]

In 1950, Truman appointed Aldrich's nephew, Nelson Rockefeller, to chair the International Development Advisory Board, the main task of which was the implementation of the Point Four program. In turn, Aldrich advised Truman fairly extensively on the Point Four program in war-torn Europe.[33]

RUSSELL LEFFINGWELL AND MORGAN'S WANING INFLUENCE

Thomas Lamont, who had run the Morgan Bank through much of the war, passed away quietly in his sleep at age seventy-seven in early February 1948.[34] His death marked the end of an era during which the Morgan Bank partners held the tightest alliances with the White House, even when presidents attacked bankers in their speeches. Lamont had negotiated war-related financing with America's allies and foes for three decades, sailing back and forth across the Atlantic dozens of times. He had stood before many congressional investigations and crossed party lines to support Democratic presidents and the ideals of internationalism, which he believed benefited the country, the presidency, and the bankers. After he died, leadership of the firm passed to longtime partner Russell Leffingwell.

A Washington insider from his days as President Wilson's assistant secretary of the Treasury during World War I, Leffingwell reigned as chairman of the Morgan Bank from 1948 to 1950 (after which he retired to a directorship position).[35] He was also chairman of the Council on Foreign Relations from 1946 to 1953, at a time when it actively promoted the Marshall Plan.

Leffingwell engaged with Truman on an array of issues, including on the tension between postwar domestic security and individual liberties. Both men believed that the Cold War was no excuse for monitoring the nations citizens, which was becoming an abrasive issue in Congress. The libertarian in Leffingwell found the notion of undue government oversight of people's lives off-putting. In general, his method of subtle sway over the Truman administration was effective, particularly regarding matters of interest rate and debt policy—though not as overwhelming as the methods of the Chase and National City Bank influencers.

Leffingwell periodically took to the press to publicize his views. In October 1948, he penned a *Fortune* article in which he argued the Federal Reserve should "drop the peg," meaning it should discontinue its artificial support of long-term government bonds (through purchasing them, which also kept rates down). The article provided Treasury Secretary Snyder, who agreed with Leffingwell, ammunition against the Fed.[36]

After the war, a battle brewed between the Treasury Department and the Federal Reserve over how to deal with rates, inflation, and reserves. Snyder's views were in lockstep with those of the bankers; excess reserve requirements would hamper banks from lending and expanding. In an August 9, 1948, statement before the House Banking and Currency Committee, Snyder said, "After careful and deliberate consideration of the proposed increase of reserves that commercial banks must carry in the Federal Reserve banks; we are firmly of the opinion that such a move will bring about a credit panic."[37]

Leffingwell agreed: "The Federal Reserve and commercial banks' reserve requirement should not be increased."[38] A true internationalist, he was also of the opinion that trade barriers should be eased as much as possible to enable international business and financial activities to thrive. This was the same view that had been held by his predecessor at Morgan for decades.

When Truman won the 1948 presidential election, the Belgrade press, reading the fusion of the bankers and the presidency correctly, dubbed the election a battle between the candidates of J. P. Morgan & Company and the Chase National Bank, giving the victory to Morgan. (Thomas Dewey, who lost to Truman, was a close friend of Chase chairman Winthrop Aldrich, though of course Aldrich was very supportive of Truman and his postwar foreign financial policies.) Truman considered the distinction a joke, writing Leffingwell on November 22, 1948: "I was very much interested in the attached report from Belgrade to the effect that the recent election was a battle between J.P. Morgan & Company and the Chase National Bank. This is merely to congratulate you on the election of your candidate."[39]

Leffingwell responded in his typical deferential manner: "Your letter of the 22nd reached me this morning. I read it promptly to our officers' meeting and we all enjoyed a good laugh. A President with so human a touch makes everybody feel good. Though you were not my candidate, you are my President, and I pledge you my support and help, and that of my colleagues, in your great task."[40] In turn, Leffingwell had made a contribution to the Democratic Campaign Fund.[41]

This would be the beginning of a friendly relationship between the two men.

MCCLOY LEAVES THE WORLD BANK

By 1949, the postwar economic recovery was waning. World exchange rates reflected this. Britain devalued the pound from $4.03 (the 1946 rate) to $2.80. Other countries followed suit. The US economy experienced its first, albeit minor, postwar recession. Loan volume declined for the first time in three years, with business loans dropping by 19 percent.[42]

Around that time, McCloy's stint as president of the World Bank was coming to an end after two short years. Truman offered him the position of US high commissioner of Occupied Germany. (As assistant secretary of war, McCloy had been situated in Germany in the spring of 1945, when Eisenhower's troops occupied 43 percent of the country.[43]) As he had done before accepting his World Bank post, McCloy gave Truman a list of requirements. Again, he asked for "a free hand in picking people" to assist him and an assurance that "no substantial decisions on Germany" would be made "without consultation with me."[44]

In addition, he demanded full authority over Economic Cooperation Administration monies dispensed in Germany and for Truman to name Eugene Black as his successor. The president agreed to his demands. Only then did McCloy send Truman a brief note accepting the job.[45]

When McCloy officially resigned from the World Bank on June 30, 1949, Snyder didn't miss a beat. He wrote Black, "I know that under your leadership the successful administration of the Bank will continue" and that "regarding matters relating to international financial programs you may be assured that at all times the Treasury will be glad to assist you in any way it can."[46]

In his new capacity, McCloy worked on the creation of the West German state from 1949 to 1952. In 1951, he controversially reduced the sentences on convicted Nazi war criminals (about which many in Europe and the United States were extremely upset).[47] McCloy retained a characteristically independent style in Germany, sending Truman reports rather than engaging in regular dialogue. Overseeing the development of Germany was one of McCloy's favorite roles, perhaps more interesting to him than running the Chase Bank, which he did afterward (though budding Middle East relationships would eventually fulfill his capacities for juxtaposing his public and private roles).

After four years in Germany, McCloy returned to New York City. In 1953, when Aldrich was nominated by Eisenhower to become ambassador to Britain, Aldrich chose McCloy to assume his slot as Chase chairman.

OLD TO NEW GUARD

Three influential men stood in the wings of the 1940s. They wouldn't emerge into the national consciousness until the 1960s, but nonetheless they were beginning their political and financial ascent. The first was John F. Kennedy, who ran for Congress for the first time in 1946 and won.

The second was David Rockefeller, whom Aldrich recruited to join Chase in 1946. Rockefeller had spent the summer of 1937 with the Chase economics department, and as a student at the London School of Economics he had devoted half a day each week as a trainee at the London branch of Chase. While traveling through Europe in 1945, Aldrich met Rockefeller in Paris and suggested that he join the bank. Rockefeller started his Chase career as an assistant manager in the foreign department.[48]

The third man was Walter Wriston, son of Henry Wriston, a conservative former president of Brown University and a friend of W. Randolph Burgess. Burgess enticed Walter to work at National City Bank in 1946.

American power unfolds more like a monarchy than a meritocracy. There are no accidents in global influence, no surprise emergences. All three young men harnessed family connections on their way to leading the country and its two biggest banks, respectively. The views of these men at the time were more alike than they would be perceived to be in later years. Before he turned more liberal on the national stage, Kennedy was critical of Truman's "soft" policy on Communism. Wriston and Rockefeller were both free-market advocates who harbored international ambitions, positions passed on by family patriarchs.

All three believed in Americas right to global expansion and the necessity of an offensive stance as a way to fight the Cold War. Likewise, the Cold War would prove a convenient excuse for making money, as well as for political posturing. The sort of patriotism that had been associated with World War II would become associated with the war against Communism and its threats, real or fabricated. This fight would allow them to consolidate their roles in the epicenter of global finance.

NSC 68

The Cold War also dictated foreign policy and budget appropriations in the White House. On April 14, 1950, a top-secret report on US objectives and programs for national security—compiled by Truman's executive secretary, James Lay Jr., and the secretaries of state and defense—was distributed to the National Security

Council, the Treasury secretary, the Economic Cooperation Administration, the director of the Bureau of the Budget, and the chairman of the Council of Economic Advisers.[49]

The report, dubbed NSC 68, opened the door for future wars against Communism, and also for the funding and financing that would come from the private bankers along those foreign policy lines. It concluded that "the gravest threat to the security of the United States within the foreseeable future stems from [the] formidable power of the U.S.S.R.," and that "the risk of war with the U.S.S.R. is sufficient to warrant, in common prudence, timely and adequate preparation by the United States."[50]

The threat, it said, "is of the same character as that described in NSC 20/4 [approved by Truman on November 24, 1948] but is more immediate than had previously been estimated. In particular, the United States now faces the contingency that within the next four or five years the Soviet Union will possess the military capability of delivering a surprise atomic attack of [considerable] weight."[51]

To mitigate that threat, the report suggested developing "a level of military readiness ... as a deterrent to Soviet aggression ... should war prove unavoidable."[52] As it said further, "Our position as the center of power in the free world places a heavy responsibility upon the United States for leadership."[53] Also, "We must, by means of a rapid and sustained build-up of the political, economic, and military strength of the free world, and by means of an affirmative program intended to wrest the initiative from the Soviet Union, confront it with convincing evidence of the determination and ability of the free world to frustrate the Kremlin design of a world dominated by its will."[54]

Bankers had a propensity to capitalize on wars, but they were equally adept at profiting from peace, especially if it could be backed by US military power and foreign policy initiatives that would augment and protect their financial expansion policies by fortifying "democratic" countries that could be their clients.

During the previous three and a half decades, the world had witnessed two major global wars, revolutions in Russia and China, and "the collapse of five empires—the Ottoman, Austro-Hungarian, German, Italian and Japanese," according to the NSC 68.[55] The report concluded that "the defeat of Germany and Japan and the decline of the British and French Empires have interacted with the development of the United States and the Soviet Union in such a way that power has gravitated to these two centers ... The Soviet Union ... is animated by a new fanatic faith, antithetical to our own, and seeks to impose its absolute authority over the rest of the world."

Six months after the report was distributed, the United States entered the Korean War. In late 1950, Truman signed a letter to Secretary of State Dean Acheson saying that recent developments required review and adjustment of certain policies and programs with respect to "international communist imperialist aggression." Truman wanted to enlist the cooperation and support of other nations in carrying this out. To the extent that US legislation, organization, and funds permitted, Truman wanted all "appropriate programs now to be adjusted and administrated in light of [those] determinations."[56]

The Korean War would find the US population less financially supportive than it had been during World War II. Thus, bankers would turn toward mergers and credit extension to grow their domestic power base, while keeping their eyes on international financial developments and their feet in the corridors of Washington.

ENDNOTES

1. Winthrop W. Aldrich, "American Interest in European Reconstruction," address before the seventy-third annual convention of the American Bankers Association, September 30, 1947.

2. Letter to Aldrich, July 2, 1946, Papers of Harry S. Truman General Files, Box 24, Folder: Aldrich, Winthrop W., Truman Library.

3. June 17, 1946, General File, Box 886, Folder: Giannini, Truman Library.

4. Ibid., Internal White House correspondence, September 26, 1946.

5. Wilson, *The Chase*, 32.

6. Oral history interview with John W. Snyder, August, 13, 1969, by Jerry N. Hess, Truman Library, at www.trumanlibrary.org/oralhist/snyder.htm.

7. "John Wesley Snyder (1895–1985)," *The Encyclopedia of Arkansas History and Culture*, at www.encyclopediaofarkansas.net/encyclopedia/entry-detail.aspx?entryID=5095.

8. "The 50th Anniversary of the Treasury–Federal Reserve Accord 1951–2001: Biographies: John Wesley Snyder," Federal Reserve Bank of Richmond.

9. Oral history interview with John W. Snyder, June 18, 1969.

10. Ibid.

11. Ibid.

12. Barry Eichengreen and Peter M. Garber, "Before the Accord: US Monetary-Financial Policy, 1945–1951," *Financial Markets and Financial Crises* (January 1991), at www.nber.org/chapters/c11485.pdf.

13. Paper from the Bank for International Settlements, Monetary and Economic Department, Basel, July 10, 1947, Papers of John W. Snyder, Truman Library.

14. Marquis James and Bessie R. James, *The Story of Bank of America: Biography of a Bank* (Washington, DC: Beard Books, 2002), 478–479.

15. "Aldrich Hopeful of Marshall Plan, Financier Back from Europe Says Proposal Is Vitally Important to World," *New York Times*, July 1, 1947.

16. Sampson, *The Money Lenders*, 92.

17. "Europe Submits Its Marshall Plan," *Life*, October 6, 1947.

18. Oral history interview with John W. Snyder, August 13, 1969.

19. Kai Bird, *The Chairman: John J. McCloy and the Making of the American Establishment* (New York, NY: Simon & Schuster, 1992), 272.

20. "Meyer Quits World Bank Helm, Saying He Was Only to Launch It," *New York Times*, December 5, 1946.

21. Charles Hurd, "McCloy Is Elected World Bank Head," *New York Times*, March 1, 1947.

22. Bird, *The Chairman*, 285.

23. Ibid.

24. Ibid.

25. Letter from Snyder to Nelson Rockefeller, March 7, 1947, Papers of John W. Snyder, IBRD-IMF and IBRD (legislation), Box 54, Folder: International Monetary Funds and Bank, publications and correspondence, 1947, Truman Library.

26. Bird, *The Chairman*, 289.

27. Sampson, *The Money Lenders*, 90.

28. Letter from Snyder to McCloy, January 10, 1949, Papers of John W. Snyder, Truman Library.

29. David Cushman Coyle, *Survey of United States Foreign Economic Cooperation Since 1945* (New York, NY: The Church Peace Union, 1957), 12.

30. Papers of John W. Snyder, 1946–1952, Box 14, Folder: Fiscal, banks 1946–1952, Truman Library.

31. "World Bank Chary on Backward Lands," *New York Times*, February 1, 1949.

32. Wilson, *The Chase*, 31.

33. Harry S. Truman, "The President's News Conference," January 12, 1950, posted online by Gerhard Peters and John T. Woolley, American Presidency Project, at www.presidency.ucsb.edu/ws/?pid=13468.

34. "Thomas W. Lamont, Banker, Dies at 77 in Florida Home," *New York Times*, February 3, 1948.

35. "Russell C. Leffingwell Is Dead; Ex-Chairman of Morgan Bank," *New York Times*, October 3, 1960.

36. Papers of John W. Snyder, 1946–1952, Box 14, Folder: Federal Reserve Bank (Interest, 1948–1950), Fiscal (banks), October 9, 1948 (sent to Secretary of Treasury by Thomas B. McCabe on October 13, 1948), "U.S. Bond Peg Still Necessary, Says F.A. Potts," *Philadelphia Evening Bulletin*, Truman Library.

37. Ibid.

38. "Russell C. Leffingwell Is Dead."

39. PFF Box 584, Folder 4316, Russell Leffingwell, Truman Library.

40. Letter from Leffingwell, November 26, 1948, PFF Box 584, Folder 4316, Russell Leffingwell, Truman Library.

41. Ibid., cross-reference sheet. Correspondence between Morris L. Ernst and President Truman between December 2, 1948, and December 9, 1948.

42. Wilson, *The Chase*, 37.

43. PSF Box 160, Foreign Affairs File, Folder: McCloy, John J., Truman Library.

44. Bird, *The Chairman*, 305.

45. Ibid., 305–306.

46. Letter from Snyder to Eugene Black, June 24, 1949, Papers of John W. Snyder, Folder: General, 1947–1952, Truman Library.

47. Bird, *The Chairman*, 363.

48. Wilson, *The Chase*, 26.

49. "A Report to the National Security Council: NSC 68," April 12, 1950, President's Secretary's File, Truman Papers, Truman Library. The report was declassified by Henry Kissinger on February 27, 1975.

50. Ibid., 60.

51. Ibid.

52. Ibid., 62.

53. Ibid., 63.

54. Ibid., 65.

55. Ibid., 4.

56. December 28, 1950, White House Central Files: Confidential Files, Box 63, Folder: Foreign Trade, Truman Library.

chapter four

CONFESSIONS OF AN ECONOMIC HIT MAN

by John Perkins

PREFACE

Economic hit men (EHMs) are highly paid professionals who cheat countries around the globe out of trillions
of dollars. They funnel money from the World Bank, the
U.S. Agency for International Development (USAID), and
other foreign "aid" organizations into the coffers of huge
corporations and the pockets of a few wealthy families who
control the planet's natural resources. Their tools include
fraudulent financial reports, rigged elections, payoffs, extor-
tion, sex, and murder. They play a game as old as empire,
but one that has taken on new and terrifying dimensions
during this time of globalization.
I should know; I was an EHM.

I wrote that in 1982, as the beginning of a book with the working
title, *Conscience of an Economic Hit Man*. The book was dedicated to the
presidents of two countries, men who had been my clients, whom I respected and thought of as kindred spirits—Jaime Roldós, president of

Ecuador, and Omar Torrijos, president of Panama. Both had just died in fiery crashes. Their deaths were not accidental. They were assassinated because they opposed that fraternity of corporate, government, and banking heads whose goal is global empire. We EHMs failed to bring Roldós and Torrijos around, and the other type of hit men, the CIA-sanctioned jackals who were always right behind us, stepped in.

I was persuaded to stop writing that book. I started it four more times during the next twenty years. On each occasion, my decision to begin again was influenced by current world events: the U.S. invasion of Panama in 1989, the first Gulf War, Somalia, the rise of Osama bin Laden. However, threats or bribes always convinced me to stop.

In 2003, the president of a major publishing house that is owned by a powerful international corporation read a draft of what had now become *Confessions of an Economic Hit Man*. He described it as "a riveting story that needs to be told." Then he smiled sadly, shook his head, and told me that since the executives at world headquarters might object, he could not afford to risk publishing it. He advised me to fictionalize it. "We could market you in the mold of a novelist like John Le Carré or Graham Greene."

But this is not fiction. It is the true story of my life. A more courageous publisher, one not owned by an international corporation, has agreed to help me tell it.

This story *must* be told. We live in a time of terrible crisis—and tremendous opportunity. The story of this particular economic hit man is the story of how we got to where we are and why we currently face crises that seem insurmountable. This story must be told because only by understanding our past mistakes will we be able to take advantage of future opportunities; because 9/11 happened and so did the second war in Iraq; because in addition to the three thousand people who died on September 11, 2001, at the hands of terrorists, another twenty-four thousand died from hunger and related causes. In fact, twenty-four thousand people die every single day because they are unable to obtain life-sustaining food.[1] Most important, this story must be told because today, for the first time in history, one nation has the ability, the money, and the power to change all this. It is the nation where I was born and the one I served as an EHM: the United States of America.

What finally convinced me to ignore the threats and bribes?

The short answer is that my only child, Jessica, graduated from college and went out into the world on her own. When I recently told her that I was considering publishing this book and shared my fears with her, she said, "Don't worry, dad. If they get you, I'll take over where you left off. We need to do this for the grandchildren I hope to give you someday!" That is the short answer.

The longer version relates to my dedication to the country where I was raised, to my love of the ideals expressed by our Founding Fathers, to my deep commitment to the American republic that today promises "life, liberty, and the pursuit of happiness" for all people, everywhere, and to my determination after 9/11 not to sit idly by any longer while EHMs turn that republic into a global empire. That is the skeleton version of the long answer; the flesh and blood are added in the chapters that follow.

This is a true story. I lived every minute of it. The sights, the people, the conversations, and the feelings I describe were all a part of my life. It is my personal story, and yet it happened within the larger context of world events that have shaped our history, have brought us to where we are today, and form the foundation of our children's futures. I have made every effort to present these experiences, people, and conversations accurately. Whenever I discuss historical events or re-create conversations with other people, I do so with the help of several tools: published documents; personal records and notes; recollections—my own and those of others who participated; the five manuscripts I began previously; and historical accounts by other authors, most notably recently published ones that disclose information that formerly was classified or otherwise unavailable. References are provided in the endnotes, to allow interested readers to pursue these subjects in more depth. In some cases, I combine several dialogues I had with a person into one conversation to facilitate the flow of the narrative.

My publisher asked whether we actually referred to ourselves as economic hit men. I assured him that we did, although usually only by the initials. In fact, on the day in 1971 when I began working with my teacher Claudine, she informed me, "My assignment is to mold you into an economic hit man. No one can know about your involvement—not even your wife." Then she turned serious. "Once you're in, you're in for life."

Claudine's role is a fascinating example of the manipulation that underlies the business I had entered. Beautiful and intelligent, she was highly effective; she understood my weaknesses and used them to her greatest advantage. Her job and the way she executed it exemplify the subtlety of the people behind this system.

Claudine pulled no punches when describing what I would be called upon to do. My job, she said, was "to encourage world leaders to become part of a vast network that promotes U.S. commercial interests. In the end, those leaders become ensnared in a web of debt that ensures their loyalty. We can draw on them whenever we desire—to satisfy our political, economic, or military needs. In turn, they bolster their political positions by bringing industrial parks, power plants, and airports to their people. The owners of U.S. engineering/construction companies become fabulously wealthy."

Today we see the results of this system run amok. Executives at our most respected companies hire people at near-slave wages to toil under inhuman conditions in Asian sweatshops. Oil companies wantonly pump toxins into rain forest rivers, consciously killing people, animals, and plants, and committing genocide among ancient cultures. The pharmaceutical industry denies lifesaving medicines to millions of HIV-infected Africans. Twelve million families in our own United States worry about their next meal.[2] The energy industry creates an Enron. The accounting industry creates an Andersen. The income ratio of the one-fifth of the world's population in the wealthiest countries to the one-fifth in the poorest went from 30 to 1 in 1960 to 74 to 1 in 1995.[3] The United States spends over $87 billion conducting a war in Iraq while the United Nations estimates that for less than half that amount we could provide clean water, adequate diets, sanitation services, and basic education to every person on the planet.[4]

And we wonder why terrorists attack us?

Some would blame our current problems on an organized conspiracy. I wish it were so simple. Members of a conspiracy can be rooted out and brought to justice. This system, however, is fueled by something far more dangerous than conspiracy. It is driven not by a small band of men but by a concept that has become accepted as gospel: the idea that all economic growth benefits humankind and that the greater the growth, the more widespread the benefits. This belief also has a corollary: that those people who excel at stoking the fires of economic growth should be exalted and rewarded, while those born at the fringes are available for exploitation.

The concept is, of course, erroneous. We know that in many countries economic growth benefits only a small portion of the population and may in fact result in increasingly desperate circumstances for the majority. This effect is reinforced by the corollary belief that the captains of industry who drive this system should enjoy a special status, a belief that is the root of many of our current problems and is perhaps also the reason why conspiracy theories abound. When men and women are rewarded for greed, greed becomes a corrupting motivator. When we equate the gluttonous consumption of the earths resources with a status approaching sainthood, when we teach our children to emulate people who live unbalanced lives, and when we define huge sections of the population as subservient to an elite minority, we ask for trouble. And we get it.

In their drive to advance the global empire, corporations, banks, and governments (collectively the *corporatocracy*) use their financial and political muscle to ensure that our schools, businesses, and media support both the fallacious concept and its corollary. They have brought us to a point where our global culture is a monstrous machine that requires exponentially increasing amounts of fuel and maintenance, so much so that in the end it will have consumed everything in sight and will be left with no choice but to devour itself.

The corporatocracy is not a conspiracy, but its members do endorse common values and goals. One of corporatocracy's most important functions is to perpetuate and continually expand and strengthen the system. The lives of those who "make it," and their accoutrements—their mansions, yachts, and private jets—are presented as models to inspire us all to consume, consume, consume. Every opportunity is taken to convince us that purchasing things is our civic duty, that pillaging the earth is good for the economy and therefore serves our higher interests. People like me are paid outrageously high salaries to do the system's bidding. If we falter, a more malicious form of hit man, the jackal, steps to the plate. And if the jackal fails, then the job falls to the military.

This book is the confession of a man who, back when I was an EHM, was part of a relatively small group. People who play similar roles are more abundant now. They have more euphemistic titles, and they walk the corridors of Monsanto, General Electric, Nike, General Motors, Wal-Mart, and nearly every other major corporation in the world. In a very real sense, *Confessions of an Economic Hit Man* is their story as well as mine.

It is your story too, the story of your world and mine, of the first truly global empire. History tells us that unless we modify this story, it is guaranteed to end tragically. Empires never last. Every one of them has failed terribly. They destroy many cultures as they race toward greater domination, and then they themselves fall. No country or combination of countries can thrive in the long term by exploiting others.

This book was written so that we may take heed and remold our story. I am certain that when enough of us become aware of how we are being exploited by the economic engine that creates an insatiable appetite for the world's resources, and results in systems that foster slavery, we will no longer tolerate it. We will reassess our role in a world where a few swim in riches and the majority drown in poverty, pollution, and violence. We will commit ourselves to navigating a course toward compassion, democracy, and social justice for all.

Admitting to a problem is the first step toward finding a solution. Confessing a sin is the beginning of redemption. Let this book, then, be the start of our salvation. Let it inspire us to new levels of dedication and drive us to realize our dream of balanced and honorable societies.

******

Without the many people whose lives I shared and who are described in the following pages, this book would not have been written. I am grateful for the experiences and the lessons.

Beyond them, I thank the people who encouraged me to go out on a limb and tell my story: Stephan Rechtschaffen, Bill and Lynne Twist, Ann Kemp, Art Roffey, so many of the people who participated in Dream Change trips and workshops, especially my co-facilitators, Eve Bruce, Lyn Roberts-Herrick, and Mary Tendall, and my incredible wife and partner of twenty-five years, Winifred, and our daughter Jessica.

I am grateful to the many men and women who provided personal insights and information about the multinational banks, international corporations, and political innuendos of various countries, with special thanks to Michael Ben-Eli, Sabrina Bologni, Juan Gabriel Carrasco, Jamie Grant, Paul Shaw, and several others, who wish to remain anonymous but who know who they are.

Once the manuscript was written, Berrett-Koehler founder Steven Piersanti not only had the courage to take me in but also devoted endless hours as a brilliant editor, helping me to frame and reframe the book. My deepest thanks go to Steven, to Richard Perl, who introduced me to him, and also to Nova Brown, Randi Fiat, Allen

Jones, Chris Lee, Jennifer Liss, Laurie Pellouchoud, and Jenny Williams, who read and critiqued the manuscript; to David Korten, who not only read and critiqued it but also made me jump through hoops to satisfy his high and excellent standards; to Paul Fedorko, my agent; to Valerie Brewster for crafting the book design; and to Todd Manza, my copy editor, a wordsmith and philosopher extraordinaire.

A special word of gratitude to Jeevan Sivasubramanian, Berrett-Koehler's managing editor, and to Ken Lupoff, Rick Wilson, María Jesús Aguiló, Pat Anderson, Marina Cook, Michael Crowley, Robin Donovan, Kristen Frantz, Tiffany Lee, Catherine Lengronne, Dianne Platner—all the BK staff who recognize the need to raise consciousness and who work tirelessly to make this world a better place.

When Plume and the Penguin Group committed to making this book available in paperback, its staff worked diligently to create this new version, including additional material. I am eternally grateful to my editor, Emily Haynes, for taking such a strong interest from the very beginning, as well as for her patience with me and her talents as an editor and diplomat; Trena Keating, Editor in Chief; Brant Janeway, Director of Publicity; Norina Frabotta and Abigail Powers, Production Editors; Aline Akelis, Director of Subrights; Jaya Miceli, designer of the powerful new cover; and Gretchen Swartley, Marketing Coordinator. The Plume and Berrett-Koehler people coordinated beatifully and, along with Paul Fedorko, dedicated themselves to the common goal of getting this message out to more people, with a special emphasis on high school and college students.

I must thank all those men and women who worked with me at MAIN and were unaware of the roles they played in helping EHM shape the global empire; I especially thank the ones who worked for me and with whom I traveled to distant lands and shared so many precious moments. Also Ehud Sperling and his staff at Inner Traditions International, publisher of my earlier books on indigenous cultures and shamanism, and good friends who set me on this path as an author.

I am eternally grateful to the men and women who took me into their homes in the jungles, deserts, and mountains, in the cardboard shacks along the canals of Jakarta, and in the slums of countless cities around the world, who shared their food and their lives with me and who have been my greatest source of inspiration.

"IN FOR LIFE"

In legal parlance, MAIN would be called a closely held corporation; roughly 5 percent of its two thousand employees owned the company. These were referred to as partners or associates, and their position was coveted. Not only did the partners have power over everyone else, but also they made the big bucks. Discretion was their hallmark;

they dealt with heads of state and other chief executive officers who expect their consultants, like their attorneys and psychotherapists, to honor a strict code of absolute confidentiality. Talking with the press was taboo. It simply was not tolerated. As a consequence, hardly anyone outside MAIN had ever heard of us, although many were familiar with our competitors, such as Arthur D. Little, Stone & Webster, Brown & Root, Halliburton, and Bechtel.

I use the term *competitors* loosely, because in fact MAIN was in a league by itself. The majority of our professional staff was engineers, yet we owned no equipment and never constructed so much as a storage shed. Many MAINers were ex-military; however, we did not contract with the Department of Defense or with any of the military services. Our stock-in-trade was something so different from the norm that during my first months there even I could not figure out what we did. I knew only that my first real assignment would be in Indonesia, and that I would be part of an eleven-man team sent to create a master energy plan for the island of Java.

I also knew that Einar and others who discussed the job with me were eager to convince me that Java's economy would boom, and that if I wanted to distinguish myself as a good forecaster (and to therefore be offered promotions), I would produce projections that demonstrated as much.

"Right off the chart," Einar liked to say. He would glide his fingers through the air and up over his head. "An economy that will soar like a bird!"

Einar took frequent trips that usually lasted only two to three days. No one talked much about them or seemed to know where he had gone. When he was in the office, he often invited me to sit with him for a few minutes over coffee. He asked about Ann, our new apartment, and the cat we had brought with us from Ecuador. I grew bolder as I came to know him better, and I tried to learn more about him and what I would be expected to do in my job. But I never received answers that satisfied me; he was a master at turning conversations around. On one such occasion, he gave me a peculiar look.

"You needn't worry," he said. "We have high expectations for you. I was in Washington recently ..." His voice trailed off and he smiled inscrutably. "In any case, you know we have a big project in Kuwait. It'll be a while before you leave for Indonesia. I think you should use some of your time to read up on Kuwait. The Boston Public Library is a great resource, and we can get you passes to the MIT and Harvard libraries."

After that, I spent many hours in those libraries, especially in the BPL, which was located a few blocks away from the office and very close to my Back Bay apartment. I became familiar with Kuwait as well as with many books on economic statistics, published by the United Nations, the International Monetary Fund (IMF), and the World Bank. I knew that I would be expected to produce econometric models for Indonesia and Java, and I decided that I might as well get started by doing one for Kuwait.

However, my BS in business administration had not prepared me as an econometrician, so I spent a lot of time trying to figure out how to go about it. I went so far as to enroll in a couple of courses on the subject. In the process, I discovered that statistics can be manipulated to produce a large array of conclusions, including those substantiating the predilections of the analyst.

MAIN was a macho corporation. There were only four women who held professional positions in 1971. However, there were perhaps two hundred women divided between the cadres of personal secretaries—every vice president and department manager had one—and the steno pool, which served the rest of us. I had become accustomed to this gender bias, and I was therefore especially astounded by what happened one day in the BPL's reference section.

An attractive brunette woman came up and sat in a chair across the table from me. In her dark green business suit, she looked very sophisticated. I judged her to be several years my senior, but I tried to focus on not noticing her, on acting indifferent. After a few minutes, without a word, she slid an open book in my direction. It contained a table with information I had been searching for about Kuwait—and a card with her name, Claudine Martin, and her title, Special Consultant to Chas. T. Main, Inc. I looked up into her soft green eyes, and she extended her hand.

"I've been asked to help in your training," she said. I could not believe this was happening to me.

Beginning the next day, we met in Claudine's Beacon Street apartment, a few blocks from MAIN's Prudential Center headquarters. During our first hour together, she explained that my position was an unusual one and that we needed to keep everything highly confidential. She told me that no one had given me specifics about my job because no one was authorized to—except her. Then she informed me that her assignment was to mold me into an economic hit man.

The very name awakened old cloak-and-dagger dreams. I was embarrassed by the nervous laughter I heard coming from me. She smiled and assured me that humor was one of the reasons they used the term. "Who would take it seriously?" she asked.

I confessed ignorance about the role of economic hit men.

"You're not alone," she laughed. "We're a rare breed, in a dirty business. No one can know about your involvement—not even your wife." Then she turned serious. "I'll be very frank with you, teach you all I can during the next weeks. Then you'll have to choose. Your decision is final. Once you're in, you're in for life." After that, she seldom used the full name; we were simply EHMs.

I know now what I did not then—that Claudine took full advantage of the personality weaknesses the NSA profile had disclosed about me. I do not know who supplied her with the information—Einar, the NSA, MAIN's personnel department, or someone else—only that she used it masterfully. Her approach, a combination of physical seduction and verbal manipulation, was tailored specifically for me, and yet it fit within the standard operating procedures I have since seen used by a variety of businesses when the stakes are high and the pressure to close lucrative deals is great. She knew from the start that I would not jeopardize my marriage by disclosing our clandestine activities. And she was brutally frank when it came to describing the shadowy side of things that would be expected of me.

I have no idea who paid her salary, although I have no reason to suspect it was not, as her business card implied, MAIN. At the time, I was too naive, intimidated, and bedazzled to ask the questions that today seem so obvious.

Claudine told me that there were two primary objectives of my work. First, I was to justify huge international loans that would funnel money back to MAIN and other U.S. companies (such as Bechtel, Halliburton, Stone & Webster, and Brown & Root) through massive engineering and construction projects. Second, I would work to bankrupt the countries that received those loans (after they had paid MAIN and the other U.S. contractors, of course) so that they would be forever beholden to their creditors, and so they would present easy targets when we needed favors, including military bases, UN votes, or access to oil and other natural resources.

My job, she said, was to forecast the effects of investing billions of dollars in a country. Specifically, I would produce studies that projected economic growth twenty to twenty-five years into the future and that evaluated the impacts of a variety of projects. For example, if a decision was made to lend a country $1 billion to persuade its leaders not to align with the Soviet Union, I would compare the benefits of investing that money in power plants with the benefits of investing in a new national railroad network or a telecommunications system. Or I might be told that the country was being offered the opportunity to receive a modern electric utility system, and it would be up to me to demonstrate that such a system would result in sufficient economic growth to justify the loan. The critical factor, in every case, was gross national product. The project that resulted in the highest average annual growth of GNP won. If only one project was under consideration, I would need to demonstrate that developing it would bring superior benefits to the GNP.

The unspoken aspect of every one of these projects was that they were intended to create large profits for the contractors, and to make a handful of wealthy and influential families in the receiving countries very happy, while assuring the long-term financial dependence and therefore the political loyalty of governments around the world. The larger the loan, the better. The fact that the debt burden placed on a country would deprive its poorest citizens of health, education, and other social services for decades to come was not taken into consideration.

Claudine and I openly discussed the deceptive nature of GNP. For instance, the growth of GNP may result even when it profits only one person, such as an individual who owns a utility company, and even if the majority of the population is burdened with debt. The rich get richer and the poor grow poorer. Yet, from a statistical standpoint, this is recorded as economic progress.

Like U.S. citizens in general, most MAIN employees believed we were doing countries favors when we built power plants, highways, and ports. Our schools and our press have taught us to perceive all of our actions as altruistic. Over the years, I've repeatedly heard comments like, "If they're going to burn the U.S. flag and demonstrate against our embassy, why don't we just get out of their damn country and let them wallow in their own poverty?"

People who say such things often hold diplomas certifying that they are well educated. However, these people have no clue that the main reason we establish embassies around the world is to serve our own interests, which during the last half of the twentieth century meant turning the American republic into a global empire. Despite credentials, such people are as uneducated as those eighteenth-century colonists who believed that the Indians fighting to defend their lands were servants of the devil.

Within several months, I would leave for the island of Java in the country of Indonesia, described at that time as the most heavily populated piece of real estate on the planet. Indonesia also happened to be an oil-rich Muslim nation and a hotbed of communist activity.

"It's the next domino after Vietnam," is the way Claudine put it. "We must win the Indonesians over. If they join the Communist bloc, well…" She drew a finger across her throat and then smiled sweetly. "Let's just say you need to come up with a very optimistic forecast of the economy, how it will mushroom after all the new power plants and distribution lines are built. That will allow USAID and the international banks to justify the loans. You'll be well rewarded, of course, and can move on to other projects in exotic places. The world is your shopping cart." She went on to warn me that my role would be tough. "Experts at the banks will come after you. It's their job to punch holes in your forecasts—that's what they're paid to do. Making you look bad makes them look good."

One day I reminded Claudine that the MAIN team being sent to Java included ten other men. I asked if they all were receiving the same type of training as me. She assured me they were not.

"They're engineers," she said. "They design power plants, transmission and distribution lines, and seaports and roads to bring in the fuel. You're the one who predicts the future. Your forecasts determine the magnitude of the systems they design—and the size of the loans. You see, you're the key."

Every time I walked away from Claudine's apartment, I wondered whether I was doing the right thing. Somewhere in my heart, I suspected I was not. But the frustrations of my past haunted me. MAIN seemed to offer everything my life had lacked, and yet I kept asking myself if Tom Paine would have approved. In the end, I convinced myself that by learning more, by experiencing it, I could better expose it later—the old "working from the inside" justification.

When I shared this idea with Claudine, she gave me a perplexed look. "Don't be ridiculous. Once you're in, you can never get out. You must decide for yourself, before you get in any deeper." I understood her, and what she said frightened me. After I left, I strolled down Commonwealth Avenue, turned onto Dartmouth Street, and assured myself that I was the exception.

One afternoon some months later, Claudine and I sat in a window settee watching the snow fall on Beacon Street. "We're a small, exclusive club," she said. "We're paid—well paid—to cheat countries around the globe out of billions of dollars. A large part of your job is to encourage world leaders to become part of a vast network that promotes U.S. commercial interests. In the end, those leaders become ensnared in a web of debt that ensures their loyalty. We can draw on them whenever we desire—to satisfy our political, economic, or military needs. In turn, these leaders bolster their political positions by bringing industrial parks, power plants, and airports to their people. Meanwhile, the owners of U.S. engineering and construction companies become very wealthy."

That afternoon, in the idyllic setting of Claudine's apartment, relaxing in the window while snow swirled around outside, I learned the history of the profession I was about to enter. Claudine described how throughout most of history, empires were built largely through military force or the threat of it. But with the end of World War II, the emergence of the Soviet Union, and the specter of nuclear holocaust, the military solution became just too risky.

The decisive moment occurred in 1951, when Iran rebelled against a British oil company that was exploiting Iranian natural resources and its people. The company was the forerunner of British Petroleum, today's BP. In response, the highly popular, democratically elected Iranian prime minister (and *TIME* magazine's Man of the Year in 1951), Mohammad Mossadegh, nationalized all Iranian petroleum assets. An outraged England sought the help of her World War II ally, the United States. However, both countries feared that military retaliation would provoke the Soviet Union into taking action on behalf of Iran.

Instead of sending in the Marines, therefore, Washington dispatched CIA agent Kermit Roosevelt (Theodore's grandson). He performed brilliantly, winning people over through payoffs and threats. He then enlisted them to organize a series of street riots and violent demonstrations, which created the impression that Mossadegh was both unpopular and inept. In the end, Mossadegh went down, and he spent the rest of his life under house arrest. The pro-American Mohammad Reza Shah became the unchallenged dictator. Kermit Roosevelt had set the stage for a new profession, the one whose ranks I was joining.[5]

Roosevelt's gambit reshaped Middle Eastern history even as it rendered obsolete all the old strategies for empire building. It also coincided with the beginning of experiments in "limited nonnuclear military actions," which ultimately resulted in U.S.

humiliations in Korea and Vietnam. By 1968, the year I interviewed with the NSA, it had become clear that if the United States wanted to realize its dream of global empire (as envisioned by men like presidents Johnson and Nixon), it would have to employ strategies modeled on Roosevelt's Iranian example. This was the only way to beat the Soviets without the threat of nuclear war.

There was one problem, however. Kermit Roosevelt was a CIA employee. Had he been caught, the consequences would have been dire. He had orchestrated the first U.S. operation to overthrow a foreign government, and it was likely that many more would follow, but it was important to find an approach that would not directly implicate Washington.

Fortunately for the strategists, the 1960s also witnessed another type of revolution: the empowerment of international corporations and of multinational organizations such as the World Bank and the IMF. The latter were financed primarily by the United States and our sister empire builders in Europe. A symbiotic relationship developed between governments, corporations, and multinational organizations.

By the time I enrolled in BU's business school, a solution to the Roosevelt-as-CIA-agent problem had already been worked out. U.S. intelligence agencies—including the NSA—would identify prospective EHMs, who could then be hired by international corporations. These EHMs would never be paid by the government; instead, they would draw their salaries from the private sector. As a result, their dirty work, if exposed, would be chalked up to corporate greed rather than to government policy. In addition, the corporations that hired them, although paid by government agencies and their multinational banking counterparts (with taxpayer money), would be insulated from congressional oversight and public scrutiny, shielded by a growing body of legal initiatives, including trademark, international trade, and Freedom of Information laws.[6]

"So you see," Claudine concluded, "we are just the next generation in a proud tradition that began back when you were in first grade."

ENTERING A NEW AND SINISTER PERIOD IN ECONOMIC HISTORY

As chief economist, I not only was in charge of a department at MAIN and responsible for the studies we carried out around the globe, but I also was expected to be conversant with current economic trends and theories. The early 1970s were a time of major shifts in international economics.

During the 1960s, a group of countries had formed OPEC, the cartel of oil-producing nations, largely in response to the power of the big refining companies. Iran was also a major factor. Even though the shah owed his position and possibly his life to the United States' clandestine intervention during the Mossadegh struggle—or perhaps because of that fact—the shah was acutely aware that the tables could be turned on him at any time. The heads of state of other petroleum-rich nations shared this awareness and the paranoia that accompanied it. They also knew that the major international oil companies, known as "The Seven Sisters," were collaborating to hold down petroleum prices—and thus the revenues they paid to the producing countries—as a means of reaping their own windfall profits. OPEC was organized in order to strike back.

This all came to a head in the early 1970s, when OPEC brought the industrial giants to their knees. A series of concerted actions, ending with a 1973 oil embargo symbolized by long lines at U.S. gas stations, threatened to bring on an economic catastrophe rivaling the Great Depression. It was a systemic shock to the developed world economy, and of a magnitude that few people could begin to comprehend.

The oil crisis could not have come at a worse time for the United States. It was a confused nation, full of fear and self-doubt, reeling from a humiliating war in Vietnam and a president who was about to resign. Nixon's problems were not limited to Southeast Asia and Watergate. He had stepped up to the plate during an era that, in retrospect, would be understood as the threshold of a new epoch in world politics and economics. In those days, it seemed that the "little guys," including the OPEC countries, were getting the upper hand.

I was fascinated by world events. My bread was buttered by the corporatocracy, yet some secret side of me enjoyed watching my masters being put in their places. I suppose it assuaged my guilt a bit. I saw the shadow of Thomas Paine standing on the sidelines, cheering OPEC on.

None of us could have been aware of the full impact of the embargo at the time it was happening. We certainly had our theories, but we could not understand what has since become clear. In hindsight, we know that economic growth rates after the oil crisis were about half those prevailing in the 1950s and 1960s, and that they have taken place against much greater inflationary pressure. The growth that did occur was structurally different and did not create nearly as many jobs, so unemployment soared. To top it all off, the international monetary system took a blow; the network of fixed exchange rates, which had prevailed since the end of World War II, essentially collapsed.

During that time, I frequently got together with friends to discuss these matters over lunch or over beers after work. Some of these people worked for me—my staff included very smart men and women, mostly young, who for the most part were free-thinkers, at least by conventional standards. Others were executives at Boston think tanks or professors at local colleges, and one was an assistant to a state congressman. These were informal meetings, sometimes attended by as few as two of us, while others might include a dozen participants. The sessions were always lively and raucous.

When I look back at those discussions, I am embarrassed by the sense of superiority I often felt. I knew things I could not share. My friends sometimes flaunted their credentials—connections on Beacon Hill or in Washington, professorships and PhDs—and I would answer this in my role as chief economist of a major consulting firm, who traveled around the world first class. Yet, I could not discuss my private meetings with men like Torrijos, or the things I knew about the ways we were manipulating countries on every continent. It was both a source of inner arrogance and a frustration.

When we talked about the power of the little guys, I had to exercise a great deal of restraint. I knew what none of them could possibly know, that the corporatocracy, its band of EHMs, and the jackals waiting in the background would never allow the little guys to gain control. I only had to draw upon the examples of Arbenz and Mossadegh—and more recently, upon the 1973 CIA overthrow of Chile's democratically elected president, Salvador Allende. In fact, I understood that the stranglehold of global empire was growing stronger, despite OPEC—or, as I suspected at the time but did not confirm until later, with OPEC's help.

Our conversations often focused on the similarities between the early 1970s and the 1930s. The latter represented a major watershed in the international economy and in the way it was studied, analyzed, and perceived. That decade opened the door to Keynesian economics and to the idea that government should play a major role in managing markets and providing services such as health, unemployment compensation, and other forms of welfare. We were moving away from old assumptions that markets were self-regulating and that the state's intervention should be minimal.

The Depression resulted in the New Deal and in policies that promoted economic regulation, governmental financial manipulation, and the extensive application of fiscal policy. In addition, both the Depression and World War II led to the creation of organizations like the World Bank, the IMF, and the General Agreement on Tariffs and Trade (GATT). The 1960s was a pivotal decade in this period and in the shift from neoclassic to Keynesian economics. It happened under the Kennedy and Johnson administrations, and perhaps the most important single influence was one man, Robert McNamara.

McNamara was a frequent visitor to our discussion groups—in absentia, of course. We all knew about his meteoric rise to fame, from manager of planning and financial analysis at Ford Motor Company in 1949 to Ford's president in 1960, the first company head selected from outside the Ford family. Shortly after that, Kennedy appointed him secretary of defense.

McNamara became a strong advocate of a Keynesian approach to government, using mathematical models and statistical approaches to determine troop levels, allocation of funds, and other strategies in Vietnam. His advocacy of "aggressive leadership" became a hallmark not only of government managers but also of corporate executives. It formed the basis of a new philosophical approach to teaching management at the nation's top business schools, and it ultimately led to a new breed of CEOs who would spearhead the rush to global empire.[7]

As we sat around the table discussing world events, we were especially fascinated by McNamara's role as president of the World Bank, a job he accepted soon after leaving his post as secretary of defense. Most of my friends focused on the fact that he symbolized what was popularly known as the military-industrial complex. He had held the top position in a major corporation, in a government cabinet, and now at the most powerful bank in the world. Such an apparent breach in the separation of powers horrified many of them; I may have been the only one among us who was not in the least surprised.

I see now that Robert McNamara's greatest and most sinister contribution to history was to jockey the World Bank into becoming an agent of global empire on a scale never before witnessed. He also set a precedent. His ability to bridge the gaps between the primary components of the corporatocracy would be fine-tuned by his successors. For instance, George Shultz was secretary of the treasury and chairman of the Council on Economic Policy under Nixon, served as Bechtel president, and then became secretary of state under Reagan. Caspar Weinberger was a Bechtel vice president and general counsel, and later the secretary of defense under Reagan. Richard Helms was Johnson's CIA director and then became ambassador to Iran under Nixon. Richard Cheney served as secretary of defense under George H. W. Bush, as Halliburton president, and as U.S. vice president to George W. Bush. Even a president of the United States, George H. W. Bush, began as founder of Zapata Petroleum Corp, served as U.S. ambassador to the U.N. under presidents Nixon and Ford, and was Ford's CIA director.

Looking back, I am struck by the innocence of those days. In many respects, we were still caught up in the old approaches to empire building. Kermit Roosevelt had shown us a better way when he overthrew an Iranian democrat and replaced him with a despotic king. We EHMs were accomplishing many of our objectives in places like Indonesia and Ecuador, and yet Vietnam was a stunning example of how easily we could slip back into old patterns.

It would take the leading member of OPEC, Saudi Arabia, to change that.

ENDNOTES

1. The United Nations World Food Programme, http://www.wfp.org/index.asp?section-1 (accessed December 27, 2003). In addition, the National Association for the Prevention of Starvation esti- mates that "Every day 34,000 children under five die of hunger or preventable diseases resulting from "hunger" (http://wvw.napsoc.org, accessed December 27, 2003). Starvation.net estimates that "if we were to add the next two leading ways (after starvation) the poorest of the poor die, water- borne diseases and AIDS, we would be approaching a daily body count of 50,000 deaths" Oittp://www.starvation,net, accessed December 27, 2003).

2. U. S. Department of Agriculture findings, reported by the Food Research and Action Center (FRAC), http://www.frac.org (accessed December 27, 2003).

3. United Nations. Human Development Report. (New York: United Nations, 1999).

4. "In 1998, the United Rations Development Program estimated that it would cost an additional $9 billion (above current expenditures) to provide clean water and sanitation for everyone on earth. It would cost an additional $12 billion they said, to cover reproductive health services for all women worldwide. Another $13 billion would be enough not only to give every person on earth enough food to eat but also basic health care. An additional billion could provide basic education for all... Combined they add up to .$40 billion." —John Robbing, author of *Diet for a New America* and *The Food Revolution*, http://www,foodrevoiution.org (accessed December 27, 2003).

5. For a detailed account of this fateful operation, see Stephen Kinzer, All the Shah's Men: An. American Coup and the Roots of Middle East Terror (Hoboken, NJ: John Wiley & Sons, Inc., 2003).

6. Jane Mayer, "Contract Sport: What Did the Vice-President Do for Hal¬liburton?'; *New Yorker*, February 16 and 23, 2004, p 83.

7. "Robert S. McNamura: 8th Secretary of Defense," http://www.defenselink.mil (accessed December 23, 2003).

chapter five

MERCENARIES ON THE FRONT LINES IN THE NEW SCRAMBLE FOR AFRICA

by Andrew Rowell and James Marriott

Private armies are increasingly part of corporate operations in the Third World. How one officer found himself defending Shell's grab for oil against the people of the Niger Delta.

"I like Nigeria. I like the pulse of Africa. It is very stimulating. I will miss it."[1] Nigel Watson-Clark always had a flair for excitement and a challenge. For twelve years, he saw active military service as a British Royal Marine, but he also had a passion for skydiving. A British national skydiving coach, he spent six years competing in championships.

Like many ex-service personnel, after leaving the Marines he took a variety of jobs, such as running a sky-diving school in Spain and working as a close protection officer—more commonly known as a personal bodyguard—in the UK. One of his friends worked on maritime security, and so Watson-Clark ended up working with Chevron in Angola. Then, in 2002, a job in Nigeria came up.

For the next three and half years, he coordinated the security needs of Shell in a strategic offshore oil field. His official job was security liaison officer for the Echo Alpha Field. His main concern was protecting Shell's orange-colored floating oil platform, the *Sea Eagle*, some seven miles offshore.[2] He was stationed on a dedicated

Andrew Rowell and James Marriott, "Mercenaries on the Front Lines in the New Scramble for Africa," *A Game as Old as Empire: The Secret World of Economic Hit Men and the Web of Global Corruption*, ed. Steven Hiatt, pp. 113-132. Copyright © 2007 by Berrett-Koehler Publishers. Reprinted with permission.

250-foot-long security vessel called the *Liberty Service* that was owned by a subsidiary of the American company Tidewater. Based in Louisiana, Tidewater owns the world's largest fleet of vessels serving the oil and gas industry.[3]

There was a simple reason for Watson-Clark to be there. The creeks and shallow waters of Nigeria's Niger Delta are strategically important to both the oil industry and the Nigerian government. In fact, oil is the lifeblood of the government, accounting for more than 80 percent of its revenues, 90 percent of the country's foreign exchange earnings, and 40 percent of its gross domestic product.[4]

Nigerian oil and gas are core assets for Shell as well as for the American companies Chevron and ExxonMobil.[5] Currently the Delta represents over 10 percent of the Shell Group's production. Meanwhile Shell controls over 50 percent of the oil and gas reserves in the country.[6] Shell's corporate fate and that of Nigeria are thus intertwined.

Vessels such as Tidewater's *Liberty Service* are an essential part of the oil industry web that stretches across continents. Shell is part of this web, and its operations in Nigeria could not exist without the web's structure of subsidiary companies, subcontractors, and consultants.

SHELL'S INTERNATIONAL WEB

The web of control is truly international: Royal Dutch Shell's global operations are controlled from the Hague and London. Its Hague-based Exploration and Production Division controls its Nigerian arm, Shell Companies in Nigeria, based in Lagos. One of several subsidiaries of Shell Companies in Nigeria is SNEPCO, the Shell Nigeria and Exploration Company. SNEPCO had engaged the company Ecodrill (itself a subsidiary of the larger Expro Group) to assist in its oil production operations. It was Ecodrill that employed Watson-Clark, who worked on one of Tidewater's vessels. Tidewater itself, though based in Louisiana, runs its West African operations not from Nigeria, but from Aberdeen, the oil capital of Scotland.

To operate effectively in a country as corrupt as Nigeria, Shell, its subsidiaries, and its contractors have to maintain extremely close contacts with several layers of government and different branches of Nigeria's military. That is the only way of doing business. Sometimes this closeness manifests itself as a revolving door between corporation and government. At other times it takes the form of a financial relationship between the corporation and the Nigerian military or Mobile Police Force (MPF). For years Shell denied that any such financial relationship existed but now admits it. Nigerians often see no difference between the government and Shell or between Shell and the military, just as they see no difference between Shell and its contractors. To the people they are all part of a governing alliance of interests.

HOSTAGES TAKEN

January 11, 2006. On board the *Liberty Service* were the ship's sixty-one-year-old American skipper, Patrick Landry, and two engineers: Milko Nichev, fifty-four, from Bulgaria, and Harry Ebanks, fifty-four, from Honduras. Also stationed on the vessel were twelve men from the Nigerian navy, who were being paid by Shell. It was Watson-Clark's job to oversee Shell's security, to look after the *Liberty Service* crew, and to train the Nigerians, who had two inflatable dinghies, known as *ribs*. "Their job was securing the field in the case of any incursion or invasion," said Watson-Clark. "We were patrolling 24/7 on the *Liberty Service*. It was quite a unique role—we never went to port, we never left the field."

Watson-Clark was essentially a front-line soldier in the web of oil exploitation—a soldier working for a private company rather than a state. Colonizing powers have always used armed forces to protect their commercial assets in the Delta. The role he was playing had changed little from that of an English mariner in the 1660s. Then soldiers were employed by the Royal Navy and sent to protect the ships of the Royal African Company, which were transporting slaves from the creeks of the Delta to the American colonies. For 150 years Britain played a pivotal role in the Atlantic slave trade. After slavery came palm oil plantations. Now the exploited resources are oil and gas.

The security liaison officer was about to be caught up in the vortex of violence that has swirled over the Niger Delta for the past four decades. The heart of the crisis is oil—who controls it, who benefits, and who suffers as a result.

For forty years the communities of the Niger Delta have been campaigning for a greater share of the oil wealth that has been pumped from under their land. They have benefited very little from it. Some people have grown rich, but rampant Nigerian corruption has meant that they were a very small elite. The oil companies have grown rich, too, but complicated tax maneuvers steered much of their profit quietly out of Nigeria before anyone realized just how much money they had made. Ordinary people have nothing to show for the oil extraction, and the communities of the Delta have remained extremely poor.

Currently the Nigerian federal government is supposed to return 13 percent of oil revenue to the Niger Delta states where the oil is extracted. In reality, a far smaller percentage makes it back to the communities. Living in the underbelly of the oil world, these states have suffered from oil's unglamorous excesses: routine air and water pollution and twenty-four-hour-a-day gas flaring that roars into the African night, rots corrugated roofs, and burns the backs of people's throats.

For forty years, the communities have complained about their plight. Often their protests have been met with ruthless military force that has left thousands dead and countless others injured or homeless.[7] Children as young as ten have been raped or tortured. Whole villages and towns have been destroyed. It is difficult to summarize the suffering of the Delta people in words. After one attack on the town of Odi in 1999, Nigerian Senate President Chuba Okadigbo said simply: "The facts speak for themselves. There is no need for speech because there is nobody to speak with."[8]

As the simmering bitterness has grown over the last ten years, the young people of the Delta have become more radical, turning to new tactics to fight back and increasingly using violence and hostage taking. Because of the violence, Watson-Clark's role was dangerous—contractors like him are often the targets of community anger in the Delta. Shell's senior executives are powerful but far away and invisible, but the contractors are very visible and extremely exposed. And using contractors, not direct employees, gives Shell a useful level of deniability.

On January 11, tensions were high. The security level on the *Liberty Service* had been increased. Just how exposed Watson-Clark and his crew were became clear that afternoon, when he spotted three speedboats with forty men on board approaching fast. The occupants wore the traditional symbols of Ijaw warriors. One of the naval ribs was sent out to intercept them. "We intercepted the three boats, but, as the navy approached, they saw that they were outmanned and out-gunned, and they retreated," recalled Watson-Clark. "There was a tactical withdrawal."

Some Nigerian navy security men were still on board the *Liberty Service*. "To be quite honest I thought we were on top of the situation, although they [the rebels] were heavily armed. I thought we would be able to handle it," said Watson-Clark. All the practice drills were put into place.

He managed to get the other supply vessels out of the area and the floating storage vessel, the *Sea Eagle*, "locked down." Then those under Watson-Clark's command began shooting with live rounds. "I believe our navy opened fire first, and then they [the rebels] opened fire with everything they had. We took heavy rounds." Bullets used against the *Liberty Service* included armor-piercing rounds. "It was very dramatic, very violent, and it overwhelmed our navy."

Watson-Clark was on the bridge. All around him instruments exploded as they were hit by bullets. Miraculously no one was hurt apart from Watson-Clark, who received only a cut on his chin. But the Nigerian navy could not repel the rebels—the men in the ribs refused to fight and those on board just hid. "Once that happened, the militants just started to board. There was no one left. We had to surrender. It was then that I thought, 'This is not good.' I don't know why, but I wasn't scared. I had never been in a firefight like that before, even in the Marines. It was like being in the middle of a movie."

Only after being taken captive did Watson-Clark realize that the attackers might not have intended to take hostages. A massive argument broke out among the rebels about whether to attack the *Sea Eagle* with rocket-propelled grenades. Within three hours the hostages had been taken into the myriad creeks that make up the Niger

Delta. To the outside world, they had disappeared into the swamps. News of the attack sent the global price of oil skyrocketing.[9]

For Watson-Clark and the other hostages, captivity was just beginning. "They identified me as the Shell representative straight away," he recalled. "They always addressed everything to me. Some of the military guys did not like what I stood for. To them I represented what they were fighting against: Shell and the federal government."

ENTER CHINA: A NEW ECONOMIC COMPETITOR

That same day—January 11—China's foreign minister, Li Zhaoxing, flew to Africa to begin a weeklong tour aimed at supplying China's growing needs for African oil and gas—a trip that, of course, included Nigeria. A seasoned diplomat—China's former ambassador to the United States—Li was sent to Africa's capitals for one reason: the continent's rich resources. China, like many countries, needed more African oil. China's consumption had risen exponentially in the past decade. By 2005 China was dependent on imports for 40 percent of its oil needs,[10] making it the world's second largest oil importer after the United States.

Two days into Li Zhaoxing's trip, China released its first-ever white paper on the continent. "Africa is abundant in natural resources which are urgently needed by China's economic development," assistant Foreign Minister Lu Guozeng told the press.[11] On his trip, Li outlined how China's plans to boost its ties with Africa were based on a "win-win" concept of economic and military cooperation.[12] China intended to access the resources and give military cooperation in return.

His visit did not go unnoticed in the oil capitals of the world. The week before, the Chinese state-controlled oil company, CNOOC, had announced that it was paying $2.3 billion for a 45 percent stake in an offshore Nigerian oil block. The decision had analysts perplexed: this block had been shunned by Shell and other Western oil majors, and even the acquisitive Oil and Natural Gas Corporation of India had refused to buy it because of the dubious legality of its ownership. China's purchase showed just how much risk it was prepared to take in its desire to buy overseas energy assets.[13]

The deal was heralded by China and Nigeria as mutually beneficial. "China is a giant market with giant needs, and we can fulfill them," said Ngozi Okonjo-Iweala, the Nigerian finance minister and a former World Bank vice president.[14] "The [Nigerian] deal gives CNOOC its first base in Africa. We will explore further opportunities in the continent," said Fu Chengyu, president of CNOOC.[15] In just six months, Chinese firms had signed oil deals worth $7 billion in Kazakhstan, Nigeria, and Syria.[16] Six weeks later CNOOC signed another oil agreement in Equatorial Guinea.

WASHINGTON'S INTEREST IN THE DELTA

Nowhere was China's interest in African oil being more closely monitored than in Washington. Ever since 9/11, the U.S. had been looking to protect its economic security through diversifying its sources of energy. For the last five years, the Bush administration and a whole host of influential right-wing think tanks had seen West Africa, and Nigeria in particular, as a counterbalance to dependence on Middle Eastern oil. Africa was the "next Gulf"—a reservoir of oil away from such troublesome countries such as Iraq, Iran, and Saudi Arabia.

Nigeria currently supplies 10 percent of America's oil, but U.S. government officials expect that amount to increase rapidly. Some 30 percent of America's oil will come from Africa in the next ten years.[17]

If West African oil is increasingly important to the U.S., its protection needs to be increasingly strengthened. Since 9/11, in conference after conference and report after report, analysts have argued that the Gulf of Guinea should be declared an area of "vital interest" to the U.S., to be protected by American military power. For example, Republican Congressman Ed Royce told an oil conference in January 2002, "I think that African oil should be treated as a priority for US national security post-9/11."[18]

Attending the same conference as Royce was Lieutenant Colonel Karen Kwiatkowski from the Department of Defense's Office of African Affairs. She, too, emphasized how "important Africa is to US defense policy and US security" and explained how the U.S. had recently developed "International Military Education and Training" in Nigeria. The number of defense attachés to Africa had doubled in the past three years. Kwiatkowski asserted that the military was keen to understand the challenges of U.S. energy companies and investors in sub-Saharan Africa: "The more we know, the more we might be able to help."[19]

Out of the symposium a working group was formed called the African Oil Policy Initiative Group. Its report was handed to the House Energy and Commerce Committee on June 12, 2002. The committee's chair, Republican Billy Tauzin from Louisiana, said, "9/11 has reawakened the awareness of the American public to our extraordinary dependence on energy from the Middle East. It has taught us the value once again of diversifying energy supplies. It is important for us to build new relations with new sources of supply … and to look toward Africa and other regions of the world."[20] One of the report's key recommendations was that "Congress and the Administration should declare the Gulf of Guinea an area of 'Vital Interest'" to the U.S.[21]

Since then, other think tanks have touted similar conclusions: "The United States has vital—indeed rising—national interests in West and Central Africa, concentrated in, but not restricted to, Nigeria and Angola," reported a task force from the Center for Strategic and International Studies (CSIS) in March 2004. This "complex, unsteady zone" was critical to the "security and diversification of U.S. energy supply."[22] In July 2005, a new CSIS task force recommended that the U.S. should "make security and governance in the Gulf of Guinea an explicit priority in US foreign policy."[23]

The same month that Watson-Clark was taken hostage, the influential Council on Foreign Relations published a report by its Independent Task Force on Africa. Once again the importance of African oil to U.S. national security was recognized. But now the threat of China competing for that oil was also realized. "By the end of the decade," said the report, "sub-Saharan Africa is likely to become as important a source of U.S. energy imports as the Middle East. China, India, Europe, and others are competing with each other and with the United States for access to oil, natural gas, and other natural resources."

One of the co-chairs of the task force was Anthony Lake, former assistant to the national security adviser in the Clinton administration and in 2002 chair of the U.S. Committee for UNICEF working on humanitarian aid. At a seminar discussing the report, Lake outlined how U.S. interests in Africa went beyond "humanitarian" concerns into three major issues: oil, China, and terrorism. "Africa will provide the largest incremental increase in oil production over the next two or three years anywhere in the world. By 2010, Africa could be providing us with as many oil imports as the Middle East."

A second interest, Lake continued, "is China. China now gets 28 percent of its oil imports from Africa. It owns 40 percent of the oil industry in Sudan. Because its government is so involved in supporting its companies, it is able to compete with American companies in very effective, not to say unfair, terms. For example, recently it made a $2 billion loan to Angola, secured by future oil deliveries, to win a bid for oil exploration there. And it is competing in similar ways for the oil resources that we need so desperately throughout the oil-rich Gulf of Guinea, including notably in Nigeria."[24]

Although Lake asserted that China was not America's enemy in Africa, it *was* "undercutting" efforts for greater transparency, better business practices, and less corruption on the continent.

Another chair of the task force was Stephen Morrison, who is also the director of the Africa Program at CSIS and another former Clinton official. Morrison was a central figure in the debate on African oil exploitation and the need for transparency in business dealings. Agreeing with right-wing think tanks in Washington that African oil should be labeled an area of vital U.S. interest, Morrison also asserted that these dealings needed to be transparent and to promote development and human rights.

A cynical observer might argue that this stance is clever: there have been so many decades of corrupt deals with little money going to the local population that the status quo cannot continue. If U.S. energy security can be guaranteed only by African oil, exploiting that oil can be guaranteed only if America can claim that Africans are benefiting from oil development. Transparency in oil deals then becomes a tool to make exploitation of African oil acceptable to the wider community.

Just as Washington and European capitals were wielding these new tools of exploitation, however, here came China advocating the same old tools: the raw power of money, with little or no regard for human rights, let alone transparency. "China has come to advance its own commercial and strategic interest on the basis of unsentimental, hard-headed logic," wrote Rory Carroll in the *Guardian*. "They have come to make money, and as much as possible."[25]

China's moves into Africa had certainly ruffled feathers in Washington. "America and its allies and friends are finding that their vision of a prosperous Africa governed by democracies that respect human rights and the rule of law and that embrace free markets is being challenged by the escalating Chinese influence in Africa," wrote the right-wing Heritage Foundation in Washington. "China's burgeoning relationship with Africa is alarming not only because it has facilitated Chinese energy and weapons dealings, but also because it is competing with U.S.-African trade."[26] A right-wing think tank that had spawned the ruthless era of Reagan economics was now bemoaning the unscrupulous behavior of China, the new economic power on the block! Just as the old hit men of Africa—the U.S. and Europe—were sporting a veneer of conscience toward the continent, the new hit man—China—was not only muscling in on their patch but also doing so with a business attitude that the old hit men had belatedly declared amoral and out of date.

At the end of the day, though, both sets of hit men are advocating exploitation no matter how it is presented. One scholar at the Chinese Academy of Social Sciences argued in an interview with the *Economist* that China's behavior was actually reminiscent of that of the old colonial powers. "Since we are mainly there to make money and get hold of their resources," he said, "it's hard to see the difference."[27]

THE MILITARIZATION OF COMMERCE

"They made it brutally clear that we weren't going anywhere for a long time. I knew we were in a very difficult situation," recalled Nigel Watson-Clark. He and the other hostages had been taken to a village somewhere in the Niger Delta. "Between the four of us there was a feeling that we were in a lot of trouble and that it was going to be very difficult to find our way out."

After two days of captivity, Watson-Clark was instructed to phone the Reuters news agency. Reading from a script, he spelled out a list of the militants' demands. These included control of oil by the local region; payment of £1.5 billion by Shell to compensate for its pollution of the area; release of Alhaji Asari, the Ijaw leader of the

Niger Delta People's Volunteer Force; release of former Bayelsa State Governor Chief Diepreye Alamieyeseigha; and expulsion of foreigners from the region.

"The main demands were more control of the resources, all ex-pats to leave, and the £1.5 billion to the Bayelsa State," Watson-Clark said. "At no point did they suggest that they wanted money themselves. They were not asking for the normal hostage-release terms." For the better part of a decade, "normal" hostage taking in the Delta had been a means of raising cash—but this was different. As soon as he read the demands, Watson-Clark's heart sank; he realized that there was no way they would be met.

He soon had another problem to deal with. His captors were monitoring CNN and the BBC to find out how much publicity their hostage taking had generated. They were annoyed at how little coverage they received. Bizarrely, the world's press was fixated at the time on a whale stuck in the River Thames in London: "That whale really, really made them angry."

Watson-Clark's captors identified themselves as MEND, the Movement for the Emancipation of the Niger Delta. They were labeled "pirates," "guerillas," and "shadowy" by the world's press but were young men from the Delta whose lives had been so blighted by oil that they had resorted to violent rebellion to raise awareness of their plight. MEND may have been a new name, but their demands were rooted in the oil conflict. To the people of the Niger Delta, particularly the Ijaw people, the demands made perfect sense. As one MEND member told a British journalist: "We have no water to drink, no schools, no electricity, no jobs." Another said: "We are not terrorists; we are freedom fighters."[28]

According to people close to the conflict, MEND represents different groups of Ijaw youth who have become increasingly radicalized over the last few years. The Ijaw are one of the largest ethnic groups in the Delta and one of the most vocal communities fighting the oil industry, along with the much smaller Ogoni. Both communities, like others in the Delta, have long demanded greater control of the wealth from the oil drilled on their land. They have also campaigned for just compensation for the pollution and degradation of their region.

It was the Ogoni who won the attention of the global media when their leader, Ken Saro-Wiwa, was murdered by the Nigerian military after a sham trial in 1995. Two of the chief prosecution witnesses at that trial later testified that they had been bribed by Shell and others to give evidence against Saro-Wiwa,[29] a claim that the company vehemently denies.[30]

The first recorded protest by the Ogoni against Shell took place in 1966, just eight years after Shell found oil in the Delta. The following year, an Ijaw named Isaac Boro, equipped with £150 and a red flag, formed the Niger Delta Volunteer Service and staged a revolt. "If we do not move," he wrote, "we would throw ourselves into perpetual slavery." He took issue with the oil companies and "their continued atrocities to our people and their wicked reluctance to improve the lot of the people." Soldiers were transported to the scene of the revolt on Shell's boats. Soon after, Boro surrendered, and the first Ijaw revolution was over.

Boro's short revolution inspired Alhaji Dokubo Asari to form the Niger Delta People's Volunteer Force in 2004 and to threaten an all-out war in the Delta. His threat sent shock waves through the oil industry, and world oil prices surged. Unsurprisingly he was arrested and charged with treason. There remains a wide-spread demand among the Ijaw people that Asari be released.

A further demand from MEND was release of Bayelsa State Governor Chief Diepreye Alamieyeseigha, who is a hero in Ijawland for demanding a greater share of oil revenue. But he had also been arrested on charges of corruption and money laundering. The final demand was that Shell comply with a recent Nigerian court order and pay $1.5 billion in compensation for pollution in the Niger Delta, especially in Ijawland. So MEND was asking for what the courts had already decreed. Indeed, the following month a Nigerian federal court upheld the judgment,[31] but Shell still refuses to pay.

Although Boro's revolution put poverty and pollution on the country's political map, the response to it set a precedent that has continued ever since: oil companies collude with the army to repress any dissent. The deadly pattern has been repeated as the people have asked for a fairer share of the oil revenues and an end to pollution. In the early 1980s the people of Iko in Andoniland were arrested and mistreated after a demonstration. In 1987 two people were killed and nearly forty houses destroyed after the Mobile Police Force (MPF), locally dubbed the Kill and Go Force, were called in.[32] In 1990, eighty died and 495 houses were destroyed when the MPF attacked the community of Umuechem; Shell had specifically requested the MPF after another demonstration against the company.[33] The list goes on. Thousands of Ogoni were killed in the early 1990s in security force retaliation for their campaign against Shell.

In May 1994 the local military commander, Major Paul Okuntimo, wrote: "Shell operations still impossible unless ruthless military operations are undertaken for smooth economic activities to commence."[34] And so ruthless military operations happened. Shell later admitted that on at least one occasion it had paid the field allowances of Okuntimo and his men.[35]

Conflicts involved not just the Ogoni and not just Shell. In the late 1990s two Illaje youths were killed after unarmed young men occupied a Chevron oil platform. Once again the MPF had been called—and arrived in Chevron helicopters. Months later, Nigerian forces, this time paid by Chevron, killed four, and some sixty-seven protesters went missing. The late Nigerian academic Claude Ake called this government–company interdependence "the militarization of commerce," the blurring of private oil company and state in oppression and violence.[36]

In December 2003, a leaked report noted that when Shell staff "and particularly senior staff, visit the community they are typically escorted by the Mobile Police."

The same report noted that the way Shell operated "creates, feeds into or exacerbates conflict" and that "after 50 years in Nigeria" Shell had become "an integral part of the Niger Delta conflict system."[37]

But other players are also poised to become part of the conflict. As Watson-Clark and the other captured contractors suffered from diarrhea and fatigue in the swamps,[38] the red carpet was rolled out at Abuja's airport for China's Foreign Minister Li Zhaoxing. In a move of diplomatic quid pro quo, Li added China's weight to Nigeria's campaign for Africa to be given a seat on the UN Security Council: "China is in support of Africa's aspirations for UN reforms," he said, forgetting to mention that China had consistently blocked UN resolutions condemning Sudan for the genocide occurring in Darfur. Now China wanted African oil.[39]

"China and Nigeria are good friends," he said. "We've a lot in common in the fields of politics, economics, sports and the exchange of students."[40] Trade, sports, and students are not all the Nigerians are looking for from the Chinese. When, in the same month, Nigerian Vice President Atiku Abubakar was interviewed by the *Financial Times*, he expressed frustration with the slow response of the U.S. to the fight against rebels like MEND. He explained that, in the absence of U.S. support, Nigeria was increasingly looking to the Chinese government to supply weapons systems. In 2005 the Chinese won a $250 million deal to supply Nigeria with twelve fighter jets, and there were reports that China would provide dozens of patrol boats to secure the creeks of the Delta.[41]

Although the Americans have increased their military presence in the Gulf of Guinea in recent years to protect their interests, once again the Chinese moved with a swiftness that surprised many. It may have been a British foot-soldier who was still hostage, but his captors could soon be facing Chinese weapons. The more China invests in oil assets in the Delta, the more it will become involved in the militarization of those assets.

As the days went on, Watson-Clark's captors came back with tales of killings and gunfights. "It became very, very difficult," he recalled. "Things became more and more desperate as every day went by. I am quite optimistic by nature, but pessimism, and this overwhelming feeling of sadness that we weren't going to get out, dominated the mood. It was real."

IN THE MEDIA SPOTLIGHT

The hostage crisis could not have come at a worse time for Dr. Edmund Daukoru. The Nigerian minister of state for petroleum resources, Daukoru had become the president of OPEC on January 1, 2006. Every New Year's Day, the oil cartel rotates the presidency, and now it was Nigeria's turn. As the minister responsible for oil, it was Daukoru who wore the coveted crown.

This was set to be his year of global fame, and the youthful-looking sixty-two-year-old had been looking forward to his first two major appearances as OPEC's president. The humble boy from the Delta had come a long way, most of it with Shell Oil Company. "I have been an oilman right from the beginning," said Daukoru. "After acquiring primary and secondary education, I was picked by Shell to go abroad for my studies; I studied geology at the Imperial College in London. On finishing my doctorate degree program, I came back to join Shell. I have thus been a Shell man right from the beginning: first as a scholar, then an employee."[42] Daukoru had worked for the company in the Netherlands, Italy, Spain, France, Switzerland, Tunisia, and, of course, Nigeria.

This Shell man "went through the ranks and became the first indigenous chief geologist in the industry, then first indigenous general manager and director of exploration." At the time this was the highest position a Nigerian could reach in Shell. Daukoru was then seconded by Shell to become the managing director of the Nigerian National Petroleum Corporation (NNPC) for eighteen months in 1992–93.[43]

However, soon after the dictator General Sani Abacha came to power in 1993, Daukoru was sacked at NNPC.[44] He retired, only to be asked six years later by President Olusegun Obasanjo to be his presidential adviser. On his appointment as minister of state for petroleum resources in 2005, Daukoru declared, "We must take our destiny in our own hands."[45]

He is not the only oil man to move from Shell to government. Chief Rufus Ada George, an ex–Shell Petroleum Development Company (SPDC) employee, was governor of Rivers State in the Delta during the Ogoni uprisings in the early 1990s. Godwin Omene, a deputy managing director of SPDC, was appointed head of the Niger Delta Development Commission in 2001. Ernest Shonekan, who briefly became Nigeria's president in 1993, was an SPDC director.

This revolving door of senior Shell staff to positions in government only adds to the belief in the Delta that Shell and the government are one. Indeed, the Ogoni activist Ken Saro-Wiwa once remarked about a forthcoming community protest, "It is anti-Shell. It is anti-Federal government, because as far as we are concerned the two are in league to destroy the Ogoni people."

Saro-Wiwa's fight against Shell cost him his life, whereas Daukoru's career within Shell took him to the heights of the oil industry. Two men born in the Delta, two men whose destiny was shaped by oil, but two very different outcomes. Both men became international news. For Saro-Wiwa the news-making event was his death; for Daukoru, his appointment as president of OPEC.

Daukoru's story personifies how the revolving door between company and state allows a tiny elite to benefit from oil exploitation. But Daukoru, as a black, is one of the few exceptions to the rule within the oil industry. Shell managing directors had all been white until 2004, when Basil Omiyi became the first Nigerian to head Shell's main subsidiary in Nigeria—Shell Petroleum Development Company.

On his OPEC appointment, Shell man Daukoru changed from having national Nigerian prominence to having international importance. He was hailed in the Nigerian press: "The move will bolster international commercial confidence in investing in Nigeria," proclaimed *Business Day*.[46]

His first appearance as OPEC president was at the World Economic Forum at Davos, Switzerland, the annual get-together of the world's business and political elite. Davos nestles snugly in the Swiss Alps; outside the conference hall, clear, crisp blue skies formed the backdrop to chalets laden with snow. Inside the hall, some 2,300 delegates had come to the ultimate exclusive networking event.

OPEC had been represented at Davos for over a decade, but this year it was putting on a special program featuring an "Energy Summit" with the theme of "Managing Tectonic Shifts." Dr. Daukoru was in high-powered company. Bill Gates, the world's richest man, was there; so, too, were political giants such as Bill Clinton, UN Secretary Kofi Annan, President of the World Bank Paul Wolfowitz, and UK Chancellor of the Exchequer Gordon Brown. Hollywood stars such as Michael Douglas whisked in and out; sports legends such as Pele and Muhammad Ali and rock star Bono all made appearances in Davos.

Inside the hall, there was heavyweight business to attend to. The growing importance of China and India featured heavily on the agenda. Having just recorded GNP growth of 9.9 percent, China was grabbing headlines. Zeng Peiyan, China's vice premier, was quick to assure the audience that the expected surge in Chinese energy consumption would not put a strain on oil and gas prices. "China is not only a major energy consumer, it is also a major energy producer," he said.[47]

Daukoru, too, was keen to soothe frayed nerves over the energy market. At a working lunch on the second day of the conference he gave his address. He started by examining the last two years of the market. "There has been the challenge of meeting exceptionally high levels of growth in oil demand from large emerging economies, especially China and India, as well as from some developed economies, such as the USA."

Daukoru continued by arguing that if there was one outstanding challenge it was the need to prevent rapid upheavals in the energy market in the future. "The century began with three years of high market stability, which was to the satisfaction of all responsible parties," he said. "But, since then, we have been experiencing a very different and much more volatile situation."

If he meant the crisis unfolding back home, he did not say. But the issue of the hostages was making other news at Davos, too. The chair of Royal Dutch Shell, Jeroen Van der Veer, talked about the hostages. Funsho Kupolokun from the Nigerian National Petroleum Corporation assured delegates that "the Niger Delta is safe." The latest unrest was just a periodic flare-up—something oil companies such as Shell were accustomed to in the Delta.

"What you are seeing now is just another round. It will be dealt with very rapidly," Kupolokun said. If anything, the hostage taking had diverted attention away from the fact that Nigeria and West Africa were developing new production faster than OPEC. "With advancing technology, reserves are not the issue," he said. "The challenge really is developing the reserves fast enough."[48] So community grievances such as grinding poverty and murderous pollution were annoyances. The real challenge was to get the oil out of the ground as fast as possible.

CNN beamed pictures of the Davos meeting to the Delta, where Watson-Clark was being held hostage. After broadcast of a meeting between Obasanjo and Brown, MEND members were delighted: "They liked that, they thought it must have something to do with them. So they would say, 'Things are working,' but then we would never get released."

WELCOME NEWS

Finally, on Monday, January 30, Watson-Clark's parents were awakened by a morning phone call from their son. Nigel had been released. "He said he's fine. We're just happy he's alive and well," his father said. The British High Commissioner in Nigeria, Richard Gozney, told the BBC Radio 4 *Today* program: "We learnt late in the night that the negotiations by the governor of Bayelsa State in the Niger Delta had been successful. We saw the hostages very early this morning, at first light, and they seemed to be safe and well."[49]

The following morning Watson-Clark flew to Heathrow, where his partner, Briony Tomkies, and their four children were waiting for him. "It is absolutely wonderful to be home. I feel great. I've got my family around me, which is very nice," he told the waiting press.[50]

Ironically Watson-Clark did not feel a huge sense of relief, just gratitude. "I was humbled by the various agencies that were there in Lagos that did get us out," he recalls. Asked who these agencies were, he replied Scotland Yard, the FBI, his bosses at the Expro Group, the Nigerian arm of Tidewater, and "there were other people involved as well who I would prefer not to go into." He added that "the whole collective effort was fantastic." If secret service agents were involved, Watson-Clark did not say. It would not be the first time that British or American agents had meddled in the affairs of Nigeria. Still Watson-Clark was glad that his moment in the media spotlight was over and that he was home.

For Dr. Daukoru, public attention was just beginning. The same day, January 31, he was in Vienna to chair the 139th Extraordinary Meeting of the OPEC Conference at the organization's Secretariat there. It was his first official meeting in charge of OPEC. The flags of the cartel's nations hung behind the delegates like silent guards watching the proceedings. Bouquets of orange, yellow, and white flowers on the main conference table added color to the otherwise drab room decor. Again concern was expressed about the "high degree of price volatility" in the oil market. Dr. Daukoru looked calm and relaxed, stylishly dressed in a gray suit with an upturned collar. If the ongoing violence in Nigeria was worrying him, he did not show it.

Asked by the press whether OPEC would increase output in the course of 2006, Daukoru said, "We have always maintained that we have more spare capacity than the market was willing to take." He revealed that OPEC had at least 2 million barrels of spare capacity, and noted that Nigeria was working to bring onstream by the first half of the year an additional output of 600,000 barrels per day on top of a base of 2.5 million barrels per day. Afterward he was mobbed by the world's oil press, eager to hear more from the most important oil leader of the moment. The price of a barrel of oil hung on his every word.

Someone else whose words can move the oil market also had a say on that day. Alhaji Dokubo Asari, the imprisoned Ijaw leader of the Niger Delta People's Volunteer Force, said that the release of the hostages was a "goodwill gesture to the international community," but he added that the attacks would continue. He singled out Britain for special mention: "We, the Ijaw and Niger Delta people, want to remind the people of the world that Great Britain has facilitated the illegal, criminal and inhuman occupation and exploitation of our lands for 112 years."[51]

It is interesting that Asari blamed the old colonial power for the problems of the Niger Delta, just as the new powers—America and China—were beginning to fight over Nigeria's oil. There is no doubt that Shell benefited from British colonial rule in Nigeria, and its continuing dominance of the Nigerian oil industry is a colonial legacy. Its monopolistic position means that, ironically, for Shell, Nigeria remains a lethal legacy, too.

In February 2006, Citigroup released an in-depth study on Nigeria. "Our analysis," it said, "suggests that Nigeria is *the* major growth region for Shell to the turn of the decade." Although much of Shell's growth will be from deepwater offshore oil fields, Watson-Clark's experience shows that operating offshore does not insulate the industry from community grievances. Citigroup concluded that Shell was "the most exposed of its peers to Nigeria. We estimate that by 2010 Nigeria will account for almost 17% of group production, up from 11% currently." More importantly, the report concluded that the region accounts for a significant proportion of Shell's expected volume growth to 2010.[52]

So the spiral of violence seems set to continue, with Shell at its center. In February, MEND took more hostages, although they, too, were later released unharmed. Two weeks after Nigel Watson-Clark was released, Nigerian military helicopters attacked the area, killing an estimated twenty people. The government claimed that it was targeting barges used for smuggling oil. MEND accused the military of targeting civilians instead. Once again, Shell was intertwined with the violence—information emerged that the helicopters had used a company airstrip—and Shell again tried to distance itself from the military action. "Armed intervention is always a decision for the proper authorities and not for private companies such as Shell," a spokesperson said.[53]

However, the following month, Charles Dragonette, a senior analyst at the U.S. Office of Naval Intelligence, admitted that Shell had asked the U.S. military for protection. Dragonette cited the Ijaw insurgency and conflict stemming from President Obasanjo's attempt to hold on to power as reasons why "Nigeria's Delta situation is not going to improve, certainly not anytime soon," and concluded that "the production of oil in Nigeria will hang precariously in the balance for the foreseeable future."[54] Forty years after Shell provided boats to put down Isaac Boro's rebellion, the company remains as intertwined with the military and oil conflicts in Nigeria as ever.

China's involvement is only just beginning. Interestingly, the Citigroup report argued that, should "Shell wish to diversify its portfolio risk" in Nigeria, potential buyers would be the Brazilian company Petrobras and CNOOC, the Chinese state oil company.

Just how important Nigeria is to China's energy plans was reconfirmed when President Hu Jintao made a state visit to Abuja as part of a weeklong tour in April 2006. To mark the occasion, Nigeria granted China four drilling licenses in exchange for a commitment to invest at least $4 billion in oil and infrastructure projects.[55]

As the red carpet was once again rolled out for a Chinese dignitary, MEND issued a warning. "We wish to warn the Chinese government and its oil companies to steer well clear of the Niger Delta," MEND wrote in an e-mail. "Chinese citizens found in oil installations will be treated as thieves. The Chinese government by investing in stolen crude places its citizens in our line of fire."[56]

One person who will no longer be in the line of fire is Nigel Watson-Clark. He handed in his resignation to Ecodrill on his return to Britain, since the only security job the company would offer him was back on the Echo Alpha field. "Everyone in Nigeria knows that there is an imbalance between what is happening in Abuja and the fabulous wealth that is coming out of Nigeria and where they are getting it from—the coastal states," he says. "I don't have a lot of sympathy for what MEND did to us, but they have been driven to that. They have been driven to doing what they are doing. There are an awful lot of people who are not benefiting from that country's wealth. They have absolutely nothing." In Africa, he points out, oil is known as the black curse.

ENDNOTES

1. Nigel Watson-Clark, telephone interview with Andy Rowell, April 21, 2006; all quotes attributed to Watson-Clark are from this interview unless otherwise stated.

2. See www.news24.com/News24/Africa/News/0,,2-11-1447_1865650,00.html.

3. See www.news.moneycentral.msn.com/ticker/article.asp?Feed=BW&Date=20060130 &ID=5457691& Symbol=US:TDW.

4. Shell Petroleum Development Company of Nigeria Limited, *2004 People and the Environment Annual Report*, May 2005.

5. M. Enfield, *The Oil Industry in the Delta*, PFC Energy, presentation to the Conference on Nigeria's Delta Region, Meridian International Center, February 15, 2005.

6. J. Bearman, "Shell Set to Rise Again with Nigerian Gas," *African Energy*, June 2005, pp. 8–9; Enfield, *The Oil Industry in the Delta*.

7. Michael Fleshman, "Report from Nigeria 2," *Nigeria Transition Watch* no. 9 (New York: Africa Fund, 1999).

8. Karl Maier, *This House Has Fallen: Nigeria in Crisis* (Harmondsworth: Penguin, 2006), p. 142.

9. "Kidnappings, Sabotage Slash Nigerian Oil Output," Agence France Presse, January 12, 2006.

10. See the Web site http://english.aljazeera.net/NR/exeres/5F9B91A6-C289-446B-A08EFF9A2BA73791.htm.

11. Xinhua Financial Network News, "China Defends African Policy, Touts Mutual Benefits following CNOOC Oil Deal," January 13, 2006.

12. "China Unveils New Partnership Plan for Africa," AFX News, January 16, 2006.

13. T. Pitman, "Chinese Foreign Minister Heads to Africa on Weeklong Tour of Oil-Rich Continent," Associated Press, January 11, 2006.

14. A. R. Mihailescu, *U.P.I. Energy Watch*, February 7, 2006.

15. See www.cnooc.com.cn/defaulten.asp.

16. J. McDonald, "China Spending Billions on Foreign Oil but Trying to Curb Appetite," Associated Press, Beijing, February 6, 2006.

17. See http://api-ec.api.org/filelibrary/BacAprr5.pdf.

18. See www.israeleconomy.org/strategic/africatranscript.pdf.

19. Ibid.

20. See his comments at http://usembassy.state.gov/nigeria/wwwhp061402b.html.

21. See www.israeleconomy.org/strategic/africawhitepaper.pdf.

22. The report is available at www.csis.org/africa/GoldwynAfricanOilSector.pdf.

23. Available at www.csis.org/africa/0507_Gulfof Guinea.pdf.

24. See www.cfr.org/publication/9371/more_than_humanitarianism.html.

25. Rory Carroll, "China's Gold Mine," *Guardian*, March 28, 2006.

26. P. Brookes and J. Hye Shin, *China's Influence in Africa: Implications for the United States*, Heritage Foundation Backgrounder no. 1916, February 22, 2006.

27. "No Questions Asked: China and Africa," *Economist* (U.S. edn.), January 21, 2006.

28. K. Houreld, "My Rendezvous with the River Rebels," *Daily Mail*, March 22, 2006.

29. M. Birnbaum, *Nigeria: Fundamental Rights Denied: Report of the Trial of Ken Saro-Wiwa and Others*, Article 19, in association with the Bar Human Rights Committee of England and Wales and the Law Society of England and Wales, Appendix 10: Summary of Affidavits Alleging Bribery, June 1995.

30. S. Buerk, e-mail to Andy Rowell, July 11, 2005.

31. See www.guardian.co.uk/oil/story/0,,1717598,00.html.

32. Environmental Rights Action, *Hell in Iko: The Story of Double Standards*, July 10, 1987; Andrew Rowell, *Green Backlash: Global Subversion of the Environment Movement* (London: Routledge, 1995), pp. 294–95.

33. Hon. O. Justice Inko-Tariah, Chief J. Ahiakwo, B. Alamina, Chief G. Amadi, *Commission of Inquiry into the Causes and Circumstances of the Disturbances That Occurred at Umuechem in the Etche Government Area of Rivers State in the Federal Republic of Nigeria*, 1990; J. R. Udofia, "Threat of Disruption of Our Oil Operations at Umuechem by Members of Umuechem Community," Letter to Commissioner of Police, October 29, 1990.

34. Lieutenant Colonel Paul Okuntimo, "RSIS Operations: Law and Order in Ogoni Etc.," Memo from the Chair of the Rivers State Internal Security Task Force to His Excellency, the Military Administrator, Restricted, May 12, 1994.

35. A. Rowell, "Shell Shock," *New Zealand Listener*, December 14–20, 1996; A. Rowell, "Shell Cracks," *Village Voice*, December 11, 1996.

36. A. Rowell, J. Marriott, and L. Stockman, *The Next Gulf: London, Washington and Oil Conflict in Nigeria* (London: Constable, 2005).

37. WAC Global Services, *Peace and Security in the Niger Delta—Conflict Expert Group*, Baseline Report, Working Paper for Shell Petroleum Development Company, December 2003.

38. Available at http://news.biafranigeriaworld.com/archive/bbc/2006/01/21/nigerian_ rebels_ vow_new_oil_raids.php.

39. "China Backs Africa for Seat on UN Security Council," Agence France Presse, FM, Abuja, January 16, 2006.

40. Ibid.

41. Reported in www.defenseindustrydaily.com/2005/09/nigeria-spends-251m-for-chinese-f7-fighters-after-oil-deals/index.php; D. Mahtani, "Nigeria Accuses US of Failure to Help Protect Its Oil Assets," *Financial Times*, February 28, 2006.

42. Quoted at www.winne.com/nigeria/topinterviews/edmund_daukoru.php.

43. Ibid.

44. P. Adams, "Nigeria's Burden of Proof: Arrests Have Been Made But the State Oil Business Has Still to Satisfy the Industry that Its Reforms Are Working," *Financial Times*, November 3, 1993, p. 34; *Economist*, "Oiling the Big Wheels," November 6, 1993, p. 107.

45. See these Web sites: http://allafrica.com/stories/200507150045.html; www.odili.net/news/source/2005/jul/17/201.html; and http://allafrica.com/stories/200507250536. html; "Oil Exploration: 'We Must Take Our Destiny in Our Hands,'" *This Day*, July 24, 2005.

46. M. Umar, "Stakeholders Applaud Daukoru's OPEC Presidency," *Business Day*, February 13, 2006.

47. Reported at www.weforum.org/site/homepublic.nsf/Content/China+Will+Rely+On +Domestic +Demand+For+Economic+Growth%2C+Says+Zeng.

48. See the Web site www.weforum.org/site/knowledgenavigator.nsf/Content/_S15722?open&event_id=1462&year_id=2006.

49. See www.timesonline.co.uk/article/0,,3-2016701,00.html.

50. Nigel Watson-Clark, quoted in www.newsandstar.co.uk/news/viewarticle.aspx? id=326757; http://news.bbc.co.uk/1/hi/england/somerset/4666186.stm.

51. Alhaji Dokubo Asari, www.timesonline.co.uk/article/0,,3-2017164,00.html.

52. Citigroup Global Markets, "Delta Force," *The Pump*, February 27, 2006.

53. "Shell Defends Use of Nigerian Airfield by Attack Chopper," Agence France Presse, February 16, 2006. Also see www.coanews.org/tiki-read_article.php?articleId=738; http://quote.bloomberg.com/apps/news?pid=10000006&sid=aEmm3EpJnEh4&refer=home; www.theallineed.com/news/0602/16185243.htm.

54. Reported at www.fin24.co.za/articles/markets/display_article.asp?Nav=ns&lvl2=mark ets&ArticleID=1518-25_1903224.

55. See www.voanews.com/english/2006-04-27-voa13.cfm.

56. See www.washingtonpost.com/wp-dyn/content/article/2006/04/30/AR2006043001022.html.

chapter six

THE WAR ON DRUGS IN ASIA: A PHONY WAR WITH REAL CASUALTIES

by Peter Dale Scott

Most well-developed heroin networks very quickly move towards a complementation of interests between the narcotics traffickers and corrupt elements of the enforcement agencies responsible for the suppression of the illicit drug trade.[1]

This chapter will show how the U.S. war on drugs, declared by Nixon on June 17, 1971, has been constrained by the political realities in the Far East to concentrate on and sometimes virtually to invent secondary targets while protecting the CIA's allies and proxies who have been the biggest Asian traffickers. This protection of the top traffickers did not happen in the Far East alone but in the Middle East and Africa as well. As we shall see in the next chapter, Dennis Dayle, a former top Drug Enforcement Administration (DEA) investigator in the Middle East, once said on television that "in my 30-year history in the Drug Enforcement Administration and related agencies, the major targets of my investigations almost invariably turned out to be working for the CIA."[2]

The results of this constrained war have been summed up by Michael Levine, the former Customs and DEA agent who was forbidden by the CIA to target a major heroin factory in Chiang Mai:

Peter Dale Scott, "The War on Drugs in Asia: A Phony War with Real Casualties," *American War Machine: Deep Politics, the CIA Global Drug Connection, and the Road to Afghanistan*, pp. 121-140, 313-321. Copyright © 2010 by Rowman & Littlefield Publishing Group. Reprinted with permission.

When Nixon first declared war on drugs in 1971, there were fewer than half a million hard-core addicts in the nation, most of whom were addicted to heroin.... Three decades later, despite the expenditure of $1 trillion in federal and state tax dollars, the number of hard-core addicts is shortly expected to exceed five million.[3]

(Three decades ago Pakistan and Afghanistan had almost no heroin addicts. Today there are an estimated 5 million addicts in Pakistan and 1 million in Afghanistan.)

This does not mean that the DEA has achieved nothing. On the contrary, billions of dollars of repressive equipment have been transferred to foreign governments, where (as we shall see) they have often been used for oppressive purposes.[4] In this way, regardless of the intentions of well-meaning DEA agents, the DEA and CIA function together today as integral parts of the U.S. war machine.

Years later, speaking of his Thai experience for Customs and that of his unit, the Hard Narcotics Smuggling Squad, Levine wrote,

> We could not avoid witnessing the CIA protecting major drug dealers. In fact, throughout the Vietnam War, while we documented massive amounts of heroin flooding into the U.S. from the Golden Triangle ..., while tens of thousands of our men were coming home addicted, not a single important source in Southeast Asia was ever indicted by U.S. law enforcement. This was no accident. Case after case ... was killed by CIA and State Department intervention and there wasn't a damn thing we could do about it.[5]

(The same would be true of the Golden Crescent in the 1980s, when Afghanistan became the world's major source of heroin.)

Douglas Valentine has now written a two-volume history of narcotics enforcement in America, based both on archival research and on interviews with scores of frustrated DEA agents. What he reports is very similar:

> The moral to the story of federal drug law enforcement is simple: in the process of penetrating organized crime, case-making agents invariably stumble upon the CIA's involvement in drug trafficking, along with the CIA's political protectors. One of the reasons the FBN [Federal Bureau of Narcotics] was abolished, was that its case-making agents uncovered these political and espionage intrigues. Adapting to this reality is perhaps the primary reason the DEA survives. It certainly has not come close to winning the War on Drugs.[6]

There are signs that Nixon intended to diminish CIA influence over drug enforcement, and he may have created the DEA to gain this important source of power for the White House.[7] But after Nixon's departure from office, it soon became clear that the CIA, having earlier placed its officers at top levels of the FBN, was now placing them in the DEA.[8]

THE ORIGINS OF NIXON'S WAR ON DRUGS

When Richard Nixon declared a war on drugs in June 1971, he did so for many reasons, a major one of which was straightforward. Nixon had good reason to be concerned about narcotics from the time of his election, partly because of the increasing rates of heroin consumption by U.S. troops but also because domestic public concern about crime made drugs a hot political issue.

In September 1969 his first major effort, Operation Intercept, targeted marijuana coming from Mexico:

> two thousand customs and border-patrol agents were deployed along the Mexican border for what was officially described as "the country's largest peacetime search and seizure operation by civil authorities." Automobiles and trucks crossing the border were delayed up to six hours in hundred-degree temperatures; tourists appearing suspicious or recalcitrant were stripped and bodily searched. Although more than five million citizens of the United States and Mexico passed through this dragnet during the three-week operation, virtually no heroin or narcotics were intercepted from the tourists.[9]

Observers commented that, while Operation Intercept aggravated an already prevalent drought in marijuana supplies, there was a consequent increase in heroin smuggling and sales on both the East Coast and the West Coast.[10] However, the White House may have considered it a success. Nixon's narcotics adviser, Egil Krogh, noted that "Operation Intercept ... received widespread media coverage" and recommended more highly dramatized crackdowns with similar code names.[11]

On June 21, 1970, the Justice Department launched Operation Eagle. One hundred fifty suspects were rounded up in cities across the country, and the Bureau of Narcotics and Dangerous Drugs (BNDD) proclaimed it to be "the largest roundup of major drug traffickers in the history of federal law enforcement."[12] Attorney General John Mitchell claimed that it had closed down "a nationwide ring of wholesalers handling about 30 percent of all heroin sales and 75 to 80 percent of all cocaine sales in the United States."[13]

Less publicized was the fact that as many as 70 percent of those arrested had once belonged to the CIA's Bay of Pigs invasion force.[14] For the first time since World War II, a CIA connection was failing to provide protection to drug traffickers.[15] It is probably relevant that Nixon, for reasons going back to his electoral defeat in 1960, mistrusted the CIA and was already seeking to diminish CIA influence in his administration. (According to Len Colodny and Tom Schachtman, "Nixon hated the CIA, believing it had misled him in 1960 about the 'missile gap,' allowing John F. Kennedy to outflank him on that issue and win the election."[16])

Those arrested in Operation Eagle were at the heart of the Trafficante- dominated "Cuban Mafia," identified by the *New York Times* in February 1970 as "for the most part previously little known underworld members employed and trained in pre-Castro Cuba by the American Mafia."[17] Arresting them contributed to the winding up of the historic French Connection because much of the heroin that had reached America via the casinos of Batista's Cuba had been refined by Corsicans in the region of Marseille.

By June 1971, Nixon had an important new reason to challenge CIA operations in Southeast Asia, which relied heavily on Nationalist Chinese Kuomintang (KMT) armies for actions in Thailand and Laos. Secretly, without advising the CIA, Nixon was having Kissinger prepare for his historic trip to Beijing in July. This would soon lead to an order in August 1971 that the CIA terminate its cross-border operations into Yunnan and other activities offensive to Beijing.[18]

These orders constituted a remarkable reversal of U.S. priorities, which up to 1971 Nixon had endorsed, not only with respect to China but in Southeast Asia as well.

THE WAR ON DRUGS AND THE SHIFT IN AMERICA'S HEROIN SUPPLY FROM TURKEY TO SOUTHEAST ASIA

At this time Nixon created an Ad Hoc Cabinet Committee on Narcotics, chaired by his national security adviser, Henry Kissinger. The next phase of Nixon's drug war was directed against opium growing in Turkey, a minor source of global opium production but the main source of supply for Corsican heroin labs and the celebrated French Connection.[19]

The oddity of choosing Turkey as a target is pointed out in Edward J. Epstein's well-informed but very one-sided account, fed with information from James Angleton and his CIA supporters, who were not disinterested:

> According to CIA estimates compiled for the ad hoc committee, India, Afghanistan, Pakistan, Thailand, Laos, and Burma all produced substantially more illicit opium than did Turkey. Moreover, after a thirteen-year prohibition, the Shah of Iran had decided in 1969 to plant 20,000 hectares with poppies, which was a 50 percent-greater area than Turkey had in

cultivation. In all, the CIA estimated, Turkey produced only from 3 to 8 percent of the illicit opium available throughout the world.[20]

Particularly noticeable was the committee's initial avoidance of the problem of Far Eastern heroin. Epstein explains this avoidance by practical rather than strategic considerations: "In the case of Burma (as well as of Afghanistan and Laos), it was recognized that the central government had virtually no control over the tribes growing and smuggling poppies, and that any American pressure or incentives given to the central government would be at best unproductive."[21]

But according to James Ludlum, the CIA's representative on the committee, both "Lebanon and the East were declared off-limits *for national security reasons.* The focus of the meeting was the flow of Turkish opium to heroin labs in Marseille."[22] It is hard not to see in this the Nixon-Kissinger strategy for Indochina, which in Laos still relied heavily on the drug-supported efforts of Vang Pao's Hmong army as well as the Royal Laotian Army.[23] To quote McCoy, "The U.S. embassy [in Laos] was well aware that prominent Laotian leaders [such as General Ouane] ran the traffic and feared that pressure on them to get out of the narcotics business might somehow damage the war effort."[24] (The war, especially in Cambodia, along with other issues, also contributed to tensions between France and America, even after de Gaulle in 1969 was replaced as president by Pompidou.[25])

BNDD agent John Cusack was largely responsible for the BNDD's targeting of Turkey, and he "produced statistics showing that Turkish opium was the raw material for 80 percent of the heroin emanating from … Marseille."[26] I shall argue later that the heroin estimate by Cusack, who is described by Valentine as an agent "with close ties to the CIA," was false and a falsehood useful to protecting the war in Laos. For now it is enough to stress that Turkey was not a major supplier to the United States, and the BNDD itself soon recognized that "a large percentage of French connection heroin came not from Turkey, but from the Golden Triangle via Manila and Hong Kong."[27]

Eventually, $35 million was supplied to the Turkish government in June 1971, resulting in a temporary drying up of Turkish illicit opium. But this had little impact on heroin supplies as opposed to the domestic political goals of Nixon's White House:

> Although this victory would cut off only a small fraction of the opium growth in the world—less than 8 percent—and even this amount would quickly be replaced by opium from Southeast Asia, India, and other sources, White House strategists realized that if the announcement were properly managed in the press, it would be heralded as a decisive victory against the forces of crime and addiction.[28]

Meanwhile, a series of major arrests and seizures in 1970–1971 made U.S. authorities increasingly aware of how serious was the direct heroin threat to America from the Far East.[29] The most spectacular of these was the April 1971 seizure in Paris's Orly Airport of sixty kilos of high-grade Laotian opium. This was found in the suitcase of Laotian Prince Sopsaisana, longtime delegate of the Asian People's Anti-Communist League/World Anti-Communist League and Laos's ambassador designate to France. Although the prince was not arrested, the seizure forced the CIA to reappraise its drug alliances in the Far East:

> According to reports later received by the U.S. [Federal] Bureau of Narcotics, Sopsai's venture had been financed by Hmong General Vang Pao, commander of the CIA's Secret Army, and the heroin itself had been refined in a laboratory at Long Tieng, the CIA's headquarters for [Hmong] clandestine operations in northern Laos.[30]

Nixon and the CIA appear to have initiated a number of measures to disengage itself from this operation and to crack down on it. As part of this crackdown, the *New York Times* temporarily broke its customary silence on CIA-drug matters. In June 1971 it published a story about heroin refineries in the Golden Triangle, based on a classified report leaked to it by the CIA when Helms was still director of the CIA.[31] A month later the *Times* also announced that the Nixon administration would crack down on Laotian, Thai, and South Vietnamese leaders involved in the drug traffic.[32]

THE U.S. WAR ON DRUGS AND COUNTERINSURGENCY IN THAILAND

Both the White House and the BNDD recognized, from the inception of Nixon's war on drugs in June 1971, that Thailand must now be their primary target. Far more resources were applied to Thailand than either Mexico or Turkey, but the results were equally futile. Even when a Thai CIA asset smuggling drugs on the side was arrested through his own carelessness, the CIA prevented the case from being tried.[33]

There were three reasons for the failure of the war on drugs in Thailand, all symptomatic of what was fundamentally wrong with the war on drugs. The first is that the top suppliers, notably the KMT generals Li Wenhuan and Duan Xiwen, were regarded as important, untouchable assets in the defense against communism by both the Thai government and the CIA. It was at this time, for example, that Customs agent Michael Levine was forbidden in 1971 to make a case against a heroin factory that was probably processing opium from Li Wenhuan. (Only a few months later, the KMT armies would be formally placed under the Thai Supreme Command.) The second was that the Teochew traffickers with whom they did business in Bangkok also had protectors in the Thai government.[34] The third is that the U.S. antinarcotics campaign was accepted by the Thai government only on condition that it maintain and develop the previous CIA support for the Border Patrol Police (BPP), the Police Aerial Reinforcement Unit (PARU), and related programs. Thus the war on drugs, far from launching an attack on the CIA's previous corrupt relationship to the drug traffic, became a means of extending and indeed expanding it. Counternarcotics became the new face for counterinsurgency, that is, repression:

> The United States enjoyed a particularly close relationship with the Thai ruling dictatorship, which agreed to cooperate with the War on Drugs in return for aid in crushing an incipient guerrilla insurrection. During the late 1960s, the OPS [Office of Public Safety] began advisory training of the 7th subdivision of the Thai national police in narcotics enforcement and intelligence gathering in an attempt to curb the source of supply reaching American GIs. They also formed a police aerial reinforcement unit, which was intended to enhance customs and border patrol, while sometimes providing a camouflage for CIA operations into neighboring Laos and Vietnam.

According to Kuzmarov, American drug war aid became diverted to the purpose of domestic oppression, just as would happen later in Burma:

> As the drug crisis in Vietnam intensified, Nixon increased the number of federal narcotics agents in Thailand from five to eleven. On August 4, 1971, Egil Krogh visited with Thai officials and issued a memo to State Department officials calling for an "all out war to disrupt those supplying American troops" with drugs.[35] On September 28, 1971, American ambassador Leonard Unger helped broker a pact, in which the United States agreed to send Black Hawk helicopters to bolster the drug enforcement capacities of the Royal Thai police, which had received previous U.S. monetary assistance under OPS programs for what it termed domestic "security purposes." A congressional investigation later uncovered that much of the American drug war aid continued to fulfill these ends and was funneled toward financing the repressive policing apparatus of the Thai government, which frequently carried out spot executions and torture.[36]

Early victims of this intensified effort were hill tribes in northern Thailand whose opium growing had earlier been tolerated but whose fields were now napalmed from the air, sometimes with approving U.S. members in the helicopters.[37] What ensued later was an organized massacre at Bangkok's elite Thammasat University of students opposing army dictatorship. In 1974 the BPP—"which was intimately connected to

CIA counter-insurgency planning—helped spawn and legitimize ... the Red Gaurs (*krathing daeng*)."[38] The Red Gaurs contained "veterans from the Thai units that fought for the US in Indochina" and who now had found new employment back home.[39] In October 1976 the BPP and Red Gaurs, along with Village Scouts (another BPP creation), were brought into Bangkok and implemented an army radio station call to kill students in Thammasat University. "A handful of students who tried to escape were brutally lynched, raped, or burnt alive outside the university. Officially, forty-three students were killed, and two policemen. Over 3000 were arrested on the day, and some 5000 later. That evening an army faction took power by coup."[40]

A year later, the military dictatorship was in the hands of the last of the Northern Army dictators, Kriangsak Chamanand, the leader of the 1976 coup and a man "heavily implicated in the [drug] trade and also a KMT client."[41]

In 1999 a Thai proposal for a book researching the source of the Thammasat massacre proved too controversial to be completed. But two Northern Army generals accused of running the drug trade at the time, Praphat Charusathien and his son-in-law Narong Kittikachorn, were later identified as

> being behind the violent crackdown on the demonstration.... One vital, unanswered question is whether there was a "third hand" behind the killings. [Some] suggest an agency was involved that wanted to discredit the dictatorship. The officer allegedly connected with this mysterious force is Maj.-Gen. Witoon Yasawat, now 74 and ailing. In a recent interview with the *Siam Post* newspaper, Witoon admitted he acted on behalf of a third party. But he refused to identify who it was, saying only that "the secret will die with me." The first shots, according to sources ... came from rooftops and were fired by Lao mercenaries in the pay of the CIA.[42]

Yasawat was a former leader of CIA-paid Thai mercenary forces in Laos, reinforcing the impression that PARU or possibly even the CIA itself was the "agency" involved.

Undoubtedly, the CIA's covert operators had helped precipitate the political crisis leading to the bloody episode at Thammasat. In 1975, after the civilian prime minister Kukrit Pramoj gave the United States a one-year deadline to begin withdrawing its troops from Thailand, "the United States together with the Thai right produced 'evidence' that the Vietnamese were planning to invade." The military mobilization in Bangkok at the time of the Thammasat incident was in response to this concocted threat.[43]

Earlier in 1975, amid "well-circulated but bogus U.S. intelligence reports detailing Hanoi's strategy to take control of all of mainland Southeast Asia"[!], Thai agents "then incited riots in the northeastern provincial capital of Nakhon Nakhon, homeland to Thailand's largest concentration of immigrant Vietnamese."[44] This instigation of anti-Vietnamese violence replicated the anti-Vietnamese pogrom accompanying the Cambodian military coup of 1970 installing Lon Nol, another coup in which some observers have seen the influence of U.S. intelligence.[45]

The story goes still further back. The Cambodian pogrom in turn reflected the anti-Chinese pogrom that followed the Indonesian coup overthrowing Sukarno in 1965, and in fact the Cambodians were allegedly advised by Indonesian "psychological warfare" experts who arrived in Phnom Penh within days of the Lon Nol coup.[46] American-trained psychological warfare experts were at the very heart of the 1965 Indonesian coup.[47]

This narrow focus on the role of the CIA, PARU, and BPP should not convey the sense that the CIA was responsible for all of the antistudent violence of that era, even in Southeast Asia. In the decade after the Paris uprising of 1968, the world in short order witnessed the 1968 Tlatelolco massacre of students in Mexico City, the 1970 killing of U.S. students at Kent State and Jackson State universities, the 1972 Kizildere massacre in Turkey, the Burmese student uprising of 1974, and the anti-intellectual Cambodian genocide of 1975. Violence has its own momentum in human history; it cannot all be laid at the door of "psychological warfare experts."

With the withdrawal of American troops from Thailand in 1976, America's experts predicted a still greater collapse into violence. But the exact opposite proved in the end to be the case. The Thammasat massacre had driven between 3,000 and 10,000 urban middle-class intellectuals into the arms of the communist resistance in northeastern Thailand. But the departure of the U.S. military was marked by a slow return of Thai politics to civilian government, for the first extended period since 1947. Assisted by the developing complexities of international politics, this led by degrees to a process of reconciliation and normalization.[48]

In short, the hopes for liberal democracy for Thailand, actively subverted by covert U.S. governmental pressures, radically improved after U.S. troops withdrew in the 1970s.

HOW THE PHONY U.S. WAR ON DRUGS PROTECTED AND HELPED CREATE THE BIGGEST TRAFFICKERS

Many observers have commented on the futility and misdirection of America's expensive drug enforcement campaigns in Southeast Asia, where the DEA was prevented from going after the real top traffickers—notably the Thai and CIA ally General Li Wenhuan of the KMT Third Army. Instead, the DEA made a point of finding secondary targets who were protected not by Thailand but by Burma. The first of these was Lo Hsing Han, the Burmese militia chief in Kokang, whom senior U.S. narcotics adviser Nelson Gross proclaimed publicly in September 1971 to be the "kingpin of the heroin traffic in Southeast Asia ... whose control, runs the gamut from poppy fields to heroin labs."

Gross's announcement was in the wake of Nixon's proclamation in June 1971 of a war of drugs. To understand it, we will have to look at the genesis of that policy and the creation of the Cabinet Committee on Narcotics Control in September, the working group of which Gross chaired.

According to Bertil Lintner, the best observer of Burma at the time,

> Nelson Gross's statement about Lo Hsing-han was dismissed by most astute observers as a media-directed exaggeration. At the same time as the drug authorities were trying to focus the world's attention on one single trafficker of moderate status and importance, two relatively unknown opium merchants in Kengtung—Shi Kya Chui and Yang Sang a.k.a. Yang Shih-li—were, in fact, trading in much larger quantities than the "kingpin" himself. From his base in Lashio in northern Shan state, Lo Hsing Han was only able to organize three to four convoys a year carrying opium, jade, and other contraband down to the Thai border at Tachilek, the apex of the Golden Triangle. Shi Kya Chui and Yang Shih-li, on the other hand, were more conveniently based at Kengtung, only 170 kilometers north of Tachilek, making it possible for them to make up to 10 trips a year.[49]

Now Valentine reveals that the idea to make Lo Hsing Han the target originated with three CIA officers who knew Southeast Asia well:

> CIA officers Jim Ludlum, Joseph E. Lazarsky and Clyde McAvoy wrote "the scenario" in Burma.... To insure that the military's interests in Southeast Asia were not compromised, Deputy Director of Central Intelligence General Robert Cushman attended the CCINC meetings where Lazarsky, Ludlum and McAvoy presented their plan of attack.... [In a meeting with General Ne Win of Burma] Gross presented the Ludlum-Lazarsky-McAvoy plan, which made Lo Hsing Han ... the fall guy.[50]

Complex negotiations ensued over a proposal from the rebels in the Shan state: that they would sell their opium crop to Lo Hsing Han, who in turn would deliver it all to the DEA. The British filmmaker Adrian Cowell, in close touch with Lo Hsing Han (and later with Khun Sa), delivered the proposal to the U.S. embassy. Soon,

Lo Hsing Han, thinking that he was about to negotiate with the Americans, naively entered a Thai army helicopter. Instead, he was taken to an army base near Chiang Mai, arrested, and extradited to Burma. "In fact, Lo's arrest had no impact on the overall flow of drugs from Burma."[51] But in America, the arrest was announced under headlines like "The Heroin King Is Captured," allegedly after a battle in which five of his followers were wounded.[52]

Gross presented the proposal to target Lo Hsing Han to Ne Win in September 1971, three months after Nixon proclaimed his war on drugs and the same month that Laos, under American pressure, made opium illegal under new laws written in the U.S. embassy. Knowing that the Thais would never give up the forces of KMT General Li Wenhuan (said to control two-thirds of the opium coming to Thailand), Gross came up with a different proposal:

> buy them out of the opium business.... Despite the cabinet committee's stated policy against preemptive buying of opium ... a deal was struck in March, 1972.... [The Chinese Nationalists] delivered twenty-six tons of brownish material that supposedly constituted their entire opium stockpile, and pledged to remain out of the opium business for several years. Unevaluated CIA reports ... leaked to columnist Jack Anderson ... said that the brownish material ... was in fact heavily weighted with cow fodder.[53]

Valentine, citing an internal report to Customs from former CIA officer William Young, writes that this idea also originated not with Gross but with the CIA base chief in Chiang Mai, Robert Brewer. Thai BNDD Chief Fred Dick also told Valentine that "I do know that the agency wrote the words and music for this opera."[54] Although the BNDD officially disputed the CIA reports, BNDD officer Dick added, "We all know they [the KMT in Thailand] never got out of the opium traffic. They probably would have been better off to give the money to the Salvation Army."[55]

With Lo's arrest, "Khun Sa's Shan national Army and the Thai-based Kuomintang picked up the slack, and Khun Sa would become an enduring target of the DEA for the next 20 years."[56] This was a continuation of the charade to avoid the top traffickers. According to Lintner, "Khun Sa, contrary to ... myths spread by many Western narcotics agencies, was not the mastermind of the international drug trade." According to Valentine, "it was common knowledge that Khun Sa moved only about ten percent of the region's opium."[57]

Khun Sa moved into his Thai base at Ban Hin Taek and regularly received visitors there, including westerners like Adrian Cowell. Lintner describes how Joseph Nellis, chief counsel of the Senate Committee on Narcotics Abuse, flew to meet him in a Thai helicopter, was greeted there by "a number of heavily armed Thai BPP policemen," and conducted an interview with Khun Sa in which the interpreter was a former "mercenary with the CIA in Laos."[58]

As with Lo Hsing Han, the war against designated target Khun Sa was a scripted charade. Author James Mills was told that

> the war being fought against Chang Chi-fu [Khun Sa] is a cosmetic one, intended only to convince Americans that the Thais are doing all they can to capture Chang and put an end to his opium business. In reality, the Thais are associated with Chang Chi-fu and share in his profits.[59]

In 1982, a new Thai government, embarrassed by Khun Sa's frequent and flamboyant press interviews, mounted a BPP attack that temporarily demolished Ban Hin Taek. (Khun Sa himself, having been given ample warning, escaped.[60]) But at Homöng, his new base in Burma, the charade continued. Bo Gritz visited him there in 1987 and, having just read of a vigorous joint Thai-Burmese military attack, was surprised to find no traces whatever of a battle:

> When I questioned Khun Sa about the matter, Khun Sa said that Thai and Burmese military officials had both come to meet him early in January [1987], and said that they stood to lose millions of dollars in US drugs suppression funds unless they made it look like they were doing something. So they worked out a deal. Khun Sa agreed to let them come up to the border and fire off their guns and a few rockets in to the air, so that they could claim that they were doing their part in fighting this "monster," whom [U.S.] Ambassador [to Thailand William] Brown had described as "the worst enemy the world has."

Khun Sa also told Gritz, truthfully, how in exchange for this theater the Thais had agreed to build a new road (Route 1285, built once again with help from USAID) out of Mae Hong Son to a point on the border facing Homöng.[61] In other words, America, by making Khun Sa the designated target in a conspiratorial charade, actually conferred on him a bargaining power he might not otherwise have had.[62]

Their status as designated DEA targets also enabled both Khun Sa and Lo Hsing Han to reach mutually satisfactory understandings with the Burmese government. With the economy suffering from Burma's isolation, Yangon relied increasingly on taxing the profits of Khun Sa and Lo Hsing Han—the two traffickers it could be confident were no longer (even if Khun Sa had once been) American assets.[63] With the gradual decline of the old KMT generals, Khun Sa had a new phase of increased importance:

Under Khun Sa's leadership, Burma's opium production soared from 550 to 2,500 tons during the 1980s—an exceptional 500 percent increase. Fueled by Burma's rising poppy harvest, Southeast Asia's share of the New York City heroin market jumped from 5 to 80 percent between 1984 and 1990. By then, Khun Sa controlled over 80 percent of Burma's opium production—making him history's most powerful drug lord.[64]

This remarkable quintupling of Burmese opium production came at a time when the Ne Win government was receiving the powerful chemical defoliant 2,4-D from the U.S. State Department for a massive but obviously ineffectual aerial spraying campaign. The $18-million-a-year program proved once again the futility of simply throwing money after an ill-understood problem in remote areas: "Instead of curbing production, narcotics officials believe the programme only inspired farmers in the poppy growing areas to increase their planting in the hope of compensating for expected spraying losses. 'We sprayed them into overproduction,' said a narcotics expert in Bangkok."[65]

It should also surprise no one that the spraying campaign was used by the Burmese military for political purposes, targeting those hill tribes like the Kachins and Wa, who were in opposition to Yangon, and allegedly sparing those like Khun Sa, who supported it. So one net result of the spraying campaign may have been to help Khun Sa increase his market share.

The 2,4-D did not reduce opium production, but it had major consequences for the hill tribes who were targeted. Edith Mirante received reports from two opposed Shan groups "that people were getting sick from it, and cattle were dying."[66] Shelby Tucker, one of the very few people to reach the Kachin areas of Burma in this period, was told that 2,4-D

> was so toxic that it killed almost everything it touched. It entered rivers and streams and spread beyond its target areas. People who drank from the rivers or ate food affected by it took violently ill. Its contaminating effects endured in the ground. It could be and was used as a tactical defoliant. It could be and was used to discourage the people from supporting the insurgents and to encourage them to support the Burma Army. It was ideal for ethnic cleansing.[67]

Then, as the flow of opium moved north and east through Kokang into China, Khun Sa and Lo Hsing Han had a new career. Thanks in part to their designation by the DEA, both men, having made peace with the State Law and Order Restoration Council, became major capitalist entrepreneurs in Yangon.

It is hard to disagree with McCoy's and Lintner's severe verdicts on the DEA's costly and at times repressive drug war in Southeast Asia:

> Khun Sa's career demonstrates the ultimate futility of Washington's war on the world's drug lords. While still central to the narcotics trade, major drug lords, protected by powerful elements within their governments, remain impervious to international pressures. Like Khun Sa, they can only be arrested when the political economy of the producing regions shifts in ways that renders them redundant—stripping them of local power, drug profits, and external support. In effect, we can only capture a drug lord when he is no longer a drug lord. This paradox raises some real questions about the nature of the global drug trade and the appropriateness of US anti-narcotics policy. More than any other man in this century, Khun Sa has shaped the world's narcotics traffic—increasing Burma's heroin production five-fold and changing the demographics of drug abuse in the United States. But even at the peak of his powers in 1990, his capture would have had little effect on the traffic. The poppy fields and urban addicts would have remained, and some other drug lord would soon reap the profit that comes from their connection. In Burma over the past 50 years, four drug lords—General Ly Wen-huan, Lo Hsing-han, Khun Sa, and, now, Wei Hsueh-kang—have, in turn, risen to extraordinary wealth and power by expanding opium output dramatically and then fallen without any perceptible impact upon supply.[68]

This drug milieu, on which not just the Hmong but the entire Laotian economy was so dependent, survived the departure of the CIA from Laos in 1975. The incoming communist government was impoverished; soon the leaders of isolated provinces and then those of the two capital cities were driven to make alliances with local traffickers.

By 1978, only three years later, a Sino-Thai trafficker, Poonsiri Chanyasak, formerly the "Mr. Big" in Thailand,[69] had successfully corrupted the new communist government in Vientiane and was now selling Laotian opium to figures who earlier had been part of the KMT network. His main Bangkok purchaser, Lu Hsu-Shui (alias Vichien Wachirakaphan), was a major DEA target, but Lu escaped arrest when the CIA decided to preempt a confidential informant in the case against him for "a high-level, sensitive national security operation."[70]

In this way the CIA precluded the arrest of a man described in the *New York Times* as someone who "was (and still may be) the leading importer of Southeast Asian heroin into the United States."[71] Thus, the Poonsiri-Lu Hsu-Shui connection constituted what I call a metagroup: a group with the ability to gain the protection of both sides in a political conflict. Mills describes how Lu Hsu-Shui and his two cousins, having escaped indictment, apparently went on to enjoy special relationships in Las Vegas, in Saudi Arabia, and with the mainland Chinese intelligence service.[72]

The anecdote again illustrates what common sense already tells us: that in a world where some high-level traffickers are used by the CIA for parastatal purposes, those traffickers, having the best protection, will rise to the top of the world trade. Drug enforcement then becomes an activity that benefits these top traffickers both by artificially boosting the price of drugs and by selective prosecution of those competitive traffickers not so protected.

This ability of drug traffickers to transcend political divisions is an important phenomenon, to be explored more deeply in a later chapter.

SOUTHEAST ASIAN AND AFGHAN OPIUM PRODUCTION: TWO STORIES OR ONE?

There are reasons to surmise that the CIA's forced departure from Laos in 1975 may have contributed to the rise of opium production in Afghanistan at the same time, soon followed by CIA destabilization of Afghanistan from as early as 1978 if not earlier. To sum up the CIA's Laotian record, the landlocked opium-growing country of Laos, the only nation in the region that never attacked another, was targeted by the Dulles brothers and the CIA for no other crime than having installed a neutralist government. The resulting decision to polarize the country backfired: what America got in the end was a resounding defeat for its proxies and the installation of their enemy the Pathet Lao as the new government.

This followed the application of maximum airpower: the tonnage of bombs dropped between 1968 and 1972 on the Plaine des Jarres alone was greater than the tonnage of all the bombs dropped by the United States in both the European and the Pacific theaters during World War II.[73] Many of these bombs are still unexploded and still cause civilian casualties. Yet after this total criminal fiasco, Brzezinski and the CIA in 1978, two years after the United States removed the last of its troops from Thailand, unilaterally decided to repeat history and destabilize another landlocked opium-growing country—Afghanistan.

To summarize what I have written elsewhere, Brzezinski was soon in contact with Pakistan's emissary Fazle Haq, a man who by 1982 would be listed by Interpol as an international narcotics trafficker.[74] The U.S. polarization resulted in a coup and new government by a Communist Party fraction so extreme that the Soviet Union (as Brzezinski had predicted) intervened to restrain it. In the next decade of anti-Soviet resistance, more than half of America's aid went to Gulbuddin Hekmatyar, who soon became "one of Afghanistan's leading drug lords." The consequences were felt in America, where heroin from the Golden Crescent, negligible before 1979, amounted in 1980 to 60 percent of the U.S. market.[75]

As we shall see, Americans were conscious of the drug implications. Jimmy Carter's drug adviser, David Musto, told the White House Strategy Council on Drug Abuse in 1980 that "we were going into Afghanistan to support the opium growers," and he asked, "Shouldn't we try to avoid what we had done in Laos?"[76]

McCoy points out that American heroin imports had decreased radically in the 1970s, whether from the success of Nixon's drug war or from Jimmy Carter's ban on major CIA covert operations from 1976 to 1978. (Another reason, of course, might have been the U.S. withdrawal from Indochina.) Acknowledging the complexities of the global drug trade, he nevertheless offers the cautious conclusion that "prohibition and protection were, on balance, significant factors—in both the decline of heroin supply in the 1970s and its subsequent increase during the 1980s."[77]

Meanwhile, through the last three decades since the first U.S. intervention in Afghanistan, there has been a dramatic decline in Southeast Asian opium and heroin production: from more than 70 percent of all the opium sold worldwide to about 5 percent. A *New York Times* article explained the dramatic change as follows:

> Economic pressure from China, crackdowns on opium farmers, and a switch by criminal drug connections to methamphetamine production, appear to have had the biggest impact. At the same time, some insurgent groups that once were financed with drug money now say they are urging farmers to eradicate their poppy fields.
>
> As a result, the Golden Triangle has been eclipsed by the Golden Crescent—the poppy-growing area in and around Afghanistan that is now the source of an estimated 92 percent of the world's opium, according to the United Nations.[78]

I suspect, however, that Afghan drug trafficking may be as much the cause as the beneficiary of the change in Southeast Asia. Just as a renewed Burmese alliance with Lo Hsing Han was the chief reason for Khun Sa's late career decline, so the new dominance of the global heroin trade by Afghanistan may have been a major factor in marginalizing Southeast Asian production. A graph produced by the UN Office on Drugs shows relative stability in global opium production between 1990 and 2005, as the decline in Burmese production was roughly compensated for by the increase in Afghan production.[79]

Does this mean that those who profited most from Southeast Asian trafficking have now been replaced by new and independent players? I very much doubt it. The entry of Afghanistan into the global drug market first dates from about 1971, the year in which opium was made illegal in Laos and the massive air communications between Indochina and America began to be wound down. Two French journalists report that it was in 1971 that a few hundred Europeans and Americans became traffickers in Kabul.[80] I suspect some of these may have come from Southeast Asia, having seen that the trafficking opportunities there were about to change.

That there was such a connection would explain why in 1985, when Burmese drugs began to flow through southern China, the Chinese People's Republic began to admit international banks to the Shenzhen economic zone bordering Hong Kong, and the second bank to be so admitted, to the astonishment of other bankers, was the Bank of Credit and Commerce International (BCCI).[81] BCCI, as we shall see, had risen to global prominence since 1980 as the lead bank transmitting CIA support to the drug-growing mujahideen in Afghanistan.

The shift in opium production between 1990 and 2007 is very like, indeed reenacts, the shift in U.S. heroin imports between 1968 and 1972:

> Between 1968 and 1972 there was a dramatic change in the pattern of international narcotics smuggling. Prior to 1968, 90 percent of the heroin coming into the United States came from opium grown in the Middle East.... By 1972, however, this pattern had changed. By then, over 45 percent of the heroin entering the United States came from opium grown in the Golden Triangle.... The heroin coming from the Middle East-French connection declined by about the same percentage.[82]

Two crucial developments may help to explain this change. The first development was Trafficante's visit in 1968 to Hong Kong, where he may or may not (as Chambliss was told by his DEA source) have met with Vang Pao. McCoy speculated plausibly that Trafficante's visit "was a response to the crisis in the Mediterranean drug traffic and an attempt to secure new sources of heroin for Mafia distributors inside the United States."[83]

The second development was Nixon's antidrug campaign in 1971, which in its first phase targeted Turkey as an opium source and ignored Southeast Asia.[84] McCoy has noted both the initial impact of the Nixon attack on Turkey and its ultimate futility:

> In the 1970s, President Nixon scored a total victory in the first U.S. drug war by destroying the Turkey-Marseille connection. During the next decade, however, American heroin dealers shifted their sources from Turkey to Southeast Asia, next to Mexico, *then to Central Asia*—remaining one step ahead of U.S. narcotics agents. By the early 1980s, it was clear that Nixon's victory was simply a down payment on defeat.[85]

In other words, three decades of the war on drugs, which has now cost American taxpayers an estimated $1 trillion, has not reduced the size of the drug traffic but rather only affected the behavior of the major controllers like Trafficante.[86] And if McCoy's analysis is correct, then the same controlling heroin connections that have dominated the traffic in the past have now shifted their supply source to central Asia—which can only mean Afghanistan.

All this leads me to a question, perhaps unanswerable, that McCoy does not ask: is it a coincidence that, both times when the drug traffic faced an impending crisis in its existing source of supplies, the interventions of the U.S. government, particularly the CIA, helped other deep forces in their efforts to create a new supply source?

DEEP FORCES, THE CIA, AND THE SHIFT IN WORLD OPIUM PRODUCTION TO AFGHANISTAN

Cusack's announcement that heroin labs in France were supplied from Turkey, and his formulation of a buyout plan to deprive Marseille's heroin labs of their opium supply, were part of a larger campaign to eliminate what was known as the French Connection. A number of books have described this campaign, but most of them have failed to point out the resulting rise in Asian opium supply and the role in the shift of both the CIA and the French intelligence agency Service de Documentation Extérieure et de Contre-Espionnage (SDECE). For all of the top traffickers had protection from intelligence agencies, and inevitably a shift in trafficking routes involved their intelligence connections.[87]

Especially after Georges Pompidou replaced Charles de Gaulle in 1969 as president of France, both intelligence agencies were changing, and change led to internal conflicts between old and new guards. The CIA, which had long been antipathetic to de Gaulle, made alliances with pro-Pompidou elements replacing the Gaullists in SDECE. Soon the chief of these was Alexandre de Marenches, an American contact since World War II whom Pompidou installed as head of SDECE in November 1970.

In November 1969 discussions began between the head of BNDD and French officials in the new Pompidou government "about how to smash the [Corsican] Orsini organization" in Marseille.[88] The Danish journalist Henrik Krüger, in a book for which I wrote the foreword, argued that this was part of a series of coordinated meetings (including Trafficante's 1968 trip to Hong Kong, Nixon's drug policy initiatives and also a Mafia summit in Italy); these meetings collectively represented a deliberate move to reconstruct and redirect the heroin trade in the United States, "from Marseilles (Corsican) to Southeast Asian and Mexican (Mafia) heroin in the United States."[89]

Krüger argued in essence that what he called this "great heroin coup" resulted in part from the "unprecedented tensions" that existed between both incoming presidents (Nixon and Pompidou) and "their old-line intelligence services."[90] A major part of his argument is the involvement of the CIA, acting through American and French anti-Gaullist, pro-Pompidou narcotics agents, in the framing and then murder of the Moroccan leftist Mehdi Ben Barka, organizer of the Havana Tricontinental Congress. (This murder was rightly seen by de Gaulle's biographer Alexander Werth as a "double operation—first against the Third World by eliminating Ben Barka and secondly against de Gaulle."[91]) According to *Time* magazine, no less than thirty-seven people disappeared in the subsequent turmoil, which Krüger attributed to the conflict between Gaullist and pro-Pompidou factions of the SDECE.[92]

McCoy also studied this shift in heroin supply. His account of it in the current edition of his book is less conspiratorial: that the drug market shift from Turkish to Asian sources simply represented a decision made by American heroin dealers to evade BNDD agents. Over the past forty years, in his words, "American heroin dealers shifted their sources from Turkey to Southeast Asia, next to Mexico, then to Central Asia—remaining one step ahead of U.S. narcotics agents."[93]

By contrast the 1972 edition of McCoy's masterpiece was closer to Krüger's thesis because McCoy too attributed the supply shift, at least in part, to a deliberate government deception program about Turkey's significance:

> As America confronted the heroin epidemic in mid 1971, government lead-
> ers and mass-media newsmen reduced the frightening complexities of the
> international drug traffic to a single sentence. Their soothing refrain ran
> something like this: 80 percent of America's heroin begins as raw opium on
> the slopes of Turkey's craggy Anatolian plateau, is refined into heroin in the
> clandestine laboratories of Marseille, and smuggled into the United States by
> ruthless international syndicates. If any of the press had bothered to examine
> this statement they might have learned that it was based largely on a random
> guess by the French narcotics police, who had eleven officers, three automo-
> biles, and a miserable budget with which to cover all of southern France.[94]

(McCoy dropped this paragraph from the 2003 edition of his book and instead accepted, as if it were an uncontested fact, that "Turkey's opium [was] the source of 80 percent of America's heroin supply."[95]) According to Doug Valentine, both the exaggerated opium statistics attributed to Turkey and also the plan to buy out Turkish opium were the work of BNDD agent John Cusack, whom he describes as "ambitious and smart, with close ties to the CIA, at times using FBN investigations as cover for CIA missions."[96] (In his earlier volume, Valentine wrote that the CIA used Cusack in the CIA murder plot against Ben Barka described by Krüger.[97])

To understand America's current involvement in Afghanistan, it would be critical to ascertain whether government policies, as Krüger argued, have helped in the past to direct shifts in heroin supply, not simply follow them. In *Cocaine Politics* in 1991,

Jonathan Marshall and I argued for a more modest government role, that is, that the CIA made alliances with the traffickers in various parts of the world rather than guiding them there.

We wrote that

> the long and sordid history of CIA involvement with the Sicilian Mafia, the French Corsican underworld, the heroin producers of Southeast Asia's Golden Triangle, the marijuana- and cocaine-trafficking Cuban exiles of Miami, and the opium smuggling *mujaheddin* of Afghanistan simply reinforces the lesson of the Contra period: far from considering drug networks their enemy, U.S. intelligence organizations have made them an essential ally in the covert expansion of American influence abroad.[98]

In this book I have presented evidence that OPC and CIA policies in the past have paved the way for opium traffic shifts and not merely followed them.[99] The emergence of Burma as a supplier of world opium resulted from Sea Supply's buildup of the KMT traffickers through Operation Paper in Burma. Laos became a major supplier of world opium as a result of PARU's ouster of a neutralist government and empowerment of General Ouane in Laos. This role for Laos was strengthened by Shackley's intervention in the 1967 Opium War and the involvement of Shackley's cohorts in the drug-trafficking bank Nugan Hand.

I would conclude that to some extent CIA policies of withdrawal from Laos and engagement in Afghanistan may have been responsible for the dramatic shift in supplies in the 1970s from the Golden Triangle in Southeast Asia to the Golden Crescent in Afghanistan. The question arises whether this shift was unintended or whether the CIA, aware of Musto's warnings, was consciously in step with other dark forces anxious to secure a zone of opium production as the United States withdrew from Southeast Asia.

This question is of the greatest relevance to another, more immediate one: why is the United States, against expert advice, now miring itself in another unwinnable war—Afghanistan?

ENDNOTES

1. Alfred McCoy, *Drug Traffic: Narcotics and Organised Crime in Australia* (Harper and Row, 1980), 30.

2. Peter Dale Scott and Jonathan Marshall, *Cocaine Politics* (Berkeley: University of California Press, 1998), x–xi. Dayle made this statement during a videotaped teleconference in the presence of Marshall and myself.

3. Michael Levine, "Mainstream Media: The Drug War's Shills" in *Into the Buzzsaw: Leading Journalists Expose the Myth of a Free Press,* ed. Christine Borjesson (Amherst, NY: Prometheus Books, 2002), 258.

4. In addition, the DEA spends millions each year on an education program, the first of whose priorities, according to its own Budget Summary, is "Anti-Legalisation Education" (Office of National Drug Control Policy, http://www.ncjrs.gov/ondcppubs/publications/policy/budget98/agency-09f.html).

5. Levine, "Mainstream Media," 265.

6. Douglas Valentine, *The Strength of the Pack: The People, Politics and Espionage Intrigues That Shaped the DEA* (Springfield, OR: TrineDay, 2009), xi–xii. Full disclosure: Both Levine and Valentine are friends, and I blurbed Valentine's important book.

7. Richard Lawrence Miller, *Drug Warriors and Their Prey: From Police Power to Police State* (Westport, CT: Praeger, 1996), 158–59; Edward J. Epstein, *Agency of Fear: Opiates and Political Power in America* (New York: G. P. Putnam's, 1977), 165–66.

8. Valentine, *Strength of the Pack,* 6–8, 32–36. Cf. the stories of James Ludlum and John Cusack later in this chapter.

9. Epstein, *Agency of Fear,* 83.

10. The *New York Times Encyclopedic Almanac,* 1972, 29: "As a result of Operation Intercept, the federal attempt to restrict the flow of marijuana from Mexico, heroin sales have jumped among children in New York city, a joint legislative committee is told"; Humberto Fernandez, *Heroin* (Center City, MN: Hazelden, 1998), 214: "In response to the shortage of marijuana, which was either seized or delayed due to Operation Intercept, an increase in heroin smuggling was noticed in southern California and as far north as San Francisco during this time." These reports are discounted by Eric C. Schneider, who writes that Operation Intercept "lasted a mere twenty days, not long enough to have an impact on anything except Mexican-American relations" (*Smack: Heroin and the American City* [Philadelphia: University of Pennsylvania Press, 2008], 148). But heroin is such an addictive drug that even a brief introduction to it may have lasting consequences.

11. Epstein, *Agency of Fear,* 84.

12. *BNDD Bulletin,* September–October, 1970; quoted in Scott and Marshall, *Cocaine Politics,* 26.

13. Warren Hinckle and William Turner, *Deadly Secrets: The CIA-Mafia War against Castro and the Assassination of JFK* (New York: Thunder's Mouth Press, 1992), 373.

14. Scott and Marshall, *Cocaine Politics,* 26.

15. When Juan Restoy, one of those arrested, "subsequently broke out of jail and was killed in a shoot-out, Little Havana [in Miami] buzzed with a rumor that he had been set up and executed by a CIA execution squad to prevent his testifying about agency involvement in the narcotics traffic" (Hinckle and Turner, *Deadly Secrets,* 373).

16. Len Colodny and Tom Schachtman, *The Forty Years' War: The Rise and Fall of the Neocons, from Nixon to Obama* (New York: Harper, 2009), 20.

17. *New York Times,* February 1, 1970; Peter Dale Scott, Paul L. Hoch, and Russell Stetler, *The Assassinations: Dallas and Beyond* (New York: Random House/Vintage, 1976), 371.

18. Alfred W. McCoy, *The Politics of Heroin* (Chicago: Lawrence Hill Books/Chicago Review Press, 2003), 341, citing *Washington Post,* August 6, 1971.

19. Epstein, *Agency of Fear,* 86–87. At the time, Epstein pointed out, the CIA estimated that Turkey produced only from 3 to 8 percent of the world's illicit opium, However, "Turkey was assumed to be the most convenient and proximate source for the European heroin wholesalers."

20. Epstein, *Agency of Fear*, 86.

21. Epstein, *Agency of Fear*, 87.

22. Valentine, *The Strength of the Packt*, 45, summarizing Ludlum's reading from his own notes of an "implementation" meeting on November 3, 1969.

23. Drugs in Lebanon were channeled largely through the Casino de Liban, where Marcel Paul Francisci was the gambling concessionaire. The casino was controlled by Yousef Beidas through the Bank Intra, which the criminal financier Robert Vesco tried but failed to take over after the death of its owner Yousef Beidas (Arthur Herzog, *Vesco: From Wall Street to Castro's Cuba* [New York: Doubleday, 1987], 150). No one has ever satisfactorily explained Vesco's mysterious connections to Nixon, his nephew Don Nixon, Nixon's aide Richard Allen, Attorney General John Mitchell, and the CIA. See, e.g., James Rosen, *The Strong Man: John Mitchell and the Secrets of Watergate* (New York: Doubleday, 2008), 228.

24. McCoy, *The Politics of Heroin*, 381.

25. Jussi Hanhimäki, *The Flawed Architect: Henry Kissinger and American Foreign Policy* (Oxford: Oxford University Press, 2004), 90; *Time*, March 9, 1970.

26. Valentine, *The Strength of the Pack*, 53.

27. Valentine, *The Strength of the Pack*, 88.

28. Epstein, *Agency of Fear*, 92, cf. 310–11. Cf. also Valentine, *The Strength of the Pack*, 46, quoting James Ludlum: Turkish "enforcement was weak, and the whole Turkish program eventually failed." This foreseeable failure raises the possibility that the $35 million was at least partly with some other goal in mind. Kissinger was simultaneously working out a deal to use Turkey as a third party to evade congressional prohibitions on aid to Pakistan (Hanhimäki, *The Flawed Architect*, 181). Negotiations with the Turks began in 1970, at a time of political chaos in Turkey resembling that in Paris two years earlier. In this crisis the CIA station chief was Duane ("Dewey") Clarridge, who worked closely with Counter-Guerrilla (the Turkish version of Gladio), and through Counter-Guerrilla, Martin Lee has associated Clarridge with the "armed bands of Grey Wolves [who] unleashed a wave of bombings and political assassinations that culminated in a coup in [March 1971].... At the same time, members of the Grey Wolves were immersed in the international drug trade" (Martin A. Lee, *The Beast Reawakens* [Boston: Little, Brown, 1997], 202). Years later Turkish Defense Minister Hasan Esat Isik "harshly criticized the subversion of Turkish sovereignty through the U.S.-sponsored Counter-Guerrilla: 'The idea came from the United States. The financing as well'" (Daniele Ganser, *NATO's Secret Armies: Operation Gladio and Terrorism in Western Europe* [London: Frank Cass, 2005], 233).

29. One of Liddy's assistants on heroin matters, Gordon Minnick, toured the Golden Triangle and came back (according to Howard Hunt) "with a report that the White House found very disturbing" (E. Howard Hunt deposition, House Select Committee on Assassinations, November 3, 1978, RIF#180–10131–10342, http://www.aarclibrary.org/publib/jfk/hsca/secclass/pdf/Hunt_11-3-78.pdf, 35).

30. McCoy, *The Politics of Heroin*, 284–85, citing interview with BNDD agent, November 18, 1971.

31. *New York Times*, June 6, 1971; McCoy, *The Politics of Heroin*, 288.

32. *New York Times*, July 8, 1971.

33. For the case of Puttaporn Khramkhruan, see Valentine, *The Strength of the Pack*, 254–56; David Corn, *Blond Ghost: Ted Shackley and the CIA's Crusades* (New York: Simon and Schuster, 1994), 300.

34. McCoy, *The Politics of Heroin*, 410–14.

35. Egil Krogh, the White House liaison with the BNDD, later went to jail for his role in overseeing the break-in by the so-called White House Plumbers into the office of Daniel Ellsberg's

psychiatrist. Krogh is described by Len Colodny as "a lawyer with a CIA background.... Krogh ... had worked for Ehrlichman's firm in Seattle before joining the White House, but he had previously been involved with the CIA in Vietnam. Krogh bragged to Ehrlichman that he had hand-carried gold for the CIA to Vietnam. Ehrlichman and Haldeman later came to believe that Krogh maintained ties to the Agency even during his time at the White House. Neither allegation was ever proven" (Colodny and Schachtman, *The Forty* Years' *War,* 101, 113).

36. Jeremy Kuzmarov, "From Counter-Insurgency to Narco Insurgency: Vietnam and the International War on Drugs," *Journal of Policy History* 20, no. 3 (2008): 358–59, citing many sources, including *Southeast Asian Narcotics,* Hearings before the Select Committee on Narcotics Abuse and Control, House of Representatives, 95th Cong., 1st sess., July 12–13, 1977 (Washington, DC: Government Printing Office, 1978), 2–3. See also Surachert Bamrungsuk, *U.S. Foreign Policy and Thai Military Rule, 1947–1977* (Bangkok: Editions Duangkamol, 1988).

37. I have read but have not been able to verify that often the tribes selected for this treatment were those not paying off the Thai police and BPP.

38. Jim Glassman, *Thailand at the Margins: Internationalization of the State and the Transformation of Labour* (New York: Oxford University Press, 2004), 67–68: "Red Gaur groups were controlled by General Withoon Yasawat, a former leader of CIA-hired Thai mercenary forces in Laos, and General Chatchai Choonhavan, son of Phin, brother-in-law of Phao, and later Prime Minister."

39. William Shawcross, "How Tyranny Returned to Thailand" *New York Review of Books,* December 9, 1976.

40. Chris Baker and Phasut Phongphaichit, *A History of Thailand* (Cambridge: Cambridge University Press, 2005), 194–95; cf. Handley, *The King Never Smiles*, 235–36: "After a free-fire order was issued by the Bangkok police chief, the campus was stormed like an enemy army's redoubt, with the ... BPP troops in front." This propaganda campaign built on earlier false reports in 1975, when Colby was still CIA chief (Handley, *The King Never Smiles*, 226). Still earlier, in the 1950s, "the CIA and the U.S. Information Service [were] manufacturing fake communist tracts in Thai that attacked the monarchy" (Handley, *The King Never Smiles,* 124).

41. Robert Harris, *Political Corruption in and beyond the Nation State* (London: Routledge, 2003), 181.

42. "The Murky Events of October 1973: A Book Proposal Reopens Thailand's wounds," *AsiaWeek,* February 3, 2000; http://www.asiaweek.com/asiaweek/magazine/2000/0128/as.thai.historyI. html). See also Benedict Anderson, "Withdrawal Symptoms," *Bulletin of Concerned Asian Scholars* 9, no. 3 (1977), in Benedict Anderson, *The Spectre of Comparisons* (London: Verso, 1998), 139–73.

43. Handley, *The King Never Smiles*, 229.

44. Handley, *The King Never Smiles,* 226. Cf. Shawcross, "How Tyranny Returned to Thailand": "When the Thai foreign minister visited Hanoi in August [1976] the army disrupted his visit by provoking simultaneous attacks upon thousands of Thailand's Vietnamese residents."

45. K. J. Clymer, *The United States and Cambodia* (London: Routledge, 2004), 22.

46. Peter Dale Scott, *Drugs, Oil, and War: The United States in Afghanistan, Colombia, and Indochina* (Lanham, MD: Rowman & Littlefield, 2003), 174, 182–83, citing, inter alia, Wilfred Burchett, *The Second Indochina War: Cambodia and Laos* (New York: International Publishers, 1970), 65.

47. See Peter Dale Scott, "Drugs and Oil: The Deep Politics of US Asian Wars," in *War and State Terrorism: The United States, Japan, and the Asia-Pacific in the Long Twentieth Century,* ed. Mark Selden and Alvin Y. So (Lanham, MD: Rowman & Littlefield, 2003), 171–98.

48. Michael Leifer, *Dictionary of the Modern Politics of Southeast Asia* (London: Routledge, 1995), 94: "With the onset of the Cambodian conflict [in 1979], the Thai Communists were driven out of sanctuaries in Laos and their cause was sacrificed by China to the need to align with Thailand to challenge Vietnam's occupation of Cambodia. From that juncture, the Thai Communist

movement began to collapse until it had ceased to exist as a viable entity by the end of the Cold War." Cf. Baker, *A History of Thailand*, 216–20.

49. Bertil Lintner, "Heroin and Highland Insurgency in the Golden Triangle," in *War on Drugs: Studies in the Failure of US. Narcotics Policy*, ed. Alfred W. McCoy and Alan A. Block (Boulder, CO: Westview Press, 1992), 296. Cf. Bertil Lintner, *Burma in Revolt: Opium and Insurgency since 1948* (Chiang Mai: Silkworm Books, 1999), 278. McCoy, relying on USG data, disagrees tacitly with Lintner and claims that while Nelson Gross's statement "was pure media hyperbole, Lo [Hsing-han] had in fact become the largest single opium merchant in the Shan states" (McCoy, *The Politics of Heroin*, 424). But Adrian Cowell, a British filmmaker who spent time first with Lo Hsing Han and later with Khun Sa, agrees with Lintner that Lo Hsing Han "was by no means one of the biggest sort of merchants in the business" (Adrian Cowell, *Frontline*, 1977, PBS, http://www.pbs.org/wgbh/pages/frontline/shows/heroin/interviews/cowell.html).

50. Valentine, *The Strength of the Pack*, 173–74.

51. Lintner, *Burma in Revolt*, 279–81; cf. Cowell, *Frontline*.

52. *San Francisco Chronicle*, July 20, 1973, 18.

53. Epstein, *Agency of Fear*, 161; James Mills, *The Underground Empire: Where Crime and Government Embrace* (New York: Dell, 1986), 777 (two-thirds). Cf. *Foreign Relations of the United States, 1969–1976* (hereinafter *FRUS*) (Washington, DC: Government Printing Office), vol. 20, 328–30, Memorandum of February 29, 1972, from the Executive Secretary of the Department of State (Eliot) to the President's Assistant for National Security Affairs (Kissinger). Egil Krogh, chairman of the White House Committee on International Narcotics Control, also traveled to the Far East and bought out heroin labs in the Golden Triangle (Epstein, *Agency of Fear*, 237; Russ Baker, *Family of Secrets: The Bush Dynasty, the Powerful Forces That Put It in the White House, and What Their Influence Means for America* [New York: Bloomsbury Press, 2009], 225–26).

54. Valentine, *The Strength of the Pack*, 172–73. There is partially declassified discussion of the proposal in *FRUS, 1969–1976*, vol. 20, 286, 297–98.

55. Valentine, *The Strength of the Pack*, 174, citing correspondence with Fred Dick.

56. Valentine, *The Strength of the Pack*, 174; cf. 399; Lintner, *Burma in Revolt*, 179.

57. Valentine, *The Strength of the Pack*, 172.

58. Lintner, *Burma in Revolt*, 313–14. James Mills hoped to fly up from Chiang Mai in a Thai helicopter to meet Khun Sa, but the project was eventually vetoed not by Khun Sa but by the DEA regional director in Chiang Mai (Mills, *The Underground Empire*, 778–79, 786–88).

59. Mills, *The Underground Empire*, 787. One of Khun Sa's many Western interviewers, Edith Mirante, wrote later that "Khun Sa was widely known to spend time in Chiang Mai and even occasionally visit his wife in Bangkok, but he was coyly going along with the Thai fiction that he was a wanted man with a price on his head" (Edith T. Mirante, *Burmese Looking Glass: A Human Rights Adventure and a Jungle Revolution* [New York: Grove Press, 1993], 170).

60. Francis Belanger, *Drugs, the U.S., and Khun Sa* (Bangkok: Editions Duang Kamol, 1989, 102–4); cf. Mills, *Underground Empire*, 1071–72; Lintner, *Burma in Revolt*, 321–23; McCoy, *The Politics of Heroin*, 418–21. Before the attack, Khun Sa "initiated terrorist missions against American officials in northern Thailand. Following Khun Sa's directives, two CIA agents were killed, a move that proved to be a big mistake. Families of U.S. officials were evacuated from the northern provinces to Bangkok for their protection, and the war against Khun Sa was stepped up dramatically.... In a few weeks [after the attack], things were back to normal for Khun Sa. When interrupted to ask why he had ordered the killings of Westerners, he replied, "Because they turned on me," he shouted. "At one time, they were my partners—them, the DEA and the CIA, both" (Belanger, *Drugs, the U.S., and Khun Sa*, 102–4).

61. James Gritz, *A Nation Betrayed* (Boulder City, NV: Lazarus, 1989), 86, quoted in Lintner, *Burma in Revolt*, 379. (Route 1285 can be seen on Google Maps.) Gritz's detailed account is erratic and unreliable, but Lintner, who was present at the time on the Thai side of the border, assures me that his overall picture is accurate. Cf. Belanger, *Drugs, the U.S., and Khun Sa*, 108–9: "The road, capable of accommodating 10-ton trucks, was ironically built by the Thai Government with manpower, time, and materials financed by U.S. taxpayers' money allocated to drug suppression funds."

62. Khun Sa fared far better in Burma after 1982, when he ceased to be subordinate to the KMT generals and began to dominate the market himself.

63. Lintner, *Burma in Revolt*, 392.

64. Alfred W. McCoy, "Lord of Druglords: One Life as Lesson for US Drug Policy," *Crime, Law, and Social Change*, November 1998, 309.

65. Lintner, *Burma in Revolt*, 392.

66. Mirante, *Burmese Looking Class*, 147: "I suspected that Ne Win wouldn't mind if it killed more than poppies in the hills of the Shan Stated". A professor told Mirante that an environmental impact assessment was done before the program started. "It made clear that spraying in Burma would be environmentally risky and of dubious effectiveness. State buried the report and went ahead with the program anyway.... The U.S. ambassador to Burma, O'Donohue, told our conference that the spraying program was the greatest success in recent U.S.-Burma relations" (148). Cf. *Mother Jones Magazine*, February–March 1989, 41.

67. Shelby Tucker, *Among Insurgents: Walking through Burma* (London: Radcliffe, 2000), 93. For similar reports on the DEA's use of 2,4-D against the FARC (Revolutionary Armed Forces of Colombia) in Colombia, see David Weir and Mark Schapiro, *Circle of Poison: Pesticides and People in a Hungry World* (San Francisco: Institute for Food and Development Policy, 1981).

68. McCoy, "Lord of Druglords," 454–55; Lintner, *Burma in Revolt*, 278, 380–81, 377–78.

69. Valentine, *The Strength of the Pack*, 70; cf. McCoy, *The Politics of Heroin*, 234.

70. Mills, *Underground Empire*, 201–3, 222 (quoting from internal DEA report on termination of Operation Durian); McCoy, *The Politics of Heroin*, 431. Poonsiri's main Bangkok purchaser, Lu Hsu-Shui, had established himself by trading opium for gold with the KMT in northern Thailand (Lintner, *Burma in Revolt*, 307). In San Francisco, Lu Hsu-shui and two of his sons paid one and a half million dollars for the Shaw Hotel, today the Renoir Hotel (Mills, *Underground Empire*, 214).

71. Christopher Lehmann-Haupt, *New York Times*, June 16, 1986.

72. Mills, *Underground Empire*, 1076–78.

73. Keith Quincy, *Hmong: History of a People* (Cheney: Eastern Washington University Press, 1995), 163.

74. Peter Dale Scott, *The Road to 9/11: Wealth, Empire, and the Future of America* (Berkeley: University of California Press, 2007), 73–75, citing Christina Lamb, *Waiting for Allah: Pakistan's Struggle for Democracy* (London: H. Hamilton, 1991), 222; cf. McCoy, *The Politics of Heroin*, 479. Fazle Haq was the governor of Pakistan's North-West Frontier Province; at the same time he was also an important CIA contact and supporter of the Afghan mujahideen, some of whom—it was no secret—were supporting themselves by major opium and heroin trafficking through the province. However, after lengthy correspondence with Fazle Haq's son, I am persuaded that there are no known grounds to accuse Fazle Haq of having profited personally from the drug traffic. See "Clarification from Peter Dale Scott re Fazle Haq," 911Truth.org, http://www.911truth.org/article.php?story=20090223165146219.

75. Scott, *The Road to 9/11*, 73–75, citing McCoy, *The Politics of Heroin*, 475 (leading drug lords), 464 (60 percent).

76. McCoy, *The Politics of Heroin*, 461; citing interview with Dr. David Musto.

77. McCoy, *The Politics of Heroin*, 462.

78. Thomas Fuller, "No Blowing Smoke: Poppies Fade in Southeast Asia," *New York Times*, September 16, 2007. Cf. United Nations Office on Drugs and Crime, "Opium Poppy Cultivation in Southeast Asia: Lao PDR, Myanmar and Thailand," 2009, 3: "Opium poppy cultivation in Lao PDR, Myanmar and Thailand combined has decreased from an estimated 157,900 hectares in 1998, the year of the United Nations General Assembly Special Session on Drugs, to only 29,400 hectares in 2007. Despite a 22% increase in 2007, this corresponds to an 81% overall reduction in only nine years."

79. "Figure 2: Global Opium Poppy Cultivation (Hectares), 1990–2007," United Nations Office on Drugs and Crime, "Opium Poppy Cultivation in Southeast Asia: Lao PDR, Myanmar and Thailand," 4. Just over 250,000 hectares of opium were planted in 1990 and just under that figure in 2007. The biggest divergence from that level was in 2001, the year that the Taliban successfully banned opium production in their area of Afghanistan. Total opium production for that one year dropped to about half the average.

80. Catherine Lamour and Michel R. Lamberti, *The International Connection: Opium from Growers to Pushers* (New York: Pantheon, 1974), 190–92.

81. Peter Truell and Larry Gurwin, *False Profits: The Inside Story of BCCI, the World's Most Corrupt Financial Empire* (Boston: Houghton Mifflin, 1992), 94–95.

82. William J. Chambliss, *On the Take: From Petty Crooks to Presidents* (Bloomington: Indiana University Press, 1988), 153.

83. McCoy, *The Politics of Heroin*, 253.

84. Cynics have wondered whether Nixon's initial overlooking of Asian drugs can be related to the funds raised for his election campaign in Asia by the previously mentioned "Committee of United States Citizens in Asia for Nixon," headed by Chennault's widow Anna Chan Chennault, for which see Renata Adler, *Canaries in the Mineshaft: Essays on Politics and Media* (New York: St. Martin's Press, 2001), 65–68.

85. McCoy, *The Politics of Heroin*, 457, emphasis added.

86. McCoy has since made this point forcefully in an interview with an Australian journal, *The Sun*: "Suddenly, as the French connection dried up, we began getting large shipments of heroin from Southeast Asia in the United States. The Vietnam War was over, the last of the GIs were gone, and Southeast Asia's producers had a surplus capacity, so they began flooding the US with heroin. So Nixon fought and won another battle in his drug war. He sent thirty DEA agents to Bangkok, where they had special relations with the Thai police, and did a very effective job of seizing heroin bound for the United States, imposing a kind of informal customs duty on heroin exports to America. So, the Southeast Asian traffickers turned around and exported to Europe, which had been virtually drug free for decades. The French syndicates had entered into something of an agreement with the government: they could manufacture heroin, but they could not sell in France and had to export it. With the French Connection out of the picture, the Southeast Asian syndicates flooded Europe with heroin. By the end of the 1970s, Europe had more heroin addicts than the United States. The syndicates also introduced significant heroin addiction to Australia" ("Tricks of the Trade: Alfred McCoy on How the CIA Got Involved in Global Drug Trafficking," *The Sun*, May, 2003, http://www.derrickjensen.org/mccoy.html).

87. Cf. my remarks about *Newsday's The Heroin Trail* in "Foreword," in Henrik Krüger, trans. Jerry Meldon, *The Great Heroin Coup—Drugs, Intelligence, and International Fascism* (Boston: South End Press, 1980), 4.

88. Valentine, *The Strength of the Pack*, 55.

89. Scott, "Foreword," 3, summarizing Krüger, *The Great Heroin Coup,* 117–29.

90. Scott, "Foreword," 4.

91. Alexander Werth, *De Gaulle: A Political Biography* (New York: Simon and Schuster, 1966), 400.

92. *Time,* December 29, 1975; Krüger, *The Great Heroin Coup,* 4–5, 59–71.

93. McCoy, *The Politics of Heroin,* 457, emphasis added.

94. Alfred W. McCoy, *The Politics of Heroin in Southeast Asia* (New York: Harper & Row, 1972), 244.

95. McCoy, *The Politics of Heroin* (2003), 393. McCoy has explained to me that the original paragraph was dropped to make space for the new material in his 2003 edition.

96. Valentine, *The Strength of the Pack,* 53: Cusack "produced statistics showing that Turkish opium was the raw material for 80 percent of the heroin emanating from … Marseille." Cf. Douglas Valentine, *The Strength of the Wolf: The Secret History of America's War on Drugs* (London: Verso, 2004), 468.

97. Valentine, *The Strength of the Wolf,* 370. Cf. Krüger, *The Great Heroin Coup,* 4–5, 59–74. Krüger is not aware of any link between Cusack and Ben Barka's murder. However, he points to other misleading statistics of which Cusack was the author. Cusack's false report that America's addict population had dropped by 200,000, when it had in fact *risen,* is dismissed by Krüger as a "giant cover-up [which] hid the fact that Nixon's heroin war was no more than window-dressing" (Krüger, *The Great Heroin Coup,* 171–73).

98. Scott and Marshall, *Cocaine Politics,* 4.

99. Scott, *Drugs, Oil and War,* 50; cf. Scott, *The Road to 9/11,* 73–75.

chapter seven

BANKING ON DICTATORSHIP

by James S. Henry

TRACKING GENERAL STROESSNER'S LOOT

In 1989, I received a call from a friend who'd been involved in the search for Marcos's assets. General Alfredo Stroessner, Paraguay's long-time dictator, had just been overthrown, and its new attorney general was in New York City looking for help. My research assistant and I agreed to meet with him. We explained that "dictator treasure hunts" usually took years, and they often only recovered a small fraction of the loot. We also explained that unless Stroessner had left behind lots of personal banking records, the search would be almost impossible. But the attorney general was determined, partly because he wanted to expose the regime's numerous crimes.

It turned out that either General Stroessner had really been very careful, or the new government wasn't sharing all its information with us. But after my assistant spent a few weeks in Asunción, we stumbled on an approach to the investigation that yielded surprising new evidence on where Latin America's longest-standing military dictator had done all his private banking...

One of the global debt crisis's few redeeming features is that it helped to rid the world of some noxious dictatorships. In some cases, like Iran, the successor regimes offered little improvement. But in other cases, human rights violations and corruption declined. At least the notion that unelected technocrats who have unfettered discretion will do a better job with economic policy has finally been discredited. General Alfredo Stroessner's regime was one of those that crumbled. The son of a Munich brewmaster and an officer in Paraguay's artillery unit, he seized power in 1954 at the age of forty-two. With the help of rigged ballots, censorship, a vigilant secret police, and graft, he and his party—the Colorados—proceeded to win the next eight elections with more than ninety percent of the vote. By February 1989, Stroessner had become the world's oldest dictator, well ahead of Indonesia's Suharto and Zaire's president-for-life Mobuto.

Stroessner's longevity was certainly not due to his tolerance and generosity. His opponents faced long prison terms, exile, torture, and death. Paraguay also became a sanctuary for all sorts of right-wing criminals on the lam, including Dr. Josef Mengele, the Auschwitz doctor who holed up there for twenty years and could often be found drinking beer with *"die Alte Kamaraden"* in Asunción's German bars; former Gestapo agents Auguste Ricord and Christian David of "French Connection" fame, who made Paraguay a key transit point for heroin; and convicted murderers of General Pinochet's opponents in Chile.[1] Despite such unsavory guests, by all the standards of the dictator's handbook—stability and enrichment, if not geographic expansion—Stroessner was a huge success. Before his regime Paraguay had had 22 Presidents in 27 years. Surrounded by Brazil, Argentina, and Bolivia, with only 3.9 million people to defend its rich cattle, cotton, and soybean farms, it was constantly at war, one of which in the 1870s had cost it four-fifths of its male population. Stroessner's internally-focused brand of fascism brought the country stability, peace and new sources of illicit income, while his German-trained secret police kept the opposition divided and voiceless. He struck profitable deals with his neighbors, including two hydroelectric projects that greatly enriched his own family as well as many Brazilian and Argentine officials. He also made himself useful to his fellow fascist regimes in Brazil, Chile, Argentina, and Bolivia, in projects like Condor. And until the very end, Stroessner was also a master at distributing the fruits of power widely enough to tranquilize potential rivals.

For example, General Andres Rodriguez, a key supporter of the 1954 coup and commander of Paraguay's US-trained First Army Corps, was permitted to acquire Cambio Guarani, Paraguay's largest exchange house; TAGSA, an air taxi service; the Aeroclub of Paraguay, which owned a valuable airstrip near Asunción; several cattle farms; and an immense white-and-yellow mansion that was built as a miniature version of Versailles. His daughter Marta married one of Stroessner's two sons.[2] Asked how he got so rich on a meager army salary of four hundred dollars per week, Rodriguez's answer was simple: "I gave up smoking."[3] In 1976, he was reported to have facilitated drug exports to the US, and in 1984, his chief of staff (and the future police chief) was accused of importing large quantities of chemicals needed to make cocaine.[4]

Under Stroessner's long reign, a growing share of the economy disappeared off the books. Paraguay never quite became the international banking haven that Panama did—it lacked Panama's central location and strong US relationship, which was rooted in the Panama Canal. But Paraguay did master most of Panama's other black arts. Officially its exports in the 1980s and 1990s averaged just $500–800 million a year and consisted mainly of cotton and soy; in fact, they averaged more than $1.5–2 billion, and consisted mainly of contraband: electronics, whiskey, soy, sugar, coffee, gold, perfume, and drugs. A huge market also developed for fraudulent passports, illicit arms, and stolen goods—Brazil's car thieves supplied half of Paraguay's eighty-five thousand cars.[5]

With the help of this invisible economy, up until the Latin American debt crisis in the early 1980s, Paraguay's legitimate economy performed rather well. Incomes grew at an average rate of 1.4 percent from 1955 to 1972 and then accelerated to 3 percent until 1982. The growth spurt took place mainly because of the $20 billion Itaipu Dam. General Stroessner became very close to the project's organizers, especially Brazil's Jose Costa Cavalcanti, the director general of Itaipu Binacional. Brazil loaned Paraguay $400 million and channeled hundreds of millions more to Paraguayan engineering, insurance, and construction companies, including several owned by General Stroessner himself.[6]

Costa Cavalcanti is hard to forget for another reason. In 1982, Chase's International Private Banking department in New York mistakenly mailed several of his bank account statements to the wrong address in Brazil. The recipient happened to be a member of the opposition PMDB Party. In 1986, the statements came into the hands of Dilson Funaro, Jose Sarney's assertive second finance minister, and eventually to me. The statements show that Costa Cavalcanti's Chase accounts contained no less than $138 million—quite a hefty sum for a former general and lifelong public utility executive.[7]

In any case, despite its vibrant underground economy, Paraguay's growth slowed considerably after 1982. Spending on Itaipu and Argentina's massive Yacyreta-Apipe Dam peaked, there were several bad harvests, and the global debt crisis crimped Paraguay's trading partners. The country also started to feel the burden of its own $2.4 billion debt. Much of this had disappeared into poorly conceived projects, like a $500 million French cement plant that failed to work.[8] About $1 billion was owed to Bank of Boston, Citibank, Chase, Lloyds, American Express Bank, Bank of America, and BNP. Another $400 million was owed to Brazil, $416 million to the World Bank, and $400 million to the IDB.[9] By 1984, Paraguay had contracted a serious capital flight problem: its foreign assets came to be worth more than half its debt.

All these problems, plus Stroessner's age and illness, eroded his political base. In the late 1980s, a succession battle erupted between General Rodriguez's traditionalists, who favored a greater role for the Colorado Party, and the "militants" led by Stroessner's oldest son Gustavo, who favored a nepotistic solution to succession. Their rivalry broke out into the open at a contentious party convention in August 1987. In late 1988, the traditionalists were propelled into action by a destabilizing series of events. Stroessner entered the hospital and appeared to be sinking fast. At that point, he appointed Gustavo, who had no piloting experience, as Air Force colonel, and the militants pressured General Rodriguez to cut the defense budget and retire more senior officers. In February 1989, General Rodriguez and the First Army launched an attack on the palace that took 250 lives and forced the Stroessner family dynasty into exile to Brasilia, where Costa Cavalcanti made everyone feel at home.[10]

The long-suffering Paraguayan opposition received the news with mixed feelings. They recalled that an earlier General Rodriguez had seized power in 1814, sealed the country off, and ruled by decree for twenty-six years. But to everyone's surprise, the new General Rodriguez made pro-democratic moves. He freed political prisoners (except those just arrested), ended censorship, invited all exiles home, and announced new elections in May. He also promised to recover Stroessner's foreign assets to "pay the external debt with this fortune."[11] The opposition had little choice but to go along, and the elections took place too soon for them to put up much of a fight. Three months later, Rodriguez won the presidency with sixty-eight percent of the vote, becoming Paraguay's first freely elected president in fifty years, notwithstanding his status as a Class-I drug dealer.[12]

For our purposes, the most interesting thing about all these events is that they opened up a rare window on the private banking behavior of Latin America's oldest dictatorship. The paper trail to Stroessner's assets was thin, but he left one important set of clues: records of all international telephone calls he and other militants made the year before they were exiled. These records aren't absolutely conclusive; we don't know what transpired during the calls. But they do show the overall pattern of the dictator's foreign banking and other foreign relationships. They also challenge the conventional wisdom about where General Stroessner did his banking.

Most observers had assumed it was Switzerland or Austria, given his German origins and his occasional public conflicts with the US. But these phone data reveal that his bankers were in fact employed by Paraguay's largest US "creditors"—a striking example of the debt-flight cycle in action.

In the year before the 1989 coup, the records show that Gustavo Stroessner placed numerous calls to Citibank International Private Banking's Miami office, specifically to the account officer in charge of Paraguayan clients. He also called the private banking departments of Banco Exterior, Riggs National, Bank of Boston, Credit Suisse, Florida governor Jeb Bush's Private Bank and Trust Company in Miami, SBC, Republic National, Hong Kong and Shanghai Bank in New York, and Arias, Fabrica, and Fabrica—Panama's leading law firm. Other members of Stroessner's inner circle made similar contacts. Cesar Romeo Costa, Paraguay's Central Bank president, apparently made numerous calls to the banker handling Paraguayan clients at American Express Bank's International Private Banking Group in New York. Manuel Gonzalez Llamas, the husband of Graciela Stroessner (the General's daughter) and a leading shareholder in Gustavo's Bancopar, placed many calls to the Miami offices of Citibank's International Private Banking Group and Credit Suisse. Jose Alberto Planas was Gustavo's former schoolmate and an investor in his Alfa Beta Construction Company. He placed calls to the New York office of Chase's International Private Banking in New York and the Miami offices of Lloyd Bank's International Private Banking, Credit Suisse, and Total Bank. Juan Enrique Nogues, the son of Stroessner's former personal secretary and an investor with Gustavo in Vipar S.A., which operated gambling casinos, placed calls to Miami's Florida National Bank. Mario Abdo Benitez, the General's personal secretary and the owner of CIE, which bought Itaipu's turbines, made calls to Bank of Boston, Lloyds, Sudameris, and Chase. He later admitted to having accounts at all of them. Delfin Ugarte Centurion, Stroessner's minister of industry, placed calls to Lloyds and Citibank and admitted to having accounts there. He was also apparently a client of Arias, Fabrica, and Fabrica.

The phone data also reveals interesting patterns in Paraguay's overall haven banking relationships. The following table, based on data obtained from Paraguay's attorney general, summarizes the destinations of 2,753 calls by seven of Stroessner's closest cronies during the year before the 1989 coup:

Table 7.1

DESTINATION	# OF CALLS	% OF TOTAL
Florida	805	29%
No. Virginia	287	10%
New York	80	3%
Wash. D.C.	67	2.5%
Missouri	52	2%
Pennsylvania	43	2%
Texas	42	2%
New Jersey	38	2%
Other US	197	7%
(Total US):	1661	61%
Switzerland	434	16%
U.K.	190	7%
Spain	155	6%
France	85	3%
W. Germany	82	3%
Other non US	146	5%
(Total Non US):	1092	39%
Grand Total	2753	100%

Overall, this evidence provides clear support for the hypothesis that the US—Miami in particular—was the Stroessner clique's main banking haven and trading post. We also note the unusually large number of calls placed to northern Virginia, a place not usually regarded as an international banking center. Was that just another kind of haven relationship?

CHILE'S "MIRACLE"

I remember the Chilean coup of September 1973 very clearly. I was attending a graduate economics course at Harvard taught by a protégé of Professor Milton Friedman. One of my fellow students, Sebastian Pinera, a member of one of Chile's oldest families and the future owner of the airline LanChile, got word halfway through the class that Allende had been ousted. He was ecstatic—"We won!" he cheered. The professor shared in his delight. Like many other US economists, he saw the overthrow as a victory for the neoliberal doctrines preached by leading University of Chicago economists like Friedman and Arnold Harberger, who both later consulted directly for Pinochet's junta. Over the next twenty years, "Los Chicago Boys" came to exert a strong influence on Chilean economic policy. The label was a little unfair to Chicago—there were also many Ivy League disciples of hard-shell free market doctrines. Dr. Jose Pinera, my classmate's brother, was also Harvard trained. He later became one of the main architects of Pinochet's labor policies, which banned strikes, closed union shops, privatized pension funds, and sharply cut real wages, jobs, and unemployment benefits. In hindsight, Pinochet conducted the first in a series of experiments by the New Right that culminated in the neoliberal programs of Margaret Thatcher, Ronald Reagan, and a lengthy list of Third World imitators. In First World democracies, their programs were moderated somewhat by the need for popular support. In countries like Chile, Mexico, and Argentina, however, where the lines between rich and poor were starker and the political systems were rigged, much less time was wasted on democratic niceties. To their credit, a few principled conservatives were bothered by the resulting alliance between dictatorship and liberal economic reform. But many others got lost in bogus distinctions between "authoritarian" and "totalitarian" regimes. In Chile's case, the resulting repression produced more than four thousand disappearances and extrajudicial killings, thousands of secret arrests and tortures, and sixteen long years without free elections, in a country that had previously been one of Latin America's most democratic countries. As Herr Friedman reportedly told General Pinochet at a Santiago audience in 1975, "When you cut the tail off a dog you don't cut it off inch by inch. You cut it off at the root."

But these points are very general, and repression is very concrete. I remember a 1974 lecture by Chilean economist Orlando Letelier, who was killed in 1976 by a car bomb planted by the DINA, Pinochet's secret police, in Washington D.C. And I remember Victor Jara, a talented Chilean folk singer and guitarist whose music I greatly admired. When the junta seized power, he was arrested and transported to a soccer stadium in Santiago where "political" prisoners were held. The police took him out in front of the crowd and they cut off his hands....

The overthrow of Salvador Allende's elected Popular Unity government in September 1973 was greeted with jubilation by Chile's propertied classes. He'd been elected with a thirty-six percent plurality in 1970, and the Popular Unity coalition's support increased to forty-four percent in the March 1973 congressional elections. But the elite was eager for a change by any means. From 1968 to 1973, at first under Christian Democrat Eduardo Frei Montalva and then Salvador Allende, government spending as a share of GNP had increased from fifteen to forty percent. A third of large farms and many private companies had been nationalized at low prices. There was seven hundred percent inflation and frequent shortages of consumer goods, and Chile's foreign debt had reached the unprecedented level of $2.5 billion. Foreign investment dried up and flight capital was pouring into accounts at Bankers Trust, Chase, and JPMorgan—Chile's leading creditors.

The CIA, multinationals like ITT, and the US government certainly played a prominent role—with a hefty dose of financial chicanery—in the 1970–73 coup activity that followed. But intervention had not started there. According to former CIA agent Philip Agee, who had been stationed in Uruguay in the early 1960s, John M. Hennessy—chairman of Credit Suisse First Boston (CSFB) from 1989 to 1996—had been assistant manager at Citibank's Montevideo branch in 1964 and reportedly helped transfer substantial funding to the campaign of Eduardo Frei Montalva, who was running for president against Allende. Frei won the election and served as Chile's president from 1964 to 1970. In the early 1970s, Hennessy became assistant secretary of the treasury for international affairs in the Nixon adminstration, in charge of coordinating economic pressures against Allende's government.[13] In 1974, Hennessy returned to Wall Street, where he became managing director of First Boston Corp., which was later acquired by Credit Suisse.

Despite the CIA's involvement, the sufficient conditions for the 1973 coup against Allende were provided by a Franco-like alliance of military officers, the Catholic Church's hierarchy, the top ten percent of landowners and industrialists, and the next twenty percent in the income distribution—the middle class. Immediately after the coup, they began to get what they thought they wanted.

The junta turned to a small band of inexperienced but supremely self-righteous economists—Los Chicago Boys—who had been mentored by University of Chicago economist and future Nobel laureate Professor Milton Friedman and Professor Arnold Harberger. After Pinochet took power, there was actually a prolonged period when several different economic camps competed for the junta's favor. But Friedman and Harberger, dean of the University of Chicago's Economics Department, tipped the balance when they visited Chile in March 1975. Since the 1950s, with help from the Rockefeller and Ford Foundations, Harberger had developed a close relationship between the University of Chicago and Chile's Catholic University, where he had taught as a visiting professor. With support from the Rockefeller and Ford Foundations, scholarships were provided for bright young Chileans who wanted to study economics. Many of these Chicago-trained economists returned to Catholic University to teach, and they later served in Pinochet's government. Their trip was sponsored by Javier Vial—head of the business group BHC, one of Chile's largest conglomerates, and the eventual owner of Banco de Chile, the country's largest private bank at the time, and sixty other companies. He was also a very strong supporter of Pinochet's dictatorship, on personal terms with the General.[14] Friedman reportedly received $30,000 for the three-day trip. His wife Rose objected to the visit because Pinochet's hard right regime and the goose-stepping Chilean military reminded her of Nazi Germany. Professor Friedman tried to assuage her guilt by re-questing the release of two Jewish political prisoners in the custody of Pinochet's police. Unfortunately, the two Jewish prisoners were never located.

Just one month after the visit, in April 1975, the junta introduced an orthodox, monetarist "shock plan," along the lines that Friedman and Harberger had recom-mended. Professor Friedman's Chicago-trained protégé Sergio de Castro replaced Fernando Leniz as minister of the economy. Other key neoliberals on Pinochet's economic team included Pablo Baraona, president of the Central Bank, Alvaro Bardon and Jorge Cauas Lama at Treasury, Rolf Lüders as treasury minister and minister of the economy, and Juan Carlos Mendez as director of the budget.

This tiny band's shared vision of Chile's future was one that later became common among neoliberal Third World governments—a Latin version of a low-wage, export-oriented Asian tiger, with weak unions, low inflation, privatized pension funds, and a minimal state apart from the police, the military, and the national copper company, most of whose income went to the military. To pursue this anti-Marxist utopia, they started out with a sharp, recessionary shock. They banned strikes, abolished price controls for food and housing, and slashed tariffs from a hundred to ten percent in just two years.

The junta also introduced Latin America's most radical privatization program ever. In 1973–74, more than 250 nationalized companies were returned to their former owners, and 200 more were sold off at bargain prices. These were not the middle-class privatizations of France, Japan, or the UK, where the buyers included millions of small investors. Like other developing countries, Chile had a very thin capital market, and hard times had made it even thinner. The big buyers at this fire-sale were a handful of closely held groups like Javier Vial's and Cruzat-Larrain's, which owned most of the local banks and had very strong ties with foreign banks.[15]

All these changes set the stage for the dictatorship's 1977–81 phase, which was described at the time by *The Wall Street Journal*'s neoconservative editorial page—in even more glowing terms than it had reserved for the Argentine junta—as "the Chilean economic miracle." Indeed, during this brief period, when the economy was recovering from the sharp recession that Los Chicago Boys had engineered, growth averaged 5–8 percent a year. But what was perhaps most miraculous was the regime's inability to foresee that its economic policies—in addition to increasing poverty and inequality—were about to cave in on each other, completely bankrupting the country and forcing the nationalization of the entire private sector.

By 1977, the junta had wiped out any organized political opposition and achieved most of its early economic goals. But the neoliberal ideologues pushed it to new extremes. Under Dr. José Pinera's radical 1979 Plan Laboral, the government abolished closed shops for unions and tried to privatize everything from health care and pensions to education. The 1980–81 pension fund privatization substituted a "fully funded" system administered by privately managed pension funds owned by institutions like Citigroup and Aetna. They came to dominate the new, highly concentrated private system that replaced the old "pay-as-you-go" government system. But this pension reform was probably the most successful of the neoliberal reforms.[16] Others succeeded only in cutting social spending, while military spending and sacred cows like the nationalized copper company were spared. The copper company was famous because of the uproar it provoked when Allende seized it from Anaconda in 1971. But Pinochet kept it nationalized—a secret law gave the military ten percent of its profits. So even under the junta, Chile's largest enterprise and exporter remained "socialist."

In any case, the junta's most important neoliberal experiments—and worst mistakes—concerned macroeconomic policy. The point man was Dr. Sergio de Castro, a Los Chicago Boy who became Pinochet's second finance minister in 1979. Like Argentina's de Hoz, de Castro was a strict believer in the monetarist view that the best way to fight inflation in small economies like Chile was by eliminating tariffs, deregulating capital and trade, and maintaining a fixed exchange rate. So he fixed Chile's peso at thirty-nine to the dollar and held it there from July 1979 until June 1982. With copper prices in a slump and the size of the state sector shrinking, this was only possible because foreign banks were willing to lend money hand-over-fist to Chile's private sector. Foreign banks were sympathetic to Pinochet's conservative economists, much as they had been to Argentina's, and they were flush with cash and very competitive, given Chile's high real domestic interest rates.

So, just as in Argentina, many domestic borrowers took advantage of fixed exchange rates and the temporary generosity of foreign bankers to make lucrative back-to-back deals. Javier Vial, the sponsor of Friedman's 1975 visit and Chile's richest man by 1978, acquired control over Banco de Chile in the late 1970s and used it as a front to borrow heavily from foreign banks like Bankers Trust and Chase. When he was its president, Banco de Chile, in turn, reloaned the dollars to Vial's other private companies, including several based in Panama, like Banco Andino. All these shenanigans became public after Vial's empire cracked in 1983. In 1997, after a 14-year investigation, he was sentenced to 4.5 years in jail for bank fraud, and former Economy and Treasury Minister Rolf Lüders, who had owned ten percent of BHC, was sentenced to 4 years.[17] Chile was stuck with Vial's debts when the bank failed and had to be nationalized. All this was no surprise to his foreign bankers. One former Bankers Trust officer, who had personally handled Vial's Panama accounts, told me, "We knew he was lending to himself, but no one wanted to pull the plug."[18]

As a result of de Castro's policies, Chile's private foreign debt boomed during the "miracle" years. In 1981 alone, $6 billion in new credits was issued by foreign banks, mainly to leading domestic private banks like Banco de Chile, Banco de Santiago, Banco International, and Banco Colocadora, whose groups owned a huge equity stake in Chile's private sector. From 1980 to 1982, private foreign debt doubled; by 1982 the total foreign debt had approached $20 billion—two-thirds of it private. The Central Bank repeatedly warned that it was not responsible for the private debt, but it allowed the spree to continue. Given all the "cheap" dollars and low tariffs, imports also soared—luxury imports became Chile's equivalent of flight capital.

The whole situation finally began to unravel in May 1981 when Crav, a leading sugar company, failed. The real crunch came in the summer of 1982 when the Latin American debt panic dried up new loans, forcing Chile to devalue and tighten interest rates—a lethal combination. By January 1983, unemployment was thirty percent, and the six top private banks and the country's two largest private groups, Vial and Cruzat-Larrain, had folded.

At this point Finance Minister de Castro began to get intense pressure from foreign banks like Chase and Bankers Trust to "nationalize" the private foreign debt. For a while, he stuck to his free-market principles, reminding them of his earlier warnings that such a move would be no more justified than Allende's nationalizations and that this was, after all, private foreign debt, freely contracted, presumably with compensation for the risks of default built into the interest rates.

But the banks were not concerned with such abstract principles. In January 1983, they quietly cut off Chile's foreign trade credit lines, to the point where oil tankers en route to Santiago started to turn around and head home. De Castro was forced to resign, and his replacement quickly declared that the junta would assume responsibility for the private foreign debt (though not its offshore flight assets.) In the words of one Chilean banker, "Pinochet achieved what Allende only dreamed of—the complete socialization of our private sector."[19]

Nor was this the end of the story. When Pinochet's fourth finance minister, de Castro protégé Hernan Buchi, took office in 1985, he had to embark on yet another, even larger round of privatizations simply to rid the government of all the debt-ridden companies that had been acquired through forced nationalization. Subsequently, foreign bankers, the World Bank, Wall Street, and the IMF all gave Buchi and the Pinochet regime rave reviews for their brilliant privatization strategy, designed to attract foreign investment, boost savings, and downsize Chile's state. But they never acknowledged why his privatization program had been necessary and possible in the first place, because in 1983, neoliberal policies had produced a disaster, and the junta had been forced by its foreign creditors to take the fall for so many bad debts.

Finally, who were the main beneficiaries of Chile's latest round of privatizations? To avoid the insider-trading outrages that had characterized many of the 1970s privatizations and helped groups like Vial and Cruzat grow quickly, Buchi offered low-cost loans to workers and pension funds to help them buy stock. By 1988, worker-owned funds comprised fourteen percent of privatized shares, not a bad achievement in worker control for an ostensibly right-wing regime. But two other kinds of investors became even more important. The first were foreign investors, especially the foreign banks. In 1986, under the Central Bank's "Chapter 19" program, foreign investors were allowed to swap their (dubious) nationalized loans for equity in state-owned companies that were privatized on very favorable terms. As a result, Bankers Trust obtained forty percent of Provida (the country's largest pension fund), plus the Pilmaiquen Power Plant for half its book value; Aetna Insurance bought the country's second largest pension fund; Chase, MHT, and Citibank also acquired major local interests. By 1990, a handful of foreign-managed pension funds controlled seventy percent of Chile's pension system, its largest pool of capital. Alan Bond, the erratic Australian investor whose financial empire later collapsed, was even permitted to buy the famous telephone company that ITT had fought Allende so hard for. COPEC, the Chilean oil company that had been privatized cheaply by Grupo Cruzat-Larrain in 1976, had since turned into a debt-ridden conglomeration of fishing, mining, forestry, and finance companies, including half of Banco de Santiago. When Cruzat-Larrain cratered in 1983, Chile's government reacquired ownership of the now-heavily indebted COPEC, which was Chile's largest private enterprise. Four years later, it reprivatized COPEC to Grupo Angelini, another leading Chilean private conglomerate, again at cheap prices, continuing the cycle.[20]

This "Chapter 19" debt-equity swap program was credited by its supporters—especially the banks—with reducing Chile's debt by more than $2 billion. It was ironic for the banks to be praising this achievement. Many others saw the program as a dead giveaway. By assuming all private foreign debt in the first place, Chile had rewarded bad lending. After a decade of tightfisted government, many of the privatized assets had actually been in pretty good shape. Except for the copper company and a few military suppliers, the only ones the government retained were assets no one else wanted. It made little sense to let foreigners trade dubious loans for such valuable assets at rock-bottom prices. It seems that Chile hadn't really eliminated state intervention; it had merely inverted its class bias.

The other key investor in Buchi's privatizations was the Chilean elite. While the government nationalized private debts, it didn't touch private foreign assets. And Buchi now offered flight capitalists a generous tax amnesty if they brought their money home. His "Chapter 18" program allowed them to buy debt from banks and swap it for government bonds or equity in state companies at very favorable prices. By 1990, this program had brought in another $2 billion. Again, the banks and their clients naturally sang Chapter 18's praises. However, it rewarded tax evasion and effectively swapped foreign for domestic debt that may well prove more costly to service in the long run. Such criticism meant little to officials in charge of the program, and some even benefitted from it personally. Soon after he left government, Dr. Jose Pinera became president of an electric utility company that had been privatized. Moreover, his brother ended up owning the privatized national airline, which he proceeded to turn into quite a profitable enterprise, even while serving in Chile's Senate.

So the circle was complete: having been bailed out of their foreign debts by the government, Chile's elite and the foreign banks now bought back their assets at 50–60 cents on the dollar or less, often with the same flight dollars that the original loans had financed. Here we have one of the purest examples of abusive banking, one that poses the question of the foreign banks' responsibility very clearly. Chile's 1983 debt crisis obviously had little to do with inefficient public enterprises, excessive public debts, Marxists, welfare-state liberals, or all the other usual suspects blamed by neoliberals. At that point, two-thirds of Chile's foreign debt was private, and the Pinochet administration had long since eliminated much of the state's inefficiency, not to mention the political opposition. Yet by the end of 1983, Chile had ended up with one of the highest per capita *public* foreign debts in the world, as well as one of the developing world's largest state sectors. This "Chicago road to socialism" was taken in part because there was no political opposition, no accountability, and no one to stop the foreign banks, the domestic elites, their unregulated domestic banks, and the generals. So perhaps democracy has its uses, after all; perhaps "free markets" alone are not sufficient.

MEXICO—COMING INTO THE PICTURE

Mexico not only became the world's largest flight market in the 1970s and 1980s, but it also housed some of the world's most corrupt senior officials. Largely because of its highly organized system of corruption, it remained a ruthless one-party dictatorship until the election of Vicente Fox in July 2000—the first opposition presidential candidate to be elected in seventy-one years. Until then it had stubbornly resisted the democratization that had already occurred in Eastern Europe, the Soviet Union, South Africa, and the rest of Latin America. The debt crisis had forced Mexico to liberalize its economy in the early 1990s. But even after that, elections were still routinely stolen; political opponents and independent journalists feared for their jobs and lives; and the police and Army remained riddled with trafficantes, torturers, and death squads. More than three dozen journalists were murdered from 1989 to 2003.[21]

Of course the world has many other brutal dictatorships, but in my experience this long-suffering US neighbor is one of the most distressing, if only because it is right next door, and in so many ways, a dependent variable with respect to "Yanqui" behavior. Once, after my research assistant interviewed a leading Mexico City economist for an article, he called in absolute terror, afraid that someone in the "ruthless" PRI government would make it impossible for him to work if he were quoted.

The case of Mexico is also important for us to understand because foreign and domestic banks have had at least as much deleterious influence there as anywhere. It also clearly presents the question of the relationship between political and economic development.

MEXICO'S 1982 CRISIS

The Mexican crisis of August 1982 was the high water market of the 1980's Third World "debt crisis," but to insiders, it not much of a surprise at all. Indeed, it had actually been greatly *over-predicted* by, as one banker put it, by "All the froggy little economists at the Fed and the Treasury," as well as by many bankers. By early 1981, it didn't take much foresight to see that a crunch was coming—interest rates were soaring, the global economy was slipping into a recession, and Poland and Turkey had already stopped paying interest on their debts. The Fed was most concerned about Mexico and Brazil, because that was where US banks had most of their loans. Mexico, in particular, accounted for more that a third of all US loans to Latin America, and its foreign debt was already $75 billion and soaring. The Fed also had private evidence that much of Mexico's debt money was taking flight, ending up in New York, Houston, and Miami.

So in February 1981, the New York Federal Reserve assigned one of its best economists to look closely at Mexico's debt situation. In September 1981, after a careful eight-month review, he presented his findings to the US Interagency Cross-border Exposure Review Committee (ICERC), a secretive panel of federal banking experts, including three apiece from the Federal Reserve, the Comptroller of the Currency, and the Federal Deposit Insurance Corporation. Their job was to rate the credit-worthiness of specific countries, as Moody's does for private borrowers. Based on the economist's work, the New York Fed recommended that ICERC downgrade Mexico's credit rating. If this recommendation had been followed, it might have slowed lending to Latin America dramatically in 1981–82. Even though debt levels were already very high, the eventual August 1982 extreme crunch might have been avoided.

But the Fed's proposal was defeated—according to this Fed economist, because of high-level political shenanigans. The problem was the President Ronald Reagan was about to meet Mexico's President Lopez Portillo in Cancun for an official state visit, and the State Department—especially Secretary of State Alexander Haig—didn't want any embarrassments. So, on the very eve of the ICERC vote, at least two members of the nine-member committee got late-night calls from the White House. The word was, "It is not in the foreign policy interest of the US to reclassify Mexico's loans at this point." Two ICERC members switched their votes and the proposal was defeated 5 to 4.

This may have had very far-reaching consequences. From October 1981 to August 1982, Mexico's debt increased by $1 billion a month, and Latin America's debt increased by $40 billion—almost twenty percent. In August 1982. Mexico's Finance Minister, Jesus Silva Herzog, was compelled to deliver his famous line to US Treasury Secretary Donald Regan: "No, *with great respect sir, I believe* we *have a problem.*" Two weeks later, Mexican officials discovered to their horror that they actually owed foreign banks more that $26 billion of *90-day paper,* including $6 billion that Mexican banks had borrowed surreptitiously. This discovery—and not Silva Herzog's warning—marked the true crisis. It wasn't revealed at the time, but if the Fed had not secretly intervened to underwrite two New York banks in September 1982, the entire global interbank loan market might have come crashing down. When the dust cleared, Mexico's 90-day paper had become *30-year* paper, debt that it is still servicing to this day.

DE LA MADRID

Mexico was in its worst economic crisis since the 1930s when President Miguel de la Madrid took office in December 1982. He'd never before held elective office. A lifelong bureaucrat with a Mexican law degree and a Masters in Public Administration from Harvard, he was appointed President by Jose Lopez Portillo, his predecessor and law professor. But until the late 1990s, it was not at all unusual for Mexican Presidents, much less senior Mexican officials, to have never held elective office. From 1929 on, the country was governed by the "revolutionary" PRI, sort of a cross between the Teamster's Union, the Mafia, and Chicago's political machine in the 1960s, under Mayor Richard Daley. Decisions about who governed the country were routinely taken behind closed doors and enforced ruthlessly. As Fidel Velazquez Sanchez, for forty years the boss of the Confederation of Mexican Workers, the PRI's largest and most loyal union, once warned an opponent, "Just remember: if you *move*, you might not come out in the *picture*."

At least de la Madrid must have known something about the country's $85 billion debt problem when he took office. After all, as Portillo's planning minister from 1976 to 1982, when the debt increased fourfold, he had been one of its main architects. Now de la Madrid lectured his countrymen on the need for "belt tightening," and in 1983, he and Planning Minister Carlos Salinas de Gortari implemented a tough IMF-type stabilization. For the already-slim-waisted "shirtless ones," this belt-tightening just meant higher unemployment and declining real wages. De la Madrid's other declared priority was a "moral renovation," an attack on the country's soaring corruption problem. The only difficulty was that much of the corruption originated right at the top of the political system: since Porfirio Diaz from 1876 to 1911, right on down through Miguel Aleman in the 1940s, and since every Mexican President has emerged from office vastly richer than when he entered. After the 1970s oil price rise, Mexico's increased oil wealth had compounded the problem, because there was now so much more to steal. De la Madrid was not eager to stray away from this tradition. So he granted his predecessor immunity, allowing former President Lopez Portillo to retire to a palatial compound just outside Mexico City. Informed observers estimate that Lopez Portillo walked away with at least $1 billion—as ordinary folks said, *"La Revolución le hizo justicia"* (The Revolution brought him justice).[22] But Lopez Portillo didn't get off completely—he was never permitted to forget his vow in February 1982 to "defend the peso like a dog," just two weeks before he devalued it sharply. After that, his compound became known as "Dog Hill," and whenever he appeared in public, someone was sure to start barking. The only other consolation was that under Mexican law, Lopez Portillo was limited to just one term. As Lopez Portillo said of

Mexico's banks when he nationalized them in September 1982 for their involvement in capital flight, "They've robbed us once … They shall not rob us again."

De la Madrid did try to punish a few of Lopez Portillo's cronies. He booted out Arturo Durazo Moreno, Mexico City's former police chief and leading dope dealer at the time, whose house—like Imelda Marcos's film center—was a full-scale replica of the Parthenon, complete with five hundred marble statues. Jorge Diaz Serrano was George H. W. Bush's former business partner in Zapata Oil and the head of Pemex—Mexico's national oil company—under Lopez Portillo. In addition to other properties, Diaz Serrano owned a mansion right on the golf course in Vail, Colorado. He was later charged with pocketing a $34 million commission on two oil tankers—actually a rather modest sum, considering the fact that up to 300 million barrels of oil were *missing* from the country's accounts during his six-year term. He only served five years in prison, which works out to be an average "salary" of $7 million a year for the tanker fee.

Apart from these two sacrifices, most other PRI magnates avoided prosecution under the de la Madrid regime. Those overlooked included Carlos "Hank" Gonzalez, the Mexico City mayor who used his position to acquire a vast business empire, an estate in New Canaan, Connecticut, and a private zoo; Fidel Velazquez, the union boss, who sold labor peace for a hefty sum to the PRI's business allies; and most interesting to us here, Joaquin Hernandez Galicia ("La Quina"), the "Director of Revolutionary Works" for Pemex's powerful oil union in the 1980s.

Hernandez Galicia, a former welder from the Gulf town of Ciudad Maderos, had been the oil workers' boss since 1961 and a personal advisor to four Mexican presidents. He was so certain of his power that in February 1982 he warned de la Madrid, "You will have to become a friend of the oil workers whether you like it or not."[23] Hernandez Galicia also had close friends who were foreign bankers, as we'll see.

Unfortunately for de la Madrid, several episodes in the early days of his administration undercut his rhetoric about "moral renovation." In May 1984, the day de la Madrid arrived in Washington DC on his first official visit, Jack Anderson leaked a CIA report estimating that de la Madrid had already accumulated $162 million abroad. Apparently some of the funds had been wired to a Cayman Islands bank and the National Security Agency was listening. Mexican diplomats labeled the story a lie, but the State Department only responded that the "US Government applauds President de la Madrid's commitment to address the issue of honesty in government."[24]

Next, in September 1985, an earthquake devastated Mexico City. Shoddy high-rise apartments built by friends of senior government officials tumbled like card houses, with thousands of people buried in the rubble and thousands more forced to camp out for weeks in squalid shelters and abandoned offices. The quake did uncover a secret burial site for political prisoners at the offices of Mexico's Attorney General.

A few months later, wealthy Mexicans got a different kind of shock. In February 1986, the US Treasury, which requires banks to identify people who deposit more than $10,000 in cash, fined the Texas Commerce Bank of Houston $1.9 million for failing to file seven thousand such reports, mainly for Mexicans. Hundreds feared their names would be revealed and started shifting their funds elsewhere. In March 1986, the Mexican periodical *Jueves de Excelsior* published a list of 575 people who had at least $1 million in US banks. De la Madrid was trying to reschedule the debt for the second time since 1982, and he'd just declared that foreign banks should "shoulder a greater part of Mexico's debt burden." The disclosure of all these *sacadolares*—"people who take out dollars"—showed that Mexico's elite wasn't any more willing to finance the country than the banks were.

Two years later, during the run up to Mexico's July 1988 presidential elections, the debt was being restructured for a third time, and a similar list of big-league flight capitalists appeared.[25] This time, the run was inspired by a candid statement from Augustin Legorreta, a Mexican banker who was very close to President de la Madrid. In a meeting of businessmen closed to the press, Legorreta admitted that despite the PRI's seventy years of revolutionary rhetoric, "Mexico is still a country run by only three hundred families."

Despite such embarrassments, de la Madrid did make some progress toward economic recovery. By the time he picked his successor in 1987, bankers were citing Mexico as proof that the one-on-one "negotiated" approach to the debt problem was working—at least for them. Off the record, they also liked Mexico's compliant debt policy, compared with other (more democratic) debtors.

THE PRECOCIOUS SALINAS

De la Madrid's anointed successor was Carlos Salinas de Gortari, a fortyish Harvard technocrat. Like his mentor, Salinas was a member of the PRI's hereditary revolutionary family. His grandfather was a prominent Monterrey businessman, and his father, Raul Salinas Lozano, also Harvard educated, had been a minister of commerce in the 1960s. Salinas was not only wellborn, but also precocious: at age four, he had picked up a pistol and shot his maid dead. He finished his Harvard Ph.D. in political science in 1978 (his dissertation was on the "impact of government spending on elections"), and by 1982, he was already minister of planning—the youngest Cabinet member ever at thirty-five.

Like de la Madrid and many other US-educated elite/technocrats in the PRI's "reform" wing, Salinas believed that Mexico's main problem was its own bloated government. He favored downsizing the state, deregulating the economy, and, if anything, *increasing* the role of foreign banks and investors. Despite a dearth of new loans, he and de la Madrid continued to pay all of Mexico's foreign interest bills on time, repeatedly restructured the debt, and experimented with almost every idea on the bankers' wish list, including debt swaps, securitization, debt conversions, and privatization. Mexico's debt emissaries spent a fortune on innumerable junkets to Paris, London, Washington, DC, and New York. Meanwhile, the country staunchly refused to be drawn into a debtors' coalition with Brazil, Argentina, and Peru.

By the end of de la Madrid's term in 1988, however, there was precious little to show for his deference to foreign bankers.[26] The debt cost more to service than Mexico earned from oil exports—tantamount to Pemex being handed over lock, stock, and barrel to the banks. From 1982 to 1988, Mexico paid over $40 billion in interest and got back only $14 billion in new loans, half of them from the IMF and the World Bank. The country transferred more than a third of its savings abroad each year. In fact, taking flight capital into account, Mexico was actually a net lender to the outside world—more than $50 billion throughout the 1980s. By 1985, the market value of its flight assets already exceeded the value of its entire foreign debt. And most of these flight capital outflows were captured by its major "creditors." One Citibank private banker—operating surreptitiously out of the fourteenth floor of Citi's office tower in Mexico City—bragged, "We could easily repay our loans to Mexico with the flight capital that we've collected here—you know, there really are quite a few fabulously rich Mexicans!"[27]

Given the banks' unwillingness to provide Mexico's government with any more loans, the skepticism that foreign investors had toward the country, and the government's reluctance to get tougher with foreign banks and its own domestic elite, Mexico had little choice but to rely on its own resources to finance investment. Since Salinas and de la Madrid wanted to shrink public spending and budget deficits and were unwilling to tax the elite, they raised interest rates to stimulate private savings. That reduced growth and unemployment, which was anathema to workers, *campesinos*, and "protected" business sectors. But the de la Madrid-Salinas program was supported enthusiastically by Mexico's top families, bankers, the bureaucratic elite, union bosses, oil workers, police chiefs, and Army officers. Given the one-party system, these were the only constituencies that really counted.

The economic program turned out to be very unpopular, and Salinas's detractors in the PRI worried that it might be a mistake to bet on an uncharismatic technocrat in a period of rising political ferment. But this argument carried little weight with de la Madrid, who'd once been an uncharismatic planning minister himself. So in September 1987, Salinas was nominated the PRI's candidate for president.

Almost immediately, the regime's policies began to misfire. The global stock crash that took place in October 1987 actually started in Mexico City, when the Central Bank suddenly lifted restrictions on investments in debt instruments, causing the Mexican stock market to lose three-fourths of its value in one week. Capital flight resumed, the government missed its budget targets, the peso sank like a stone, and by year's end, inflation was at fifteen percent a month and rising. De la Madrid was forced to implement yet another round of "belt tightening," squeezing credit and freezing wages and prices. Since 1981, Mexico had experienced seven years of negative growth. Real incomes for everyone but the elite had fallen by a quarter, and there were incipient signs of social unrest all over the country. The country stagnated under the weight of its foreign debt, which totaled $101 billion by 1988.[28]

THE 1988 "ELECTION"

The July 1988 presidential elections were the greatest challenge to the PRI's hegemony in its history—at least until Vicente Fox won in 2000. In the party's first deep split since 1929, Cuauhtemoc Cardenas, the PRI's governor of Michoacan State and the son of President Lazaro Cardenas, who nationalized the oil industry in the 1930s, joined forces with disenchanted leftists and nationalists to form the "National Democratic Front." The Front's radical rhetoric gave voice to widespread discontent. It also claimed to support democracy, but had a few strange bedfellows of its own, including Luis Echeverria Alvarez —Mexico's president in the 1970s and one of Mexico's wealthiest men—and Hernandez Galicia. But at least it supported a popular job creation program, which it intended to pay for with a repudiation, or radical restructuring, of Mexico's foreign debt.

Just a few weeks before the 1988 election, Cuauhtemoc Cardenas had been doing very well in the polls. Salinas, on the other hand, would have nothing to do with such irresponsible policies. The consummate planning bureaucrat-turned-free marketeer, he saw himself as continuing the tradition of authoritarian top-down reforms begun by Porfirio Diaz—the tough nineteenth-century dictator who ruled Mexico for thirty-five years with the support of the landowning elite, foreign bankers and investors, and his own well-heeled entourage.

Evidently many Mexicans did not share Salinas's enthusiasm for Porfirio Diaz or for the neoliberal agenda. To them, he was still just another in a long series of little-known, remote members of the *Priista* technocracy who came down from the temple every six years and went through the motions of seeking their mandate. Despite massive advertising on his behalf by the PRI's machine (with help from Hill and Knowlton, the renowned PR firm whose clients had also included Duvalier and BCCI), as of election eve, non-government polls found that he and Cardenas were still running neck and neck. Of course many voters viewed all Mexican elections with skepticism, because of the PRI's long history of election fraud. But Salinas and his predecessor, Miguel de la Madrid, had sworn this time would be different.

On July 6, 1988, when the polls closed and the government started tallying the count at its central computing office in Mexico City, the country eagerly awaited the results. There was much disappointment when Manual Bartlett, the PRI's interior minister in charge of administering the vote, announced the next morning that the Federal Election Commission's computer system had crashed and that the results would be delayed. When they finally emerged a week later, Salinas was declared the victor by a wide margin. Officially, the PRI received fifty-two percent of the vote, compared with the PRD's thirty-one percent, and the business party PAN's seventeen percent.

Opposition leaders have claimed that the computer crash was contrived to buy time for rigging the vote once it became clear that Cardenas was winning. Despite widespread rumors, these claims were not easily confirmed. Many of those on the inside were too scared to talk, and Salinas's foreign supporters, including leading newspapers like *The Wall Street Journal* (whose parent company, Dow Jones, added President Salinas to its corporate board, where he remained until April 1997) and *The New York Times* did not investigate too deeply. They believed that a compliant, technically-competent neoliberal would serve the mutual interests of Mexico and its trading partners better than Cardenas.[29]

In June 1994, before Mexico's August 1994 Presidential election, *Computing*, a UK magazine that focuses on technology, became interested in the computer failure aspect of the 1988 elections. It tracked down several data entry operators who had worked on the election and obtained the following eyewitness account of what had actually happened in July 1988:

> We arrived at work on the morning of July 6, election day, at the central computer and statistic official. When we got there we discovered that the rooms were empty and our computers weren't there. We were ordered into a minibus and taken to the Government House (in Mexico City), to a room with blacked-out windows. Our computers had been set up there, complete with the voter database. We started to enter the data. As the supervisors saw that Salinas was losing, they ordered us to leave aside votes for the PRI and only enter opposition votes. Then, at about 3 A.M. on July 7, the supervisor called a halt, and with tears in his eyes, he told us: "If you care for your families, your jobs, and your lives, enter all votes from now on in favor of the PRI. I went back to work and did as I was told. I wanted to cry, but I had to do it.
>
> They kept us there until five or six in the evening the following day. When I'd finished my work, I called up the voting record for my uncle, and to my astonishment the computer record showed that he, an opposition supporter, had voted for Salinas. That was when I realized why we had been told only to enter opposition votes in the beginning. While we were away

from the computers, they had reversed all the data from the first session of data capture so all those votes showed up as Salinas votes.[30]

To the consternation of the Salinas government, these details were confirmed in July 1994 by a former director of Mexico's Federal Electoral Institute. But when *Computing* tried to verify them with Unisys, the US multinational that had supplied the computers used in the election, it responded that the 1988 "fault reports" for its Mexico subsidiary had been destroyed and that Unisys had "not been involved in the electoral process."

In December 1994, Adolfo Onofre, the courageous computer consultant who had cooperated with the investigation of the Unisys computer "failure," was arrested and badly beaten by Mexico's Federal Police when he returned to Mexico City from Britain, where he had sought political asylum.[31]

LA QUINA'S PRIVATE ARMY

Salinas not only lost Mexico City by a landslide in 1988, but most independent observers now believe that he also lost the whole country. Without an army of its own, most members of the opposition decided to recognize his "victory," which the Reagan Administration and the domestic and foreign business community lost no time in doing.

A few powerful dissidents like Hernandez Galicia refused to do so, however. Hernandez Galicia had already battled Salinas over the Pemex union's contract, and there was much more to fight about. For forty years, oil workers had been Mexico's best-paid workers. Under a 1947 agreement that was still in force, they received 2.5 percent of all drilling contracts as "dues," plus 10 percent for the union's Fund for Social Works, which Hernandez Galicia happened to administer. Under a 1977 agreement with Lopez Portillo, the union also controlled forty percent of all drilling contracts and half of all other Pemex contracts. The standard gambit was for union bosses to set up intermediary companies, subcontract work, and pocket 10–25 percent spreads. The union even had its own contractors, owning a whole fleet of oil tankers and two drilling platforms that employed *pelones* (nonunion workers). At Salinas's insistence, the bidding reservation was abolished for onshore bids in 1985, but offshore work remained with the union. There was also rampant overmanning. The contracts gave the union exclusive power over hiring, and Hernandez Galicia openly sold the jobs. There were also thousands of "ghost workers" on the payroll. Not surprisingly, Pemex's output per worker was only a third as high as that of PDVSA, Venezuela's state oil company.[32] When oil prices plummeted in the mid-1980s, the company chose to cut exploration rather than take on the union. By the late 1980s, Pemex was pumping four times as much oil as it was finding, and Mexico's reserves had fallen below Venezuela's.[33]

By then, Hernandez Galicia's union really became a state within a state, with more than nine hundred full-time officials and three thousand "enforcers" on call. In addition to the tankers and drilling companies, his Fund for Social Works controlled movie theaters, service stations, a watch factory, 130 supermarkets, a fleet of airplanes, the Alameda Hotel in Mexico City, the Emiliano Zapata Ranch in Tamaulipas (with three thousand cattle), and at least five other ranches. Hernandez Galicia also owned a stake in the Continental Performance and Construction Company, a Texas drilling company and Pemex subcontractor. In 1983, he estimated the value of all these assets at $670 million.[34] They were managed for him by Sergio Bolaños, a Mexican businessman. Collectively, they were known as Grupo Serba.

Despite all the corruption, while Hernandez Galicia was powerful, foreign bankers were quite happy to support him. In the 1970s, for example, Bank of America, Pemex's leading creditor, had loaned nearly $500 million to Grupo Serba, Bolaños, and Hernandez Galicia. The loans were arranged by Bank of America's influential Mexico City representative Pepe Carral, a former schoolmate and close friend of Presidents Luis Echeverria and Lopez Portillo. Bank of America was also Pemex's largest lender. And after he retired from Bank of America, Carral set up an investment fund that managed assets for several of these friends.

So even after Salinas took office in late 1988, he still had very powerful enemies. On the eve of his inauguration, Hernandez Galicia tried to embarrass Salinas, charging that Mario Ramon Beteta, de la Madrid's Pemex director, had pocketed a commission on a tanker deal just like Diaz Serrano, his predecessor.[35] Hernandez Galicia also warned Salinas that his union would strike if the government disposed of "even one millimeter of the petroleum industry to the private sector." And the union secretly started to buy automatic weapons. That was serious—Hernandez Galicia really did have his own private army. His union's 210,000 members were disbursed all over the country, and they outnumbered the Mexican Army by two to one.

The upshot was that in January 1989, just a few days after Hernandez Galicia visited the National Palace to pay his respects to Salinas, a bazooka blew down his door in Cuidad Madero at 9 A.M. in the morning, and Mexican Army troops dragged him off to jail in his underwear. Hernandez Galicia, Bolaños, and forty-three other union officials were charged with crimes that ranged from murder and arms trafficking to "gangsterism." The police confiscated several hundred Uzi machine guns and fifty thousand rounds of ammunition. A week later, Mexico's attorney general asked the US Federal Reserve to freeze all US bank deposits owned by these union officials. They turned up more than *$3.2 billion* stashed in accounts at Citibank, Chase, MHT, and Bank of America.[36]

So it was not only could Mexico's capitalists and corrupt officials who could employ private bankers, but "Directors of Revolutionary Works" as well. If Salinas hadn't acted as quickly as he did, Hernandez Galicia's stash might have bankrolled a second Mexican revolution. This was by no means the only union leader jailed by Salinas. He also jailed the head of Aeromexico's union, the head of the social security system's union, and the heads of a Mexico City bus line's union—all of whom were protesting the privatization of their respective enterprises.

Salinas wasted no time with amenities when it came to civil liberties. In 1994, Amnesty International described some of the methods used by Mexican security forces against the Indians in Chiapas who were protesting the extraordinary concentration of land ownership:

> Hundreds of people were tortured and ill-treated by the army and other security forces in Chiapas. In other parts of the country the frequent use of torture by law enforcement agents, particularly the state judicial police, continues to be reported. Torture methods included beatings; near-asphyxiation with plastic bags; forcing peppered water into the nose; electric shocks and burning. Some detainees died as a result. Confessions extracted under duress continued to be admitted as evidence in courts, and medical treatment for detainees who suffered torture was frequently not available. By the end of the year none of those responsible for any of the hundreds of cases of torture reported in Chiapas and throughout the country had been brought to justice.[37]

LA CONTRA-REVOLUCIÓN

Having stolen the election and demolished his remaining political opponents with brute force, Salinas proceeded with what opposition leaders called his "neo-Porfirista" reforms. Porfirio Diaz had been overthrown by *La Revolución* in 1912. Now, from 1989 to 1994, Salinas introduced a dramatic neoliberal *Contra-Revolución*.

His first step was to undertake Mexico's fourth foreign debt restructuring since 1982. In March 1989, when US Treasury secretary and former investment banker Nicholas Brady announced the "Brady Plan," Mexico volunteered to be its first guinea pig. Unlike the 1985 Baker Plan, the Brady Plan seemed to recognize the need for debt reduction, underwritten with aid from First World governments.

The basic idea was that banks would trade their Mexican loans in for new government-backed bonds that were issued at steep discounts from face value, backed by US Treasury bonds. But it soon became clear that the actual aid available was small. After all, the US government had debt problems of its own. Furthermore, by 1989–90, many foreign private banks were too worried about their shaky domestic portfolios to put much new money into Mexico—Citibank, for example, came within a hairsbreadth of having to be bailed out by the Federal Reserve.

So the July 1989 Mexican rescheduling—concluded only after great pressure from the US Treasury—merely reduced Mexico's debt by $7 billion, enough to cut its interest bill just ten percent. Like all such "voluntary" approaches to the debt problem, the Brady approach ended up being mainly a complex, time-consuming substitute for a real solution—although it generated nice fees for investment bankers!

Partly because this "free market-based" approach to debt reduction produced such meager results, Salinas had to redouble his strategy of liberalizing the economy while holding on tight to the reigns of power. Given his reluctance to raise taxes, he turned to relying on attracting foreign investment and flight capital back to Mexico with a major privatization and liberalization program.

Soon Salinas became one of Latin America's most vocal advocates in the neoliberal movement that swept through Latin America's elites in the aftermath of the 1980s debt crisis. Following in the footsteps of Pinochet's Los Chicago Boys, its followers professed an almost religious faith in the virtues of unfettered private markets and free trade. Their agenda included the sharp retrenchment of government borrowing and social spending, the rejection of state intervention in favor of privatization and lower taxes, and the deregulation of markets for capital, labor, land, traded goods, and even environmental rights. Support for this agenda soon became almost as prevalent among the elites and their business and banking friends as their dizzy optimism about state-led development had been in the 1970s. Indeed, its supporters included many who had dined heartily on the debt-heavy meals of that period.

The result was a proliferation of free-market reforms in the early 1990s. Under Salinas, Mexico became a vanguard and a policy laboratory for the whole global neoliberal movement, as Marcos' Philippines had been for development planning. This was a crucial conquest. While Chile's free-market experiments had been interesting, that country was, at best, an industrious copper exporter with thirteen million inhabitants located at the ends of the earth. Mexico was a real player—it boasted a $250 billion diversified economy, fabulous oil and mineral wealth, the world's third largest metropolis, and ninety-two million poor people who shared a two thousand-mile border with the world's richest country. Depending on how this relationship was managed, Mexico could be a very useful neighbor—a supplier of low-cost labor, goods, and energy, and a major market for First World loans, investments, and exports. Or it could be a time bomb.

As we saw, even before his "election," Salinas was already the favorite son not only of Mexico's oligarchs and party bosses, but also of multinational investors like GE, Allied Signal, Alcoa, and GM; commercial banks like Citibank and JPMorgan;

investment banks like Goldman Sachs and Morgan Stanley; the US media; press; and, the US government and its financial acolytes—the IMF and World Bank. During the two years before the 1988 elections, the IMF and the World Bank had provided Mexico with $4 billion in new credits, and private banks had helped out by rescheduling $43 billion of Mexico's outstanding debt.[38] Before and after the election, a parade of First World leaders, including George Bush Sr. (a friend of Salinas's father, Raul Sr.), Paul Volcker, Citibank chairman John Reed, newly elected World Bank president Lewis B. Preston (formerly of JPMorgan), IMF director Michel Camdessus, and many lesser officials and bankers descended on Mexico to encourage its newfound passion for free markets. They praised the quality of the PRI's Ivy League-educated economists and touted Mexico as a model of stability and growth—much as they had done with the Philippines two decades earlier.

After the election, foreign investors also stepped forward to ratify Salinas's agenda. From 1988 to 1994, Mexico became the darling of the international investment community, attracting more foreign investment than any other developing country except China. It accounted for nearly half of the $175 billion in new foreign direct and portfolio investment that poured into Latin America during this period.[39] In the wake of the debt crisis, "foreign" investors—including members of the domestic elite who secretly repatriated their flight capital to avoid taxes and conceal their investments—replaced foreign bankers as the leading suppliers of finance to Mexico and other "emerging markets," providing more than three-fourths of Mexico's entire capital budget. Much of this capital was attracted by Salinas' privatization program, one of the most aggressive in Latin America. It involved selling public assets in key sectors like telecommunications, steel, airlines, and banking, including the reprivatization of all the banks that Lopez Portillo had nationalized in the early 1980s, and then using the proceeds to finance the budget. By 1994, this fire-sale had raised $24 billion, more than any other Latin American country.[40]

Salinas introduced many other sweeping changes, like a new investment law that opened many sectors to foreigners and a tax amnesty for returning flight capitalists. He slashed government spending as a share of GDP and opened up Mexico's capital markets to foreign banks, brokerages, and insurance companies. He sanctioned an amendment to Mexico's constitution that effectively put an end to restrictions on private landholding, an attempt to undermine the communal farms that had been the cornerstone of Lazaro Cardenas's agrarian reform in the 1930s and 1940s. With the help of high real interest rates, he reduced inflation from 130 percent to around 20 percent in two years and strengthened Mexico's peso. In 1989, he also declared that drug trafficking was a threat to the nation, presided over the seizure of a record amount of cocaine, and signed a new drug enforcement cooperation treaty with the US. Finally, he negotiated the NAFTA treaty, a new "free trade" zone with his powerful neighbors—the US and Canada—that opened doors to their markets, exports, and investors. For good measure, he even had Mexico join the GATT and the OECD. Porfirio Diaz himself could not have designed a more complete deconstruction of the PRI's statist heritage.

All these moves were greeted enthusiastically by Salinas's allies, especially the three hundred top families, the US government, the banks, foreign investors, and the neoliberal intelligentsia. Combined with the 1990 oil price rise, this helped set off a foreign investment boomlet from 1991 to 1995.

The result was a vast feeding frenzy on the part of the private elite. Far from simply opening up the economy, this actually consolidated their hold on many sectors. Sweeping privatizations of the banking, telecommunications, media, mining, agriculture, and airline industries provided numerous sweetheart deals, especially for a dozen or so key insiders, like Carlos Slim, Carlos Hank Gonzalez, and Roberto Gonzalez Barrera—all of whom were close to the President and his family. Other private groups that held dominant positions in export industries like glass, beer, cement, tourism, and mining or were able to offer investment opportunities and partnerships to foreigners, also benefited immensely from NAFTA, which was concluded by Salinas and President George H. W. Bush in late 1992 and strong-armed through the US Congress by President Bill Clinton in late 1993.

So it is not really surprising that inequalities of wealth and income in Mexico rose dramatically from 1988 to 1994. The number of Mexicans on *Forbes Magazine's* annual survey of the world's billionaires increased from one in 1988 to twenty-four in 1994, placing Mexico in fourth place, just ahead of France and the UK.[41] It also earned Salinas de Gortari many personal tributes. As noted, he became a member of Dow Jones' corporate board. On December 7, 1994, he was treated to a $400 per plate testimonial dinner in his honor at the Jeane J. Kirkpatrick's American Enterprise Institute in Washington, DC, for his "contribution to improved public policy and social welfare."[42] In 1995, just before the scandals involving his brother Raul broke, his name was briefly put forward by the Clinton adminstration as a candidate for the new head of the World Trade Organization.

Salinas's political opponents complained that all these tributes overlooked the huge surge in corruption and drug dealing that had also accompanied his liberalization programs, as well as his "unelected" status. They saw his policies as basically returning Mexico to its old role as an appendage of the US economy, a place where labor was cheap and "anything goes," and where domestic farmers and industry would be wiped out by cheap US imports. After seventy years of "revolutionary" government, the country still didn't accord its workers basic labor rights like effectively enforced maximum hours, minimum wages, child labor laws, or occupational health and safety. Despite all the excitement about free trade, there were no free trade unions. Despite Salinas's new environmental law, Mexico's environment was poorly protected. And despite high nominal taxes, private income and wealth went largely untaxed.

Most importantly, the PRI was still unwilling to allow free elections except when it served its own interests. It had permitted some candidates from the right-wing PAN party to win state governorships for decorative purposes, but when Cardenas had threatened to win, the elections were stolen in plain view. When workers at Mexico's largest copper mine protested their privatization, Salinas sent in the Army. Critical journalists were routinely intimidated, fired, or assassinated. And senior members of the Salinas family had been cultivating some interesting sidelines of their own, which made Hernandez Galicia's business practices look clean by comparison.

FREE TRADE—IN "BADS"

The other side of liberalization was that it really unleashed Mexico's burgeoning underground economy, especially drug trafficking. For the first time, Mexico acquired a world-class international drug cartel in the 1990s, complete with accounts at Citibank's Swiss subsidiary and personal protectors in the office of the presidency. Mexico's role in drug exports had been growing ever since the mid-1980s, when Colombia's traditional supply routes through Florida were pressured, Colombia cracked down on its own crime bosses, and new Mexican gangs developed their own supply routes and political connections. Like all other exporters to the US, the dealers were aided by NAFTA's increasingly open borders. As the traffickers' wealth grew, so did the opportunities for official corruption. One investigation showed that in 1994–95, more than thirty tons of cocaine confiscated by Mexico's Federal Police simply disappeared.[43] According to a report by a former senior Mexican drug enforcement official, the traffickers were simply given a green light by President Salinas to generate foreign exchange.[44] The crisis in the legal economy increased the supply of human "mules" willing to risk border crossings, even as Mexico's enforcement efforts suffered budget cutbacks. So it is not surprising that during the 1990s, illegal drugs and illegal immigrants became the country's largest exports, next to oil and debt service payments.

But for corrupt PRI officials, neoliberalism had an entirely new meaning—more opportunities to make money quickly, launder it, and stash it. Among the chief beneficiaries was the president's brother, Raul Salinas Jr. In late 1995, his primary bank accounts at Citibank New York, Citibank's Swiss subsidiary, Pictet, Rothschild, Julius Baer, Banque Genevoise de Gestion, Bank Cremi, and a network of dozens of other banks in Mexico, the Cayman Islands, London, New York, Germany, and Luxembourg were revealed to be involved in laundering and concealing $130 million to $400 million of unexplained wealth.[45] Paulina Castañon, Raul's wife, was halted by

Swiss authorities on November 15, 1998, when she tried to withdraw $84 million from an account at Bank Pictet in Geneva. A Swiss prosecutor who worked on the investigation for seven years concluded that at least $70 million had come from drug deals.[46] Raul Salinas claimed that the money came from undocumented loans or investment funds that he was given to manage by wealthy Mexican businessmen, like Carlos Hank Rhon, Gonzalez's son.

But Swiss authorities found his explanation dubious. They uncovered evidence of payments by Juan García Abrego, the head of the Gulf cartel, whom other witnesses claimed had met with both Carlos and Raul at a Salinas family ranch.[47] There were also many other allegations of high-level drug dealing and money laundering. Furthermore, both the Bush and Clinton administrations were probably aware of some of these links to organized crime, but did nothing, because they were concerned it might jeopardize Salinas's support for the NAFTA treaty. The head of the US Drug Enforcement Agency's Dallas office from 1984 to 1994 said, "The intelligence on corruption, especially by drug traffickers, has always been there. But we were under instructions not to say anything negative about Mexico—it was a no-no since NAFTA was a hot political football."[48]

Eventually, in January 1999, after a four-year trial, Raul Salinas was sentenced to fifty years in prison—later reduced to twenty-seven years—for his role in the 1994 murder of his brother-in-law, the PRI's general secretary Jose Francisco Ruiz Massieu.[49] Carlos Salinas, afraid that he might be murdered or prosecuted if he remained in Mexico, fled to Ireland, which had no extradition treaty with Mexico, until the late 1990s. The US Department of Justice briefly launched a money laundering investigation of Citigroup, based on the fact that it handled more than $100 million in the scheme; Raul had claimed that Amy Eliot, a vice president in Citigroup's International Private Banking Group, had "'devised the whole strategy."[50] However, the Clinton adminstration never brought money-laundering charges against Citibank. By 2000, the five-year statute of limitations on this offense had probably expired. It was pure coincidence that former US Treasury secretary Robert Rubin joined Citigroup as its vice chairman after October 1999 and that Citigroup also hired the Federal Reserves top expert on money laundering, Richard Small, as its director of Global Anti-Money Laundering.

TEQUILA SUNRISE

In August 1994, Ernesto Zedillo, a Yale economist and another lifelong PRI bureaucrat who had never before held elective office, was elected to succeed Carlos with 50.2% of the official vote. Zedillo was nominated only after Salinas's first choice, Luis

Donoldo Colosio, was mysteriously assassinated in March 1994 in Baja, Zedillo's home state. The PRI had its work cut out for them to make Zedillo—theretofore Colosio's campaign manager— a credible candidate in just four months. But the PRI succeeded with the help of a massive advertising campaign, which featured the slogan, "Welfare for your family!" The curious appearance of the "guerrilla" movement in Chiapas in January 1994 and an epidemic of political violence probably also convinced some voters to support the "stable" PRI.

Because the PRI had generously renounced paying for elections with government money in 1994, it had to find its campaign funding in other ways. But since it was the ruling party, that was no problem. Salinas simply invited thirty of Mexico's top business moguls to dinner at a private mansion in Mexico City's fashionable Polanco district—including Carlos Slim, who owned a significant part of Telmex, the formerly state-owned telephone company; Robert Hernandez, owner of Banamex, which had been privatized in 1991; Emilio ("El Tigre") Azcarraga, a TV and media czar; and Lorenzo Zambrano, owner of Cemex, which controlled sixty-five percent of Mexico's cement market.[51] It was "payback" time: everyone in the room had benefitted enormously from Salinas's reforms in the last six years, especially from privatization, and they were about to profit even more from the liberalization of trade. As Don Emilio Azcarraga reportedly told them,

> I, and all of you, have earned so much money over the past six years that I think we have a big debt of gratitude to this government. I'm ready to more than double what has been pledged so far, and I hope that most in this room will join me. We owe it to the president, and to the country.[52]

Evidently this sentiment was widely shared. At the end of the evening, the PRI had reportedly collected pledges of $25 million a head, for a grand total of $750 million. Since these business moguls were not in the habit of giving away so much money for nothing, the amount raised was also an indication of how much they expected to benefit from government favors that would flow from a PRI victory.

Another factor that aided Zedillo's 1994 victory was an economic "card trick." As of mid-1994, the country was riding the crest of a temporary economic boom, created by the policy of opening the doors to foreign investors. Their willingness to provide a substitute for bank loans meant that the whole issue of Mexico's foreign debt appeared to have long since passed. Moreover, Salinas's economic team decided to defer an overdue but unpopular devaluation of the peso until after the 1994 elections, because it would have boosted inflation. The team also secretly boosted government spending by more than was disclosed in official statistics. These politically-motivated policies were maintained, despite numerous warnings from independent economists, the US Treasury, and even the IMF

To sustain the pre-election spending, Mexico had to take on a huge amount of short-term debt—mainly in the form of interbank loans and new issues of Mexican bonds sold to US investors through Wall Street investment banks. The debts of Mexico's domestic banks to international banks nearly doubled from 1991 to 1994 (from $8 billion to $15.5 billion)—all of it denominated in dollars. And the Mexican banks, also newly privatized, rapidly expanded their loans to Mexico's private sector. Many of these bank loans were wasted on poor projects or on "loans" to their owners' other companies. Bank of Mexico's former vice governor Francisco Gil-Diaz wrote later that many of the private investors who took over banks in the 1989–92 privatizations were political insiders with little banking experience. They took on credit risks they did not understand.[53] Also at work was something economists call "moral hazard," a fancy way of saying that—in the absence of effective bank regulation, the presence of insider influence, and the likelihood of a government bailout for their lending errors—the "novice" Mexican bankers had discovered that they could essentially write themselves blank checks.

Once again, hasty privatization and weak banking regulation, the twin Achilles' heels of neoliberal finance, were influential. Since it was clear that Mexico could not sustain this level of borrowing, investors started to speculate that the pegged value of the peso had to give. But until it did, the Central Bank continued dishing out reserves, delaying the inevitable.

Another key component of Mexico's $100 billion foreign debt was short-term Mexican dollar bonds, or *Tesobonos*. By 1994, these had increased from almost nothing in 1988 to $28 billion, more than a quarter of Mexico's total foreign debt.[54] About $18 billion of the $28 billion had been sold through Wall Street firms to their favorite big-ticket investors, and the other $10 billion was held by wealthy Mexicans. All of them had been well compensated for inducing investors to bear the risk of holding Mexican debt with high yields. Combined with Mexico's weak non-oil exports and its high propensity for imports, this policy of depending heavily on short-term foreign finance and then delaying the necessary adjustments brought the chickens home to roost. But in the short run, it basically allowed the PRI to manipulate its way to another electoral victory. Indeed, in August 1994, the threat from the left temporarily evaporated. Cardenas's PRD splintered, managing just seventeen percent of the official vote. The conservative PAN party got twenty-six percent. And this time the computer system was supplied by IBM and Booz Allen Hamilton, not Unisys.

THE TEQUILA CRISIS

Not long after the 1994 elections, however, these macro-economic policies came completely unglued. In December, there was a disastrous attempt by Zedillo's finance minister and Yale economist Jaime Serra to make up for lost time, finally devaluing the peso. The problem was that it did not stabilize—it kept falling. Its value fell by more than fifty percent in one week, precipitating a massive wave of capital flight that caused it to sink even lower.

The crisis marked the return of capital flight and foreign borrowing. Large capital outflows had been reported in the months since the assassination of presidential candidate Colosio in March 1994 and just before the December peso float. Apparently some high-level domestic investors had had advance warning.[55] Foreign investors trailed behind a little, but they also quickly lost confidence. The devaluation then triggered the largest wave of capital flight since 1982. About $8 billion in reserves had already fled the country from March 1994 to the end of October. In the following two months, Mexico lost the rest of the $25 billion in reserves that Salinas had carefully accumulated during the previous five years. Even as real wages were plummeting, the government was compelled to boost real interest rates—the "wages" of capital—to more than thirty percent a year in a desperate effort to woo investment capital. Just like the 1920s, however, when Mexican and Argentine bonds experienced a similar loss of confidence, Mexico learned the hard way that foreign bondholders can be even more fickle than foreign bankers.

Mexico's capital flight problem marked the beginning of its deepest economic crisis since the 1930s. Over the next year, as the new Zedillo government took office, there was no bailout for ordinary Mexicans. Unemployment tripled to twenty-eight percent and real national income fell by more than seven percent. At a time when the labor force grew at the rate of a million new workers each year, 1.6 million jobs were lost. Real wages—already below their 1980 levels—fell by another twenty-five percent. Taking the government's claims about continued prosperity at its word, many people had gone heavily into debt. Forty percent of Mexico's eighty-six thousand small businesses, several hundred thousand individual debtors, and several large industrial companies now went bankrupt.[56] Two million small farmers lost everything and were forced to migrate to find work. Meanwhile, to help pay for this fiasco and satisfy the IMF's demands for lower deficits, the government raised sales taxes and prices for gasoline, electricity, and foodstuffs by fifty percent.

For those in the bottom eighty-five percent of the income distribution who still produced mainly for the domestic market, the consequences of all this were catastrophic: an unprecedented combination of soaring inflation, interest rates, and job losses, yielding, in turn, a sharp rise in suicides, divorces, malnutrition, "voluntary" blood sales, kidnappings, political murders, land conflicts, homelessness, and day-to-day street violence. NAFTA may well have helped to generate $250 billion in cross-border trade since its adoption in 1993. But given the economic crisis, the vast majority of Mexicans were seeing very few of its benefits. By the year 2000, more than half the country's population was surviving on less than four dollars per day, and the traditional "middle class" had been emptied out, as inequality and poverty both soared. If this was "conservative reform," many ordinary Mexicans wondered how radical alternatives could possibly have been any worse.

And this was not Chile's distant little laboratory. There were ninety-nine million potential Mexican immigrants right on the US border. Mass unemployment and the plunge in real wages, combined with the adjacent US boom, encouraged Mexican laborers to leave the country in droves. The years 1995–2003 proved to be record years for illegal emigration. Detentions by the US Border Patrol increased by sixty-six percent, despite a quadrupling of patrols, the adoption of harsher penalties for US employers who hire illegal immigrants, sophisticated new detection technologies, and the enactment of tough new anti-immigrant legislation, like California's Proposition 187.[58] More than one out of every seventeen professional class workers had left Mexico since 1980.[59]

THE BAILOUT … AND THE BUYBACK

In the ensuing 1995 Tequila Crisis, all of the country's top ten private banks, which had stoked the borrowing spree with careless loans and excessive foreign borrowing, might have failed, were it not for the $50 billion bailout provided to them and to the holders of Mexican bonds by former Goldman Sachs investment banker and US Treasury Secretary Robert Rubin and the IMF.[60] Of course, these were the very same banks that had been nationalized by President Portillo back in 1982. Among them were Mexico's largest private bank, Bancomer, which had been acquired by Eugenio Garza Lagüera, and the second largest, Banamex, which had been sold to well-connected non-bankers Roberto Hernández Ramírez and Alfredo Harp Helú in 1991 for $1 billion. The source of all this investment was not clear. But within a year, the bank had registered a $500 million profit, enough to pay back half the investment.[61] Banco Serfin, Mexico's third largest commercial bank, had been sold to non-banker Adrián Sada González. All told, Salinas had sold all these banks back to the private elite for only $12 billion.

Now, in effect, their loan portfolios had to be renationalized. The "cleanup" cost to taxpayers turned out to be at least a whopping twenty-two percent of Mexico's GDP, or $80 billion, payable at the rate of $15–20 billion a year plus interest.[62] The ultimate amount will probably be even greater, since it depends on the "recoverability" of assets used to secure the loans. Interestingly, FOB APROA, Mexico's deposit insurance agency, refused to identify the precise list of funds that would be paid to reimburse the banks for uncollected debts. In 1999, Michael Mackey, a Canadian auditor hired by the Mexican Congress to examine precisely what had become of all the bank loans that FOBAPROA insured, discovered that at least $7.7 billion in loans absorbed by the bailout involved "highly irregular or plainly illegal" conduct, where bank executives had made billion-dollar loans to themselves that they never repaid, loaned millions of dollars to investors to buy shares in their banks, or made huge "loans" to their friends and family without credit analysis.[63]

It turned out that the holders of $29 billion in Mexican bonds were also "not without influence." After all, these bonds were issued with the help of leading investment banks like Goldman Sachs, Morgan Stanley, and Citibank. Just as in the 1920s, these banks had helped organize the bond issues and place them with private clients and institutional investors. When the peso crisis struck in December 1994—reportedly aggravated when Salinas's family started moving their capital into dollars in the wake of the growing scandal involving Raul Salinas—Mexico ran out of reserves to preserve the peso and service its bonds. About a third of them were owned by wealthy Mexicans. The other two-thirds were owned by the clients of Wall Street firms like Rubin's old employer, Goldman Sachs. Clearly, Rubin understood what was at stake—he was Goldman Sachs's vice chairman from 1989 to 1992, in charge of international currency operations. He was also reportedly involved with Carlos Slim's Telmex financings. And Goldman Sachs was one of a handful of Wall Street firms that had dealt heavily in Mexican bonds. From 1992 to 1994, it had purchased $5.2 billion of Mexican bonds on behalf of its clients or its own portfolio, one-fifth of the total. These were the very bonds that Rubin's bailout was about to salvage.[64]

This time around, *unlike* during the 1920s, the banks worked closely with the Mexican government, mounting a successful lobbying campaign to get the Clinton administration and the IMF to bail out all these wealthy bondholders and Mexico's private banks, *in full*. One investment banker said that Mexico's elite "pulled its usual act, pointing a gun to its head and threatening to pull the trigger," unless it got another bailout.[65]

Against the opposition of most Americans, President Clinton decided to bail out his friends on Wall Street and in Mexico. This was the fourth Mexican bailout since 1982. To do so, Clinton had to behave in a somewhat extra-democratic way. To circumvent Congress, Secretary of the Treasury Robert Rubin drew on a US Treasury Emergency Stabilization Fund (ESF) that had originally been intended to support the US dollar. Clinton argued that the dollar might somehow be vulnerable to a speculative run on the peso. The argument was strained at best, but it is not surprising that Rubin was sympathetic.

The result was a $50 billion injection of First World taxpayer money, almost all of which went directly into the pockets of wealthy bondholders and the banks. About $20 billion came from the IMF, $20 billion from the special US Treasury's ESF, and

$10 billion from Europe's Bank for International Settlements. At the end of the day, however, these lenders all demanded their money back, with interest, from the Mexican government. So the costs ended up being borne by Mexico's taxpayers—mainly the millions of ordinary Mexicans who bear the brunt of the country's taxes.

For a select few, therefore, the economic crisis that followed the peso collapse was not without its compensations. In fact, there was never a better time to be a speculator, a buyer of undervalued government assets, or a flight banker. The elite were effectively insured against the effects of the crisis they had helped to create. With the help of the US, the Mexican government relieved the largest banks of many bad loans. The US also bailed out wealthy foreign and domestic investors who had bought Mexican bonds. Finally, the elite had their own life preserver. Even after Salinas's reforms, most of them had still kept at least half their private wealth outside the country in dollars, much of it in secret trust and foreign bank accounts. So it was no accident that in 1995–96, even as the peso was losing half its value, new sales of Mercedes and other luxury cars in Mexico City's affluent neighborhoods set new records.

At the time, there were many in the financial community, including Citibank's former CEO Walter Wriston and many European bankers, who disagreed with the position taken by Clinton and Rubin. They argued that this "crisis" was very different from 1982—since no major international banks (e.g., Citibank) were at risk this time. The public interest in bailing out this crowd of relatively sophisticated, well-healed owners of Mexican bonds and banks was negligible.[66] Moreover, there were serious questions about what the Mexican banks had done with all their "loans" the first place. Despite all their promotional rhetoric about free markets, when their own pocketbooks were at stake, these powerful transnational interests decided to opt for state intervention—just as Chile's bankers had done in 1983. One is reminded of the line from Auden: "When there was peace, he was for peace. When there was war, he went."

In less than a month, the resulting bailout added $50 billion to Mexico's public foreign debt, undoing a whole decade of tedious debt restructuring. By the end of 1995, Mexico's foreign debt had ballooned to more than $160 billion—the highest of any developing country, higher in real terms by fifty percent and larger relative to GDP than it had been the year of Mexico's first debt restructuring in 1997. To service this debt, Mexico had pay more than $56 billion in interest and principle in 1995 alone, and very high continuing debt, service costs. After a decade of "reform," it was the worst year ever for the growth of Mexico's foreign debt and capital flight.

At the same time, nearly half a million Mexican individual debtors and small businesses managed to organize their own nationwide union, El Barzon, seeking relief from the extraordinary interest rates that Mexican banks were charging. They had some success, but ultimately the government and banks responded harshly, breaking up their demonstrations and throwing several of their leaders in jail.[67] In 2000, over their stalwart protests, the new Mexican president Vicente Fox decided to both honor the FOBAPROA obligations to the banks and to keep the list of government bailout recipients a secret. Like many other things in Mexico, debt relief was distributed in inverse proportion to need and in direct proportion to influence.

Despite all the bailouts for the elite and bondholders, the peso's value hit an all-time low in November 1995, and the government raised interest rates again, prolonging the crisis. As its domestic banking industry cratered, for a while it appeared that Mexico might even need another increase in its credit line with the US and the IMF. But in December 1995, it received a stay of execution from the Federal Reserve, which lowered US interest rates to prevent the US economy from sinking into its own recession.

Yet, the turbulence continued for quite a while. One day the peso fell five percent on rumors of a military coup against Zedillo; another it tumbled four percent on reports that peace talks with the ELZN guerrillas had been called off; the next, it was roiled by the discovery of Raul Salinas's foreign accounts. Because of Mexico's heavy dependence on foreign finance, the economy remained hostage to events and expectations beyond its control. Meanwhile, in addition to bondholders and Mexican bank owners, there was at least one other group that profited from the Mexican crisis. In the aftermath of the crisis, to reduce FOBAPROA's costs of repairing the damage to Mexico's banking system, Mexico decided to open up its banking system to foreign ownership. Prior to the crisis, there had been severe restrictions on the rights of foreign banks to own a controlling position in Mexican banks. In fact, Citigroup was the only bank in Mexico City—having opened early in the twentieth century—that was "grandfathered" in. But now this barrier was dropped, and the buyers wasted no time in capitalizing on the opportunity. By 2001, Citigroup was the proud owner of Banamex. Banco Bilbao, Spain's largest financial group, purchased Bancomer; and Banco Santander, another leading Spanish bank, purchased Banco Serfin.

In 2003, Mexico's economy is stalled again, waiting for the US to recover. When the US does so, Mexico's economy undoubtedly will also rebound in the next few years. After all, it has one of the world's richest endowments of human and natural resources, and its labor costs are relatively low. But more than twenty years after the so-called "Third World debt crisis" began and more than a decade after it was supposed to have ended, Mexico is far from healthy, NAFTA and neoliberal reforms notwithstanding. It has massive, unsolved corruption and narco-trafficking problems, a huge supply of surplus labor, and a gargantuan foreign debt. While technical policy errors, bad luck, and local conditions all played a role in this outcome, it is hard to place the systemic blame anywhere but on authoritarian neoliberalism and its correlates: overborrowing, capital flight, corruption, money laundering, and dependent development.

In the last twenty years, Mexico ceded more and more control over its economic destiny to global markets, international bankers and their internal collaborators. Like other countries that have allowed themselves to become too far dependent on these transnational interests, Mexico still lacks a coherent, long-term economic strategy and an authentic democratic culture. It also lacks a solution to the basic problem of generating the five percent growth—or the one million plus new jobs—that it needs each year to lift its people out of poverty and become something more than a servants' quarters, oil reserve, illicit drug store, and vacation spot for its more affluent northern neighbors.

ENDNOTES

1. For Paraguay's role in the Ricord story, see Nathan M. Adams, "The Hunt for Andre," *Readers Digest*, May 1973, pp. 225–59; Alfred W. McCoy, *The Politics of Heroin in Southeast Asia*, New York, Harper & Row, 1972, p. 216; James Mills, *The Underground Empire*, New York, Dell, 1986, pp. 554–55; Henrik Krüger, *The Great Heroin Coup*, Boston, South End Press, 1980, pp. 83–86. For Paraguay's role in "Operation Condor" and its role as a refuge for General Viaux, see John Dinges and Saul Landau, *Assassination on Embassy Row*, New York, McGraw-Hill, 1980, pp. 181–87; Taylor Branch and Eugene M. Propper, *Labyrinth*, New York, Viking/Penguin, 1982.

2. "Colombian Journalist," May 21, 1989; *Financial Times*, February 6, 1989; Nathan M. Adams, "The Hunt for Andre," *op. cit.*, pp. 238–42.

3. *Financial Times*, February 4, 1989.

4. Nathan M. Adams, "The Hunt for Andre," *op. cit.*; James Brooke, *New York Times*, May 1, 1989, p. A3.

5. *Financial Times*, February 8, 1989.

6. *ABC Color*, April 5, 1989; Paraguayan Attorney General's depositions of Mario Abdo Benitez and Juan Martin Villalba de los Rios, May 1989.

7. This episode was outlined in *Jorno do Brazil*, August 28, 1988. Teodomiro Braga, April 14, 1989.

8. *ABC Color*, April 31, 1989.

9. The World Bank, World Debt Tables (1989). IDB, Statement of Loans (1986).

10. *Financial Times*, February 4, 1989, February 8, 1989; Roett, *op. cit.; New York Times*, May 1, 1989.

11. Judge Eladio Duarte Carballo was quoted in *ABC Color*, "*US $40 million en el exterior*," April 15, 1989.

12. *New York Times*, May 1, 1989.

13. See Morton Halperin, Jerry Berman, Robert Borosage, and Christine Marwick, *The Lawless State. The crimes of the US Intelligence Agencies*, New York, Penguin Books, 1976, p. 16.

14. For more about Vial, see "La Nueva Derrota," *Que Pasa*, November 10, 1997; S. Rosenfed and J.L. Marre, "Chile's Rich," *NACLA Report on the Americas*, May/June 1997.

15. See "*Milton Friedman: Gurú a regañadientes*," *Revista Qué Pasa*, February 28, 1998. For the account of the 1973–78 period, see Paul E. Sigmund, "Chile: Privatization, Reprivatization, Hyperprivatization," Princeton University, unpublished, July 1989.

16. See Rodrigo Acuña R. and Augusto Iglesias P., "Chile's Pension Reform After 20 Years," The World Bank—Social Protection Discussion Paper No. 0129, December 2001.

17. For Vial's and Lüder's October 28, 1997 sentences, see "*La Nueva Derrota*," *Que Pasa*, November 10, 1997, available at *www.quepasa.cl/revista/1386/18.html*.

18. "Chile Military Analyst," Sao Paulo, February 21, 1989;"Miami Banker," May 1991.

19. Raul Fernandez, former director of Public Credit for Costa Rica, International Bank of Miami, April 22, 1988.

20. See S. Rosenfeld and J. L. Marre, "Chile's Rich," *NACLA Report on the Americas,* May/June 1997.

21. See The Inter American Press Association, "IAPA welcomes study of putting crimes against journalists under federal jurisdiction," February 20, 2003, *http://www.impunidad.com/pressreleases/ iapa_ news2_20_03E.html.*

22. Jack Anderson, *The Washington Post,* June 5, 1984.

23. Alan Riding, *Distant Neighbors,* New York, Alfred A. Knopf, 1985, p. 176.

24. Jack Anderson, *The Washington Post,* May 15, 1984, p. C15.

25. *Proceso,* April 1988.

26. Banco de Mexico, The Mexican Economy—1988, p. 144.

27. "Mexican Banker #1," July 7, 1988.

28. The World Bank, World Debt Tables, 1991, v. II, p. 264.

29. "The Overselling of Carlos Salinas," *New York Times,* February 24, 1996, p. 20.

30. *Computing,* July 7, 1994.

31. *Computing,* December 8, 1994.

32. Dan La Botz, *The Crisis of Mexican Labor.* (New York: Praeger, 1988), pp. 146–148; Francisco Ortiz, "A cambio de contratos, el STPRM cede su exclusividad en la perforacion de pozos," *Proceso,* 10. 24. 77; Alan Riding, *op. cit.*

33. *Business Week,* October 17, 1988, p. 102.

34. Alan Riding, *op. cit.,* p. 173; *Financial Times,* January 11, 1989; "Mexican Banker #1," March 21, 1989.

35. *Financial Times,* January 12, 1989; October 31, 1989.

36. *Financial Times,* January 18, 1989, repeating the article by *Excelsior,* January 17, 1989.

37. Amnesty International (1994), quoted by The Irish Mexico Group, February 1997, available at *http://flag.blackened.net/revolt/mexico/img/salinas_state.html.*

38. World Debt Tables, *op. cit.*

39. World Bank, World Debt Tables, 1995; ECLA; author's calculations, including gross portfolio, direct, and bondholding investments for 198–94.

40. *Reuters,* January 23, 1996.

41. *Forbes Magazine,* July 8, 1994.

42. See "Heritage of a Thief," *Counterpunch,* vol. 1, no. 24, December 1, 1994.

43. *El Financiero,* February 9, 1996.

44. Eduardo Valle Espinosa quoted by *Spotlight Magazine, April* 17, 1995.

45. *Reuters,* December 2, 1995.

46. See Juan Gasparini, "Switzerland Delegates to Mexico the Task of Finishing the Salinas Investigation," IPI Agency, May 15, 2002.

47. See the article on the alleged meeting by Andreas Oppenheimer, *Miami Herald*, February 17, 1997.

48. See the Dallas Morning News, February 26, 1997.

49. See Agathe Duparc, "Salinas: End of the Criminal Saga in Geneva," *L'Hebdo*, May 15, 2002.

50. See "Citi and the Mexican Millions," *Euromoney*, May 1997, p. 12; *New York Times*, October 31, 1997, p. Al.

51. See the detailed description of this invent in Andres Oppenheimer, *Bordering on Chaos—Guerrillas, Stockbrokers, Politicians and Mexico's Road to Prosperity*, New York, Little, Brown and Company, 1996.

52. Ibid.

53. See Francisco Gil-Diaz, "The Origin of Mexico's 1994 Financial Crisis," *Cato Journal*, vol. 17, no. 3, 1998.

54. See Trond Gabrielsen, "Case Study: Banking Crisis in Mexico," Institute for Policy Dialogue (2003), available at *http://www-1.gsb.columbia.edu/ipd/j_bankingMXN.html*.

55. *The Independent*, August 22, 1995.

56. For the plight of Mexico's small businesses in the crisis, see the statement by Canacintra in the *L.A. Times*, November 16, 1995.

57. See Ginger Thomson, "Free-Market Upheaval Grinds Mexico's Middle Class," *New York Times*, September 4, 2002.

58. *La Jornada*, February 6, 1996.

59. Ginger Thomson, *New York Times, op. cit.*

60. *La Jornada*, February 1996.

61. See *www.narconews.com/fraud1994.html*, 1994.

62. The 22 percent of GDP estimate for the cost of the Mexican bailout is from World Bank Online Data, "Crisis Management Mexico, 1994–1995," June 2001. See *Financial Times*, January 23, 1996; *Reuters*, December 15, 1995.

63. See Julia Preston, "Bailout Audit in Mexico Cites $7.7 Billion in Dubious Loans," *New York Times*, July 20, 1999.

64. For the role of Rubin and Goldman's stake in Mexican bonds, see SourceMex—Economic News & Analysis on Mexico, March 8, 1995, available at *http://ssdc.ucsd.edu/news/smex/h95/smex.19950308.html SourceMex*.

65. Investment banker from Morgan Grenfall, quoted by *Reuters*, October 13, 1995.

66. See Walter Wriston, *Stern Business Magazine*, Spring 1995.

67. For the crackdown on El Barzon leaders, see *La Jornada*, December 24, 1995.

chapter eight

GET RID OF THIS STINKER

by Stephen Kinzer

The most heavily attended funeral in Guatemalan history was for a man who had been dead twenty-four years. More than 100,000 people filled the streets of Guatemala City and jammed the cemetery. Many threw red carnations at the cortege and chanted, "Jacobo! Jacobo!" Some, especially those old enough to remember the statesman they were burying, were overcome with emotion.

"All I know is that there was no persecution during his government," said a seventy-seven-year-old man in the crowd who struggled to hold back his tears. "Afterwards, people began dying."

Jacobo Arbenz Guzman was the second of two presidents who governed Guatemala during the country's "democratic spring," which lasted from 1944 to 1954. For decades after the CIA overthrew him and chased him from his homeland, it was dangerous to speak well of Arbenz or lament his fate. He died alone and forgotten. Only when his remains were finally brought home to Guatemala and buried, on October 20, 1995, did his people have a chance to honor him. They did so with a fervor born of unspeakable suffering.

Arbenz took office in 1951, the same year another nationalist, Mohammad Mossadegh, became prime minister of Iran. Each assumed leadership of a wretchedly poor nation that was just beginning to enjoy the blessings of democracy. Each challenged the power of a giant foreign- owned company. The company howled in protest, and charged that the government was Communistic. Secretary of State John Foster Dulles agreed.

Few private companies have ever been as closely interwoven with the United States government as United Fruit was during the mid-1950s. Dulles had, for decades, been one of its principal legal counselors. His brother, Allen, the CIA director, had also done legal work for the company and owned a substantial block of its stock. John Moors Cabot, the assistant secretary of state for inter-American affairs, was a large shareholder. So was his brother, Thomas Dudley Cabot, the director of international security affairs in the State Department, who had been United Fruit's president. General Robert Cutler, head of the National Security Council, was its former chairman of the board. John J. McCloy, the president of the International Bank for Reconstruction and Development, was a former board member. Both undersecretary of state Walter Bedell Smith and Robert Hill, the American ambassador to Costa Rica, would join the board after leaving government service.

During the first half of the twentieth century, United Fruit made great profits in Guatemala because it was able to operate without interference from the Guatemalan government. It simply claimed good farmland, arranged for legal title through one-sided deals with dictators, and then operated plantations on its own terms, free of such annoyances as taxes or labor regulations. As long as that system prevailed, men like John Foster Dulles considered Guatemala a "friendly" and "stable" country. When a new kind of government emerged there and began to challenge the company, they disapproved.

For thirteen years during the 1930s and 1940s, United Fruit thrived in Guatemala under the patronage of Jorge Ubico, a classically outsized Latin American *caudillo*. According to one historian, Ubico "called anyone a Communist whose social, economic and political ideologies were more progressive than his own" and "trusted only the army, wealthy indigenous landowners and foreign corporations." The most important of those corporations was United Fruit, which provided tens of thousands of full- and part-time jobs in Guatemala. Ubico showered United Fruit with concession agreements, including one in 1936 that his agents negotiated personally with Dulles. It gave the company a ninety-nine-year lease on a vast tract of land along the rich Pacific plain at Tiquisate, and guaranteed it an exemption from all taxes for the duration of the lease.

Guatemalans became restive as Ubico's harsh rule wore on. An emerging middle class, inspired by the democratic rhetoric of World War II and the examples of reformist presidents Lázaro Cárdenas in Mexico and Franklin D. Roosevelt in the

United States, began agitating for change. During the summer and fall of 1944, thousands of demonstrators, led by schoolteachers, launched a wave of street protests. As they reached a peak, young officers staged a lightning uprising and toppled the old regime. Guatemala's own "October Revolution" was won at the cost of fewer than one hundred lives.

A few months later, Guatemalans went to the polls in their country's first democratic election. By an overwhelming margin, they chose a visionary young schoolteacher, Juan José Arévalo, as their president. In his inaugural address, delivered to an expectant nation on March 15, 1945, Arevalo cited Roosevelt as his inspiration, and vowed to follow his example.

> There has in the past been a fundamental lack of sympathy for the working man, and the faintest cry for justice was avoided and punished as if one were trying to eradicate the beginnings of a frightful epidemic. Now we are going to begin a period of sympathy for the man who works in the fields, in the shops, on the military bases, in small businesses.... We are going to add justice and humanity to order, because order based on injustice and humiliation is good for nothing.

President Arévalo laid a solid foundation for Guatemala's new democracy, and did much to bring his country into the modern age. During his six-year term, the National Assembly established the country's first social security system, guaranteed the rights of trade unions, fixed a forty-eight-hour workweek, and even levied a modest tax on large landholders. Each of these measures represented a challenge to United Fruit. The company had been setting its own rules in Guatemala for more than half a century, and did not look favorably on the surge of nationalism that Arévalo embodied. It resisted him every way it could.

Arévalo's term ended on March 15, 1951. As thousands watched, he handed the presidential sash over to his elected successor, Jacobo Arbenz. It was the first peaceful transfer of power in Guatemalan history. Arévalo, though, was not in a celebratory mood. In his farewell speech, he lamented that he had not been able to do more for his people:

> The banana magnates, co-nationals of Roosevelt, rebelled against the audacity of a Central American president who gave to his fellow citizens a legal equality with the honorable families of exporters.... It was then that the schoolteacher, ingenuous and romantic, from the presidency of his country, discovered how perishable, frail and slippery the brilliant international doctrines of democracy and freedom were. It was then, with the deepest despondency and pain, that I felt, with consequent indignation, the pressure

of that anonymous force that rules, without laws or morals, international relations and the relationships of men.

The incoming president was destined to feel that pressure even more intensely. Arbenz was a thirty-seven-year-old colonel who had helped lead the 1944 uprising against Ubico, but he was by no means a typical Guatemalan army officer. His father was a pharmacist who had emigrated from Switzerland and had committed suicide while Jacobo was still a boy. That ended his hope of becoming a scientist or an engineer, but a friend in the tight-knit Swiss community arranged for him to be given a place at the Military Academy. There he compiled a brilliant academic record and excelled at boxing and polo. He was also strikingly good-looking, blue-eyed and fair-haired but with a Latin profile. At a Central American athletic competition, he met a young Salvadoran woman, María Cristina Vilanova, who, despite her upper-class background, was a passionate leftist. After their marriage, she encouraged him to develop a social conscience and political ambition. He showed both in his inaugural address, setting out "three fundamental objectives" for his presidency:

> to convert our country from a dependent nation with a semi-colonial economy into an economically independent country; to convert Guatemala from a country bound by a predominantly feudal economy into a modern capitalist state; and to make this transformation in a way that will raise the standard of living of the great mass of our people to the highest level.

This was a sweeping agenda, and as soon as President Arbenz began to press it, he found himself at odds with all three of the American companies that dominated Guatemala's economy. First he announced plans to build a publicly owned electric system, which would break a highly lucrative monopoly held by Electric Bond & Share. Then he turned his attention to International Railways of Central America, which owned nearly all the country's rail lines, including the sole link between the capital and the Atlantic port of Puerto Barrios—most of which it also owned. Arbenz proposed to build a new deepwater port, open to all, with a highway connection to the capital. Then, confronting the cruelly unbalanced system of land ownership that was and is at the root of poverty in Guatemala, he won passage of a landmark law that threatened United Fruit itself.

The Agrarian Reform Law, which the National Assembly passed on June 17, 1952, was the crowning achievement of Guatemala's democratic revolution. Under its provisions, the government could seize and redistribute all uncultivated land on estates larger than 672 acres, compensating owners according to the land's declared tax value. This was a direct challenge to United Fruit, which owned more than 550,000 acres, about one-fifth of the country's arable land, but cultivated less than 15 percent of it. The company said it needed these vast, fertile tracts for future contingencies. To citizens of a country where hundreds of thousands went hungry for want of land, this seemed grossly unjust.

The three interlocking companies most affected by Arbenz's reforms had controlled Guatemala for decades. United Fruit was by far the country's largest landowner and largest private employer. It held 46 percent of the stock in International Railways of Central America, thereby securing freight service and access to Puerto Barrios at highly favorable rates. Electric Bond & Share supplied power for the railways and banana plantations. Together, the three companies had more than $100 million invested in Guatemala. Arbenz subjected them to a host of new regulations, and many of their executives and stockholders came to detest him. So did the New York lawyer who represented all three of them, John Foster Dulles.

Early in 1953, the Guatemalan government seized 234,000 uncultivated acres of United Fruit's 295,000-acre plantation at Tiquisate. It offered compensation of $1.185 million, the value the company had declared for tax purposes. United Fruit executives rejected the offer, asserting that no one took self-assessed valuations seriously. They demanded $19 million.

Most Guatemalans considered land redistribution a welcome step in a nation where democracy was beginning to bloom. It looked quite different from Washington. Many old friends of United Fruit had assumed influential positions in the Eisenhower administration just as the Guatemalan government was seizing the company's land. They considered these seizures not only illegal and outrageous but proof of Communist influence. Since Guatemala is the traditional leader in Central America, they also worried that any reforms allowed to succeed there would quickly spread to other countries. In their minds, defending United Fruit and defeating Central American Communism fused into a single goal. They could achieve it only by overthrowing Arbenz.

United Fruit rose to its mythical status in Guatemala under the leadership of Sam Zemurray, the visionary "Banana Man" who had organized the overthrow of President Miguel Dávila of Honduras in 1911 and gone on to become one of the most powerful figures in Central America. Soon after Guatemala turned democratic, in 1944, Zemurray sensed that its reformist government would give the company trouble. The stakes were high, and he wanted to be sure that American public opinion was with him. He decided to hire an outside public relations expert. The new man was Edward Bernays, a nephew of Sigmund Freud and the dominant figure in his young profession.

Bernays was one of the first masters of modern mass psychology. He liked to describe himself as the "father of public relations," and no one disagreed. His specialty was what he called "the conscious and intelligent manipulation of the organized habits and opinions of the masses." He proposed to Zemurray that United Fruit launch a campaign to blacken the image of Guatemala's government. That, he argued, could decisively weaken it and perhaps set off events that would trigger its collapse.

"I have the feeling that Guatemala might respond to pitiless publicity in this country," Bernays surmised.

Never before had an American corporation waged a propaganda campaign in the United States aimed at undermining the president of a foreign country. Zemurray was reluctant to make United Fruit the first. Then, in the spring of 1951, Bernays sent him a message with alarming news. The reformist leader of faraway Iran, Mohammad Mossadegh, had just done the unthinkable by nationalizing the Anglo-Iranian Oil Company. "Guatemala might follow suit," Bernays wrote in his note.

That was all Zemurray needed to hear. He authorized Bernays to launch his campaign, and the results soon began to show. First were a series of articles in the *New York Times*, portraying Guatemala as falling victim to "reds"; they appeared after Bernays visited *Times* publisher Arthur Hays Sulzberger. Next came reports in leading magazines, most of them written, like the *Times* series, with helpful advice from Bernays. Then Bernays began organizing press junkets to Guatemala. They produced glowing dispatches about United Fruit and terrifying ones about the emergence of Marxist dictatorship in Guatemala.

Prominent members of Congress echoed these themes. Most outspoken among them was a Massachusetts senator with a familiar name, Henry Cabot Lodge, scion of two families that United Fruit had helped make rich. In the same chamber where his grandfather and namesake had helped secure American control of Cuba and the Philippines more than half a century before, Lodge delivered vituperative speeches depicting Guatemalan leaders as crypto-Communists. Meanwhile, in the House of Representatives, the majority leader and future speaker, John McCormack—also from Massachusetts, where United Fruit had sustained generations of prosperity— rose regularly to deliver chilling warnings that Guatemala's democratic leaders had become "subservient to the Kremlin's design for world conquest" and were turning their country into "a Soviet beachhead."

This rhetoric reached a new peak after the Agrarian Reform Law was passed. Powerful officials in Washington, products of the international business world and utterly ignorant of the realities of Guatemalan life, considered the idea of land redistribution to be inherently Marxist. "Products of the Cold War ethos," the historian Richard Immerman has written, "they believed it axiomatic that no government would take such a radical measure against a United States business if it were not dominated by communists."

Guatemala's communist party was actually a modest affair. Even at its peak it had only a few hundred active members, no mass base, and no support in the foreign ministry or army. Communists never held more than four seats in the sixty-one-member National Assembly. None sat in Arbenz's cabinet, although two gifted young

Communist firebrands, one the leader of a labor federation and the other a charismatic peasant organizer, were among his closest advisers.

Arbenz was a leftist and intrigued by Marxist ideas. Often he irritated the United States with symbolic gestures, like allowing an official newspaper to charge that American forces were using germ warfare in Korea, or permitting the National Assembly to observe a minute of silence when Stalin died in 1953. He may have considered these incidents trivial. Officials in Washington, however, seized on them as proof that he had become an enemy.

If the first American error in assessing Arbenz was to believe that he was leading Guatemala toward Communism, the second was to assume that he was doing so as part of a master plan drafted in Moscow. Secretary of State Dulles in particular had not the slightest doubt that the Soviet Union was actively working to shape events in Guatemala. The fact that the Soviets had no military, economic, or even diplomatic relations with Guatemala, that no delegation of Guatemalans had ever visited Moscow, and that a study by the State Department itself had found the few Guatemalan Communists to be "indigenous to the area" interested him not at all. In the spring of 1954, he told a South American diplomat that although it was "impossible to produce evidence clearly tying the Guatemalan government to Moscow," American leaders were acting against that government "based on our deep conviction that such a tie must exist."

No evidence ever emerged to support that "deep conviction." Not in the vast archive of files the CIA captured after its coup, nor in any other document or testimony that has surfaced since, is there any indication that Soviet leaders were even slightly interested in Guatemala during the 1950s. Dulles could not have fathomed that. He was convinced to the point of theological certainty that the Soviets were behind every challenge to American power in the world. So was the rest of the Eisenhower administration. It believed, as one historian has put it, "that it was dealing not with misguided, irresponsible nationalists, but with ruthless agents of international communism."

Dulles and his colleagues came into office determined to rid themselves of the troublesome regime in Guatemala, but without a clear idea of how to do so. Kermit Roosevelt's triumph in Iran showed them the way. They decided to design a Guatemalan version of Operation Ajax. To reflect their confidence, they code-named it Operation Success.

On December 3, 1953, the CIA authorized an initial $3 million to set the plot in motion. It would start with a propaganda campaign, proceed through a wave of destabilizing violence, and culminate in an attack staged to look like a domestic uprising. This operation, though, would be much larger in scale than the one in Iran. Allen Dulles's idea was to find a suitable opposition leader among Guatemalan exiles; equip him with a militia that could pose as a full-scale rebel army; hire American pilots to bomb Guatemala City; and then, with the country in chaos, have the American ambassador tell military commanders that peace would return only if they deposed Arbenz.

The ambassador that Secretary of State Dulles chose for this job was John Peurifoy, a West Point dropout from South Carolina who had failed the foreign service examination and, eager to work in government, took a job as an elevator operator at the Capitol. He made friends easily and with the help of home-state connections landed a job at the State Department. In 1950 he became ambassador to Greece, where he showed himself to be a flamboyant figure, happiest when driving fast cars or denouncing leftists. His passion for the latter attracted Dulles's attention, and at the end of 1953 he was named the new United States ambassador to Guatemala. The *New York Times* speculated that this choice would mean "a change in the asserted passivity with which the United States has watched the growth of Communist influence."

On the evening of December 16, Peurifoy had his first and only meeting with Arbenz. It lasted for six hours, over an extended dinner at Arbenz's official residence. When Arbenz began to discourse on United Fruit's abuses, Peurifoy interrupted to say that the real problem in Guatemala was "commie influence." The next day he sent Dulles a curt assessment of the man they had targeted: "If he is not a communist, he will certainly do until one comes along."

"Normal approaches will not work in Guatemala," Peurifoy added ominously. "The candle is burning slowly and surely, and it is only a matter of time before the large American interests will be forced out entirely."

These were just the words Dulles wanted to hear. He brought the cable to Eisenhower, who read it gravely. By the time he finished, according to his own account, he had decided to give Operation Success his final approval.

Eisenhower's order set the CIA off on its second plot against a foreign government. It was run autonomously within the agency, meaning that its coordinator, Colonel Al Haney, a former college football star who had run CIA guerrillas behind enemy lines in Korea, could report directly to Allen Dulles. Haney established a clandestine headquarters at a military airfield in Opa-Locka, Florida, on the outskirts of Miami; a transshipment post for weapons at France Field in the Panama Canal Zone; and a network of remote airstrips in Honduras and Nicaragua, both of which were ruled by dictators who fervently wished to see Arbenz overthrown. Allen Dulles found all of this "brilliant," but Colonel J. C. King, the head of Western Hemisphere operations for the CIA's directorate of plans, which carries out covert action, spoke up to dissent. King had no use for nationalists like Arbenz, but he worried about the long-term impact of Haney's ambitious plan.

"He'll be starting a civil war in the middle of Central America!" King protested.

Allen Dulles responded by inviting both King and Haney to his Georgetown estate, Highlands. Over cocktails, he told them they had no more reason to argue.

The president and secretary of state had ordered that Arbenz be overthrown. It was the CIA's job to carry out that order.

"Go to it, my boy," Dulles said as he slapped his hands on Haney's broad shoulders. "You've got the green light."

Operation Success was now fully approved in Washington, and fully funded—with $4.5 million, more than the CIA had ever spent on a covert operation. It lacked only one essential element: a Guatemalan to play the role of rebel leader. After several false starts, the CIA settled on a former army officer, Carlos Castillo Armas, who had led an abortive uprising in 1950 and had become a familiar figure in Guatemalan exile circles. Agents found him in Honduras, flew him to Opa-Locka, told him they were working with United Fruit on an anti-Arbenz project, and proposed that he become its putative leader. He accepted immediately.

During the spring of 1954, Castillo Armas waited in Honduras while the CIA hired fighters, requisitioned planes, prepared bases, and secured the cooperation of Honduran and Nicaraguan officials. The CIA station on the fourth floor of the American embassy in Guatemala City buzzed with activity. So did the operational base at Opa-Locka.

One of the agents assigned to Operation Success, Howard Hunt, who later became notorious for his role in the Watergate burglary, came up with the idea of using the Roman Catholic clergy to turn Guatemalans against Arbenz. Catholic priests and bishops in Guatemala, as in other Latin American countries, were closely aligned with the ruling class, and they loathed reformers like Arbenz. Hunt visited the most powerful Catholic prelate in the United States, Francis Cardinal Spellman of New York, and asked him if he could bring his Guatemalan counterparts into the coup plot. Spellman assured him that would be no problem. Soon, as Hunt later recalled, CIA agents "were writing scripts or leaflets for the Guatemalan clergy, the Catholic clergy, and this information was going out in [pastoral letters] across the country and in radio broadcasts." The most important of these pastoral letters, read in every Catholic church in Guatemala on April 9, warned the faithful that a demonic force called Communism was trying to destroy their homeland and called on them to "rise as a single man against this enemy of God and country."

While the CIA was busily laying the groundwork for a coup in Guatemala, Secretary of State Dulles intensified his diplomatic campaign. In March he traveled to Caracas, Venezuela, for a meeting of the Organization of American States. Some foreign ministers came to Caracas with hopes of discussing economic development, but Dulles insisted that their "major interest" must be Communism. He introduced a resolution declaring that if a country in the Western Hemisphere fell under the control of "the international communist movement," any other nation in the hemisphere would be legally justified in taking "appropriate action." Guatemala's representative, Foreign

Minister Guillermo Toriello, called this resolution "merely a pretext for intervention in our internal affairs."

> The plan of national liberation being carried out with firmness by my government has necessarily affected the privileges of foreign enterprises that are impeding the progress and economic development of the country.... They wanted to find a ready expedient to maintain the economic dependence of the American Republics and suppress the legitimate desires of their peoples, cataloguing as "communism" every manifestation of nationalism or economic independence, any desire for social progress, any intellectual curiosity, and any interest in liberal and progressive reforms.

More than a few delegates sympathized with this view, but Dulles was determined to win passage of his resolution. He remained in Caracas for two weeks, sitting through long meetings during which he fended off no fewer than fifty amendments. Finally and inevitably, he was successful. Sixteen countries supported the "Declaration of Caracas." Only Guatemala opposed it, with Mexico and Argentina abstaining.

This outcome was a great success for the United States, and it deeply shook Arbenz. The Dulles brothers agreed to intensify their pressure on him until the time seemed right to strike him down. Before they could do so, he made an unexpected misstep that delighted them.

Until Guatemala turned to democracy, in 1944, the United States had been its main arms supplier. After the transition, the Americans stopped sending weaponry. They also pressured Denmark, Mexico, Cuba, Argentina, and Switzerland to back out of arms deals with Guatemala. When the CIA began arming Guatemalan exiles, Arbenz became alarmed at the poor state of his defenses. He looked urgently for a country that would sell him weapons, and finally found one. On May 15, 1954, a freighter called the *Alfhelm* docked at Puerto Barrios and workers began unloading crates labeled "Optical and Laboratory Equipment." Inside were arms and ammunition from Czechoslovakia.

Czech arms makers had demanded payment in cash, and most of the weaponry they shipped turned out to be obsolete, impractical, or nonfunctional. Still, they could not have sold weapons to Guatemala without approval from Moscow. The symbolism of the *Alfhelm* shipment was overwhelming. A vessel loaded with Soviet-bloc arms had landed in Guatemala. To Representative McCormack, this was "like an atom bomb planted in the rear of our backyard." Secretary of State Dulles declared it proof of "communist infiltration."

"That is the problem," he told reporters in Washington, "not United Fruit."

From that moment, it became almost impossible for anyone in Washington to defend Arbenz. Some might have tried if they had known what the State Department and CIA were intending to do. The coup in Guatemala, though, like the one in Iran, was conceived in great secrecy. No one outside a handful of men knew about the plan, so no one could object, warn, or protest. This attraction of covert "regime change" operations was not lost on the Dulles brothers.

Some doubts about the administration's policy toward Guatemala did emerge, publicly and privately, but they were easily brushed aside. One came on the pages of the *New York Times*, where the reporter Sydney Gruson wrote several articles after the *Alfhelm* incident suggesting that Guatemalans were rallying around their government and that they were caught up not in Communism but in "fervent nationalism." This was not what United Fruit and the Eisenhower administration wished Americans to hear. Allen Dulles arranged a dinner with his friend Julius Adler, the business manager of the *Times*, and complained. Adler passed the complaint on to *Times* publisher Arthur Hays Sulzberger. A few days later, Gruson's boss pulled him out of Guatemala.

Allen Dulles also had to deal with a problem at his CIA station in Guatemala. The station chief, Birch O'Neill, did not like the idea of a coup. Like his counterpart in Tehran a year before, Roger Goiran, he warned that it would not work out well in the long run. Dulles responded by transferring O'Neill out of the country.

As Allen Dulles was removing these potential obstacles, his brother faced dissent from several State Department officials. One of them, Louis Halle, a member of the policy planning staff, circulated a lengthy memorandum asserting that Guatemala was in desperate need of social reform, that its government was "nationalist and anti-Yanqui" but not pro-Communist, and that the entire crisis was of United Fruit's making. Another official, Deputy Undersecretary of State Robert Murphy, found out about Operation Success by accident and fired off an angry note to Dulles telling him that the idea was "wrong" and would probably be "very expensive over the long term."

"To resort to this action confesses the bankruptcy of our political policy vis-à-vis that country," Murphy wrote.

Secretary of State Dulles had long since made up his mind to overthrow Arbenz, and did not bother to reply to dissenters in his ranks. News of their protests, though, filtered through higher echelons of the State Department. Ambassador Peurifoy was concerned enough to ask his superiors if there had been a change in plans. In a return cable, Raymond Leddy, the State Department's policy director for Central America, assured him that Operation Success was still on.

"We are on the road to settling this problem," Leddy wrote. "There is a 100 percent determination, from top down, to get rid of this stinker and not to stop until that is done."

Haney's operation was already in full swing. He had recruited a miniarmy of nearly five hundred Guatemalan exiles, American soldiers of fortune, and assorted Central American mercenaries and had sent them to camps in Nicaragua, Honduras, and

Florida, where they were being given rudimentary training. His clandestine "Voice of Liberation" radio station, supposedly transmitting from "somewhere in Guatemala" but actually based in Opa-Locka, was broadcasting a stream of false reports about popular unrest and military rebellions. It was time for Haney to send his handpicked "liberator," Colonel Castillo Armas, into action.

Soon after dawn on June 18, Castillo Armas summoned his men, packed them into jeeps and trucks, and led them northward in his command car, a battered old station wagon. They crossed the Honduran border without incident. Then, following the orders his CIA handlers had given him, Castillo Armas led his motorcade six miles into Guatemalan territory. There he stopped. This was the invasion.

Arbenz placed his army and police on alert but, on the advice of Foreign Minister Toriello, did not send troops to the border area. Toriello hoped to resolve this matter diplomatically. He wanted to show the world that foreign-sponsored troops were on Guatemalan territory, and did not want any government soldiers there to muddy the issue.

By mid-morning, Toriello was writing an urgent appeal to the United Nations Security Council. He asked the council to meet immediately and condemn an invasion of Guatemala launched "at the instigation of certain foreign monopolies." While he wrote, the "Voice of Liberation" was broadcasting breathless reports of Castillo Armas's supposed swift progress through the countryside. Two CIA planes buzzed low over the main military barracks in Guatemala City, firing machine-gun rounds and dropping a fragmentation bomb that set off a series of loud explosions. Ambassador Peurifoy, one of the few people in the country who knew exactly what was happening, heard them in his embassy office. He looked out his window, saw smoke billowing up from the barracks, and dashed off a gleeful cable to Dulles.

"Looks like this is it," he wrote.

The air raids continued for several days. One plane shot up the airport in Guatemala City. Others hit fuel tanks and military posts across the country. They led to several injuries and some property damage, but their purpose was not military. Like the bogus radio broadcasts, they were aimed at creating the impression that a war was under way. Each time a plane strafed another town, Guatemalans became more insecure, confused, and fearful—and more willing to believe what they heard on the "Voice of Liberation."

Secretary of State Dulles was receiving almost hour-by-hour reports on these events, from his brother and from Ambassador Peurifoy. His position, however, required him to dissemble in public. On the afternoon of June 19, the State Department issued a disingenuous statement saying it had news of "serious uprisings" and "outbreaks of violence" in Guatemala. Then it declared the lie that was at the heart of Operation Success.

"The department has no evidence that indicates this is anything other than a revolt of Guatemalans against the government," it said.

Arbenz knew that was untrue. He had come to realize that the United States was behind this rebellion, which meant that he could not defeat it with armed force. This realization drove him first to drink, and then to a decision to address his country by radio. In his speech he declared that "the arch-traitor Castillo Armas" was leading a "United Fruit Company expeditionary force" against his government.

> Our crime is having enacted an agrarian reform which affected the interests of the United Fruit Company. Our crime is wanting to have our own route to the Atlantic, our own electric power and our own docks and ports. Our crime is our patriotic wish to advance, to progress, to win an economic independence that would match our political independence....
>
> It is completely untrue that communists are taking over the government.... We have imposed no terror. It is, on the contrary, the Guatemalan friends of Mr. Foster Dulles who wish to spread terror among our people, attacking women and children by surprise with impunity from pirate airplanes.

In the days after that speech, things began looking better for Arbenz. The army remained loyal to him, and his popularity among ordinary Guatemalans was unbroken. At a meeting of the Security Council in New York, France introduced a resolution calling for an end to "any action likely to cause bloodshed" in Guatemala and directing all countries to refrain from "rendering assistance to any such action." Castillo Armas was making no military progress. Most important, the air raids, which had driven much of the country to near-panic, were tapering off because one of the CIA's four P-47 Thunderbolts had been shot out of action and a second had crashed.

From his command post at Opa-Locka, Al Haney sent an urgent cable to Allen Dulles. It said that Operation Success was on the verge of collapse and would probably fail without more air support. Dulles went immediately to the White House to ask President Eisenhower for permission to dispatch two more planes. Eisenhower readily agreed. Later he told one of his aides that he had seen no realistic alternative.

"If at any time you take the route of violence or support of violence," he said, "then you commit yourself to carrying it through, and it's too late to have second thoughts."

Arbenz, who of course knew nothing of this, pressed his diplomatic offensive. He dispatched Toriello to New York, and there the foreign minister urged the Security Council to send an investigating team to Guatemala immediately. This was exactly what the Americans wished to prevent. The new United States ambassador to the United Nations—none other than former senator Henry Cabot Lodge—worked feverishly behind the scenes, and in a pivotal decision on June 25, the Security Council voted not to investigate what was happening in Guatemala.

While Lodge was holding the diplomatic fort, Haney sent his two new planes into action. His first round of raids had been for psychological effect, but now they took a more serious turn. For three days and nights, the planes strafed military bases, shot up fuel tanks, and dropped incendiary bombs on ammunition dumps. These attacks spread alarm and led hundreds of people to flee from their homes. On the day of the Security Council vote, in a last-minute appeal that was poignant almost to the point of pathos, Toriello sent a long cable to Dulles.

> I regret to inform your Excellency that a savage attack with TNT bombs took place yesterday on the civilian population of Chiquimula, as well as the strafing of that city and the cities of Gualán and Zacapa.... Guatemala appeals urgently to your Excellency to communicate to you this painful situation, and asks that your enlightened government, always respectful of the human rights of which it has been the standard-bearer, be good enough to intercede with the Security Council.

Dulles ignored this appeal. He could afford to, because events were now turning his way. No outsider had discovered the great ruse of Operation Success. Most Guatemalans believed what the "Voice of Liberation" told them: that Castillo Armas was leading a rebel army through the countryside, that many Guatemalan soldiers had risen up to join him, and that the government was powerless to stop the juggernaut.

As the bombing campaign intensified, Arbenz began to lose his grip. At one point he considered calling the peasantry to armed resistance, but his military commanders would not hear of it. He was out of options. At midday on Sunday, June 27, he sent Toriello to the American embassy to arrange the terms of his surrender.

Ambassador Peurifoy, who had taken to wearing a flight suit and brandishing a pistol, told Toriello that if there was a "clean sweep" at the National Palace, he might be able to persuade "insurgent forces" to end their campaign. A few hours later, the army chief of staff, Colonel Carlos Enrique Díaz, invited Peurifoy to his home. When Peurifoy arrived, the four other senior Guatemalan military commanders were also there. Díaz began by complaining bitterly about what the United States was doing in his country. Peurifoy, by his own account, "replied sharply that if he had brought me to his house to make accusations against my government, I would leave immediately." That reminded the Guatemalans who was in the stronger position. They reluctantly agreed to confront Arbenz and demand his resignation, but indignantly told Peurifoy that under no circumstances would they negotiate with Castillo Armas or bring him into a new government.

At four o'clock that afternoon, the commanders called on Arbenz. They told him they had constituted themselves as a military junta and were deposing him. He had no choice but to agree. His friends promised him two things: that they would never deal with Castillo Armas, and that they would allow him to deliver a farewell message over the radio. At nine-fifteen in the evening, Arbenz addressed his people for the last time.

> Workers, peasants, patriots, my friends, people of Guatemala: Guatemala is enduring a most difficult trial. For fifteen days a cruel war against Guatemala has been underway. The United Fruit Company, in collaboration with the governing circles of the United States, is responsible for what is happening to us....
>
> I have not violated my faith in democratic liberties, in the independence of Guatemala and in all the good that is the future of humanity.... I have always said to you that we would fight regardless of the cost, but the cost should not include the destruction of our country and the sending of our riches abroad. And this could happen if we do not eliminate the pretext that our powerful enemy has raised.
>
> A government different from mine, but always inspired by our October Revolution, is preferable to twenty years of fascist bloody tyranny under the rule of the bands that Castillo Armas has brought into the country.

After Arbenz finished his broadcast, he left the studio and walked forlornly to the Mexican embassy, where he asked for and was granted political asylum. Colonel Díaz took the microphone. He officially accepted the reins of power, and then promised Guatemalans, "The struggle against mercenary invaders will not abate." Ambassador Peurifoy's jaw tightened as he listened over the radio. When Díaz was finished, the ambassador slammed his hand onto his desk.

"OK," he spat, "now I'll have to crack down on that s.o.b."

The broadcast also upset the two principal CIA operatives in Guatemala, station chief John Doherty and agent Enno Hobbing, who had been sent from Washington to help oversee Operation Success. As soon as it was over, they agreed that their work was not yet complete. They decided to depose Díaz that very night and replace him with an officer they knew and trusted, Colonel Elfegio Monzón.

Doherty and Hobbing drove to Monzón's home, gave him the good news that he was about to become president, and packed him into their backseat. Together the three drove to Díaz's headquarters. It was midnight when they arrived.

Díaz, who had been in power for only a few hours, feared the worst. He began by trying to defend Arbenz's reforms, but Hobbing cut him off.

"Let me explain something to you," he said. "You made a big mistake when you took over the government."

There was a long moment of silence as Díaz absorbed this message. Then Hobbing spoke again. "Colonel," he told Díaz, "you're just not convenient for the requirements of American foreign policy."

"But I talked to your ambassador!" Díaz protested.

"Well, Colonel, there is diplomacy and then there is reality. Our ambassador represents diplomacy. I represent reality. And the reality is we don't want you."

"Can I hear it from the ambassador?" Díaz asked plaintively.

It was four o'clock in the morning when an irritated Peurifoy arrived at Díaz's headquarters. They had a tense meeting. Díaz insisted that he would not resign without a guarantee that Guatemala would not be turned over to Castillo Armas. Peurifoy refused to give it. Finally he stormed out. Back at the embassy at dawn, he composed a pithy cable to Haney.

"We have been double-crossed," it said. "BOMB!"

That afternoon, at a clandestine airstrip in Honduras, a CIA pilot named Jerry DeLarm stepped into the cockpit of a P-47. Accompanied by a fighter escort, he headed to Guatemala City. There he dropped two bombs on the parade ground of the main military base and several more on the government radio station.

Reality was closing in on Colonel Díaz. He summoned Peurifoy in the predawn hours of Tuesday, June 29, but as soon as they started talking he was called into a side room to consult with other officers. A few minutes later he emerged, with a tommy gun pointed at his ribs. Beside him was Colonel Monzón.

"My colleague Díaz has decided to resign," Monzón said suavely. "I am replacing him."

Monzón formed a three-man junta and, a few days later, flew to El Salvador for negotiations with Castillo Armas. They met under Ambassador Peurifoy's supervision. His influence brought them to a speedy agreement. Within a few days, the two subsidiary members of the junta, reportedly encouraged by payments of $100,000 apiece, accepted diplomatic posts abroad. On July 5, Monzón followed them into retirement. Castillo Armas replaced him and proclaimed himself president of Guatemala. Soon afterward, Secretary of State Dulles addressed Americans by radio and told them that a great victory over Communism had been won.

The Guatemalan government and Communist agents throughout the world have persistently attempted to obscure the real issue—that of Communist imperialism—by claiming that the U.S. is only interested in protecting American business. We regret that there have been disputes between the Guatemalan government and the United Fruit Company.... But this issue is relatively unimportant.... Led by Colonel Castillo Armas, patriots arose in Guatemala to challenge the Communist leadership and to change it. Thus the situation is being cured by the Guatemalans themselves.

Dulles knew he was being untruthful when he asserted that "Guatemalans themselves" were responsible for overthrowing Arbenz, but he did not realize that the other claim he made in his victory proclamation was also false. He truly believed that Arbenz was a tool of "Communist imperialism" rather than what he actually was: an idealistic, reform-minded nationalist who bore Americans no ill will. By overthrowing him, the United States crushed a democratic experiment that held great promise for Latin America. As in Iran a year earlier, it deposed a regime that embraced fundamental American ideals but that had committed the sin of seeking to retake control of its own natural resources.

ENDNOTES

1. People began dying: Reuters dispatch from Guatemala City, Oct. 20, 1995. United Fruit tied to United States government: Ambrose, Stephen E., *Ike's Spies: Eisenhower and the Espionage Establishment* (Garden City, R.Y.: Doubleday, 1981), p. 223; Immerman, Richard H., *The CIA in Guatemala; The Foreign Policy of Intervention* (Austin: University of Texas Press, 1982), p. 125; Marchetti, Victor, and John Marks, *The CIA and the Cult of Intelligence* (New York: Knopf, 1964), p, 376.

2. Ubico called anyone a Communist: Immerman, p. 33. Ubico showers United Fruit with concessions: Ambrose, p. 218; Immer¬man, p. 124; Schlesinger, Stephen, and Stephen Kinzer, Bitter Fruit: The Untold Story of the American Coup in Guatemala (Garden City, N.Y.: Dou¬bleday, 1982), p. 70; Rabe, Stephen G., Eisenhower and Latin America: The Foreign Policy of Anticommunism (Chapel Hill: University of North Car¬olina Press, 1988), p. 45.

3. Arévalo's inaugural speech: Schlesinger and Kinzer, p. 34. Arévalo's farewell: Schlesinger and Kinder, p. 47.

4. Arbenz inaugural address: Schlesinger and Kinzer, p. 52.

5. Dispute over compensation for United Fruit: Gleijeses, Piero, *Shattered Hope: The Guatemala Revolution and the United States*, 1944-1954 (Princeton: Princeton University Press, 1991), p. 164.

6. Bernays on public relations: Bernays, Edward, *Biography of an Idea: Memoirs of a Public Relations Counsel* (New York: Simon and Schuster, 1965), pp. 745, 761. Bernays on Guatemala: Bernays, pp. 9, 31. Press campaign: Immerman p. 113.

7. Lodge and McCormack: Immerman, p. 117. Products of the Cold War ethos: Immerman, p. 81. Communists in Guatemala: Rabe, pp. 48, 57.

8. Such a tie must exist: Department of State, Foreign Relations of the United States 1952-54, vol. 4: The American Republics (Washington: Government Printing Office, 1984), doc. 30. Ruthless agents: Rabe, p. 46.

9. Change in passivity: New York Times, Nov. 8, 1953. Normal approaches will not work: Schlesinger and Kinzer, p. 139. Start a civil war: Schlesinger and Kinzer, p. 117.

10. Toriello speech in Caracas: Schlesinger and Kinzer, pp. 143-44.

11. Arms from Czechoslovakia; Schlesinger and Kinzer, pp. 147-58; Immerman, pp.155-60. Gruson pulled out of Guatemala; Salisbury, Harrison, Without Fear or Favor (New York: Times Books, 1980}, pp. 478-80. O'Neill transferred: Wise, David, and Thomas B. Ross, The Invisible Govern¬ment (New York: Random House, 1964), p. 194.

12. Murphy opposes coup: Immerman, p. 159. We are on the road: Immerman, pp. 157-58.

13. Looks like this is it: Schlesinger and Kinzer, p. 15. State Department statement: New York Times, June 20, 1954. Arbenz radio speech: Schlesinger and Kinzer, pp. 19-20.

14. Eisenhower approves more planes: Ambrose, p. 230; Eisenhower, Dwight D., Mandate for Change: The White House Years, 1953-1956 (Garden City, N.Y.: Doubleday, 1963), pp. 425-26; Wise and Ross, pp. 178-79.

15. Toriello cable to Dulles: Phillips, David A,, The Night Watch: Twenty-five Years of Peculiar Service (New York: Atheneum, 1977) p. 46; Schlesinger and Kinzer, p. 184; Wise and Ross, pp. 190-91.

16. Arbenz radio speech: Schlesinger and Kinzer, pp. 199-200. Peurifoy will crack down, arranges new regime: Schlesinger and Kinzer, pp. 205-16. Dulles radio address: Department of State, Intervention of International Communism in the Americas, Publication 5556 (Washington: Department of State, 1954), p. 32.

chapter nine

CONSIDERATIONS FROM OUT OF THE MAINSTREAM

by Aref N. Hassan

I t is our hope that so far the readings in this book have impressed upon you the realization that there is more to world politics than meets the eye, and certainly more than is taught in mainstream classes and courses. In line with this theme, this last chapter of the book presents an alternative narrative to world politics.

Things in world history and world politics are not what they seem and our understanding of these things can be further enhanced by considering alternative perspectives on them. Why? Because certain entities want us to be misguided, they want to inform us only of things that intend not so much to inform and tell the truth about history and current events as much as to serve a certain purpose. There is a deliberate and concerted effort to convey a narrative that is of service to some entity (for example, empire, kingdom, nation, corporation, bank). Certain facts are deliberately omitted and others are deliberately fabricated. The distortion started from the earliest days of history and recordkeeping and continues to this day (now it is much worse). This narrative is reinforced by perpetuating a communal mind-set, a communal set of values, an educational system, and an economic cycle that facilitates and then demands submission.

FROM THE EARLIEST DAYS

The question is this: How have we humans been bamboozled into this? Three things have been at work here. Coercion and fear (oppressive apparatus); collusion (those who see a benefit for themselves in this big lie go in on it); and co-optation, where people are convinced to agree, submit, sign up, believe through the constructed norms and values (forms of intellectual hegemony).

Before the emergence of the rich and powerful global elite, we had the rich and powerful non-global elite. They were the merchants, land owners, slave owners, guilds, and ruling classes. In time, with the emergence of empires, these elites became global to varying degrees. During the earlier periods of history, it was relatively easier to control the masses, the public, or the serfs and peasants. There were ideologies that demanded submission to the ruling king or emperor relying either on divine right or on religious doctrine. With the age of enlightenment and science and skepticism, people started to question all the schemes of control and global enslavement. Enlightened movements started to emerge asking for freedom and equality. In the face of these demands, a solution started to take shape that would be a response to the demands of the masses and at the same time would satisfy the masses. The elites realized that they could not keep running the same scheme, so they came up with the idea of reintroducing the principle of democracy (the ancient Greeks had come up with the original concept) as a modern way to bring the global populations into submission (if they weren't already under some authoritarian elite rule, that is). This democracy solution did not come instantaneously as the solution to the demands of the masses for freedom, but rather was a response that the elites crafted as the demands of the masses strengthened. Democracy was the perfect solution to the dilemma faced by the elites and below is the reasoning behind it.

Democracy satisfied the demands of the masses for equality, participation, a voice, and a yearning for freedom. Democracy satisfied the elites in that it kept real power in their hands. The masses were given the illusion that they can determine things and that they are really free to rule themselves, but the elite knew better than that. They knew that the way a democracy was to function would inevitably yield power to them. Only those with money and connections ever come to power, all the while convincing the masses that they now have rule of the people by the people. What people? The common man? No, the rich man.

A historical examination of all elected leaders in modern democracies since the American Revolution will reveal that for the most part—the few exceptions were allowed to occur to try to show that anyone can make it—the leaders came from the elites or were joining the elites.

What does it mean to join the elites and how does one join the elites? You are either born into the elites or you join them intellectually and socialize with them before you become rich. You either truly believe or cynically pretend to believe in the elite paradigm that the elites are trying to propagate at the time. You show your commitment to the elite cause and you prove your loyalty to it.

There have always been and will always be leaders or figures who started off as common men and made it to the elite. This is for many reasons. Every once in a while, the elite need to allow for such exceptions to come to power, as long as they are beholden to these elites and their agenda. It should be noted that the elite have sometimes miscalculated the commitment of their puppets to their interests, as when they allowed Hitler to come to power, thinking he would protect private wealth from the dangers of communism, only to discover that he was uncontrollable and had his own genocidal agenda.

Intellectual hegemony emerged as the most powerful tool of enslavement in the modern age. No need for force if you can hypnotize the masses and control them that way. The tools of the mass hypnosis of the global populations in modern times are things such as pop culture, education, and social networks. The key to keep this hypnosis going is to keep some decent level of living for the masses. As long as the masses are housed, well fed, and have some time and money to play around with, they are happy in their state of hypnosis. They also need to have some individual personal liberties. As long as these are provided, the masses are happy to go along for the ride.

The working formula right now is the following: The top one percent of the world elite are getting richer by the day and the ninety-nine percent are working harder and harder every day to maintain their lifestyle (not improving it much, but just maintaining it with the constant illusion of upper mobility, of course).

The problem is that the one percent are getting very greedy and are forgetting that they need to keep throwing some crumbs to the masses to keep them quiet. There is a tipping point that will come when too many people have fallen from the middle class. These people will then awaken to the reality and will demand change. Absent a change, democracy will collapse. But has democracy been a good thing?

Democracy is certainly better than the systems of centuries past. People are not thrown to the lions for entertainment or stoned to death for committing adultery or burned at the stake for disagreeing with dominant religious doctrine. Democracy has also produced a system that serves the public good in terms of using some of the tax money collected from the masses to build schools, roads, airports, and other infrastructure. Democracy has also produced a societally stable situation where there is a fair system (in some manner) of justice.

So what are the faults of democracy? At the core it is still a system that brings mostly the elites to power and serves in perpetuating the interests of the elites. It is becoming a system that is increasingly bad for the masses and the middle class.

Democracy is a system that is increasingly being corrupted by greedy, out-of-control savage capitalism.

Capitalism or private ownership to serve private needs has been the economic rule that has governed human interaction since early times. Kings and emperors owned land and people for their personal benefit and enjoyment. This was always the case before the modern system of capitalism came into being. It seems that world history can be seen as these constant attempts by the elite to keep ownership and control over global wealth and power. Everything that has happened in human history has been new systems intended to quiet the masses but at the same time keep the wealth and power in the hands of the elite.

Communism and socialism were a blip in the history of mankind. The reason they failed is that the global elites united their efforts to bring down these two systems of government that, if done correctly, could have threatened the global control of the world by the elite. Communism's problem was that it took away the control of the economic elites and handed that power over to the new communist party elite. This new party elite was now in charge of both economic and political power and they abused and mismanaged both. At least in capitalism we have two subsets of elites, economic and political, each good at what they do in running the show (they are also clearly in collusion).

It is simply human reality that we are ruled by an elite class of humans who perpetuate control over the masses. The way greed and capitalism work in this day and age is that it creates a technology-driven, surveillance-controlled world that also controls media and education. We are increasingly living in a system in modern western society where real change is impossible and where revolutions are also practically impossible.

THE DANGER OF A CONNECTED AND TECHNOLOGICALLY ADVANCED WORLD

This is where we get to the really scary thing; whereas in the past real change through revolutions (peaceful and non-peaceful) could happen, in the modern technological age, the system as controlled by the global elite has solidified its hold and it is now practically impossible to start a revolution or even a movement similar in scope and impact as the civil rights movement.

This is how technology has contributed to the end of any possibility of real change in the world. The iron grip of the financial-corporate-intelligence-military-industrial complex is now close to being complete. After that all human beings and even political movements are just data points that are under constant surveillance and can be manipulated or deleted if need be. Do you think George Washington could start a revolution now or that the French working class can start a revolution? Can revolutionaries even move or communicate before the system is aware of them and arrests them? The system knows what the public, the opposition figures, and revolutionaries are reading, what they are watching on TV, what they are google searching, what opinions they are expressing on social media, what places they are frequenting, and on and on. If Dr. King were to try his civil rights movement today (assuming racism was as prevalent now in government and society), how long do you think before the racists in power figure out what he is up to and break into his email or use the media to tarnish his reputation? Would a modern Dr. King have Facebook and email accounts from a young age? The system and elites who monitor them (and can certainly manipulate them if they wanted to) would know what he may become and would work to thwart his ideas before they mature.

In the world we live in today, where the global elite-owned and elite-controlled corporations control most if not all major media outlets (TV stations, major newspapers, Facebook, YouTube, Twitter, etc.), real mass movements will not be given coverage or even the proper public space on social media. Both the global elites and governments around the world can very easily choose not to cover stories or to shut down accounts under various guises from violating the policies of these outlets to threatening national security. Thus, very easily, any true movement that aims to liberate the global masses from the control and grip of the global elite can be choked in its infancy by denying it access to the necessary mediums to spread its message.

Technology has given the system and the elite absolute control; the rise of the surveillance state under the guise of protecting people from terrorism and threats to national security has been very convenient in allowing the global elite to keep a watchful eye over everyone.

There are many attempts to raise awareness and raise consciousness about all of this, but it is all failing. Why? The elites have used the capitalist democratic system to serve their greed for money and power and this has corrupted everything. They have also used capitalism to further enslave the masses. This enslavement does not happen by force but rather by co-optation and seduction. People are seduced with the materialist consumerist lifestyle; falling into that trap is how they are enslaved.

People are indoctrinated by media and advertisement and pop culture into accepting materialist and technological gadgets. Society and life evolve in a way that makes it a necessity to be part of this scheme so that you need to have email to apply to college and to jobs; you need to have a credit card to buy things online; you need to have a smart phone to be accessible for your employer and customers. People do not have an option of staying outside of this system if they want to be integrated and functional in modern society. Of course everyone can go live in the woods if they want to, but that is pretty much the only way to avoid entrapment and enslavement by the system.

The other method of entrapment is the cool and convenient factor. Everyone wants to be fashionable and in tune with the times and everyone wants the convenience and efficiency that comes from using technology. People are consciously making and accepting the tradeoff of the benefits of these technological advances at the expense of their privacy and freedom. The system knows this very well and it keeps developing itself in a way that further gives it the advantage and makes it less and less possible and feasible for people to break out of this web of technological enslavement. If you notice, it is very hard to do anything in the world today without leaving a digital footprint. So many things have moved completely online or are impossible to do if you do not have an active email account, Facebook page, and smart phone.

We see therefore that technology has emerged as the biggest culprit in the modern enslavement scheme. Technology is just like the communist party in promising wonderful things to everyone and in the process delivering to them (among some wonderful things-delivered by technology not communism) systemic tyranny and enslavement. In fact many thinkers are arguing that the rise of the machines is inevitable and that artificial intelligence could be the most dangerous thing we ever face.

Globalization has also accelerated and become much more enshrined (again thanks to technology) that we have the emergence of global enslavement on so many levels not seen before in human history. The Roman Empire enslaved people but not to the levels we see in modern days. The Romans did not know what you were reading every minute, what you were saying to your friends on Facebook, where you are located every single minute due to the various GPS chips in your phone, car, and other devices.

Can you imagine the means at the disposal of the modern nation-state and modern private entities to track people and their activities and even their thoughts? If someone like George Washington were trying to accomplish now what he accomplished in his day, do you think he stands a chance against the status quo of this powerful system with all its means of surveillance and obfuscation and even oppression? How early in the infancy of Washington's movement would the system have known about him and his potential and then moved to quiet him or get rid of him?

The existence of this amount of power, like never before in history, is something to be concerned about, even very scared of. The mere existence of such absolute power is scary; it is only a matter of time before such power will be used arbitrarily and unjustly on a large scale. We know power creates a rationale for exercising itself whether it is needed or not.

Given the corporate-intelligence-military-industrial-technological-pharmaceutical-financial-banking interests that collude with each other, it is practically impossible to see a reversal of or even a break in the trajectory and growth of this system. The system is simply too strong and too entrenched. Just like no one could break Saddam's or Kaddafi's hold from the inside, only shock and power used from the outside could bring them down because nothing on the inside of their systems had the means or ability to do so. The West is in no way similar to these defunct savage regimes but the nature of the power structure in the West is similar in its hold on power (due to the many reasons we outlines above) that only exogenous shock can destroy the system, something like a world war or a catastrophe of global proportions that breaks down all the global elites' systemic capabilities (something like a meteor hitting planet Earth or a major drastic and debilitating or destructive climate change event).

ON THE SUBJECT OF WARS

This brings us to the subject of wars. Why do they happen? History and political science give us much information as to why wars happen, but really wars are always about wealth, trade, and money. It is only when the elite have a dispute or get greedy and want what the other elites have that we have wars. Wars are always about land, trade routes, natural resources, control of credit, and so on. They are never about protecting people or about God or nation.

Can we see war happening in the near or distant future? Probably so. There is no doubt that there has been a convergence of interests of the global elite where they can all benefit from working together, but there are still sub-classes of elites in the emerging world who may try to get more or challenge the system. It is also possible that some demagogical leader will escape the leash of the elite and then an unexpected or uncalculated war happens.

Depending on the place and size of such possible war, this may bring about a global situation where enough damage is done to the system that something new needs to emerge (think how the Napoleonic wars disrupted the global system of colonialism and allowed the colonies to get their independence because of the massive disruption going on at the core of the system in Europe). The question then is, will this new "something" be only a reiteration of the old system that puts the elite back in power just as it has been throughout history? This will remain the open question.

What we can say is this: Technological innovation and the direction of evolution of society to more online everything and less human-to-human contact is inevitably leading to concentration of power and money and commerce and communication in fewer and fewer hands. This can only be a recipe for tyranny (though not obvious) and can be undone only by a conscious reversal of this type of development. Is it possible that this kind of change (reversal) will come voluntarily? This is unlikely, seeing as there is so much money to be made and power to be had and there are so many forces that have an interest in perpetuating this system. Unfortunately, the future seems to show a very bleak world where we are controlled and under surveillance.

ADDITIONAL MEANS AND METHODS OF SUBDUING THE GLOBAL POPULATION

In the not-too-distant past, families in the developed world lived comfortably. Men worked and saved their money to buy a house and a car and when they did, they were ready to find a bride and get married. After marriage, dad worked and his salary was enough to pay for all the family's expenses while mom stayed home and took care of the kids and the house. Today if we were to look at the lives of common people, what would we see? We see that given the increased cost of living and the stagnant wages, no common man is able to work and save enough money for a house and a car before marriage (unless he was postponing his marriage by a few decades, that is). We see that young men and women are finding themselves in credit card debt and college debt even before they start their post-college careers. Soon after college, if they decide to buy a house and a car, they will have to do it with credit and this only adds to their debt. We see that when young people do form families, both parents are working to make ends meet and still it is not enough. We see that kids of middle-class families are in search of income because they cannot rely on their parents to give them allowances. As soon as kids are off to college, they get part-time or full-time jobs in addition to taking classes. We also find, despite the fact that everyone in the family is working, the money that is being earned is still not enough to make ends meet (and thus the growth of credit card, second mortgage, and other forms of debt).

The proper trajectory of history would have had a proper increase in wages to accommodate the increase in the cost of living. That, of course, does not take into account the ploy of the global elite to further enslave the global masses. Instead, the elite figured out that instead of raising wages, they can simply extend credit and with that further their control of the common person. The result is that the common person (or the "peasants" of the modern capitalist system if you want to call them that) is now indebted to global banks and corporations from the day they leave college or even before. Of course as we know, credit is power, and to those whom you owe money, you are beholden.

One can see human life transformed into nothing but a debt curve with a price tag on it. From the time babies are born and until they turn 18, there is debt created in association with them and that debt is held by their parents. Estimates are every child will cost their parents around half a million dollars to raise, and that is only until age 18. Given stagnant wages, regular working-class parents are going to have to carry debt associated with raising their children, particularly if they have more than one child. Once the kids are off to college, then they will start their own debt cycles. Fresh college graduates, young families, and even mid-career professionals live the life of the hamster on the wheel. They run and run, only to find themselves still in place. They work and work to pay interest and principal on their loans, only to find they need to take out more loans and work even harder to pay the interest and principal on both new and old loans. What we end up with is a global population that is overworked and underpaid, global masses that are so overwhelmed with their financial obligations that they have no time for anything else in life. No time for family and friends, no time for leisure in life, and certainly no time for being politically informed and active. This is exactly what the global elite want: the global population to be nothing but quiet and compliant machines ready to work whatever jobs the global economy demands from them and submissive to living the lives that the global elite, through their control of the global political order, demand from them.

The plan of the global elite has worked perfectly. They don't need to gain the submission of the global population by espousing things like divine right or rely on oppressive military regimes; instead, they do that by utilizing the power of credit. They sink people in so much debt that no one has time or energy after a 50- or 70-hour workweek to learn about politics or be engaged in the political system. If there is any time left in the week, people want to spend it taking care of life affairs and trying to enjoy themselves as opposed to thinking and learning about politics or being active. The last point we will mention here is that the consumerist culture that has grown over the last few decades, fueled by the global elite-owned media and pop culture, has clearly played a significant role in feeding this cycle.

Not surprisingly, what complements this global system of enslavement is the dumbing down of both education and media. The defunding of public education on all levels is a big part of this ploy. They don't want intellectual college graduates who will question the system; they want technically trained workers who can work the jobs demanded by the corporate global economy the elites are commanding. They have eliminated jobs or job postings that require liberal arts degrees, thus reducing the demand for these majors and resulting in these majors losing enrollment and being eliminated from many universities. For the majors that they weren't able to eliminate with their games of demand and supply, they worked hard at manipulating their curricular specialization so that they start focusing on matters that do not question or threaten the global elite. If you look at the totality of the fields of political science, international relations, and economics, you see that the bulk of work has focused on very narrow sets of topics to the exclusion of many others. The push for quantitative methods is also interesting given that, as we all know, there are no data sets out there that can help us study or analyze the global control of the elite.

The global elites want us to understand history and world politics in a manner that perpetuates their interests. The narrative that is taught in K–12 and in universities is the one the elites want us to be taught. They expect, sometimes demand, to teach certain things in these intro classes (such as theories, levels of analysis, and concepts such as balancing). In fact, there are no introductory books available to teach introductory world politics classes except the ones that are made by big publishers that all adhere to the same story lines. Those who say or think differently are mocked as loony, crazy, not serious, and conspiracy theorists. The ones who want to present an alternative perspective on world politics will find it very hard to find publishers; if they do get their books published, they will find it hard to get bookstores to carry their books. That is how the global elite, through their control of the publishing and book sales companies, control the message and block that which they don't like.

To ensure that the population as a whole does not get a good view of the full picture of global enslavement, the global elites, through their control of the media, make sure that news and political coverage is reduced to a minimum and, if it is covered, it is manipulated and dumbed down as well. In fact the downward spiral of the quality and integrity of international news is not accidental. It is an intended outcome of the global elite plan. Even local coverage has been dumbed down and reduced to a minimum and has to compete for air time with entertainment and gossip news about celebrities or murderers or athletes. After completing their control of broadcast and digital media, the global elite are trying to do away with the printed medium and working toward replacing it with only digital productions. It was hard for the global elite to control the global flow of information that came from printed newspapers, magazines, journals, and books. The death of printing presses and brick-and-mortar bookstores has not been accidental. The shift of most newspapers and journals and magazines to digital has been underway for quite a while and is almost complete in some parts of the world. The focus now is on books; the idea is to do away with paper books and that effort is underway. Once the printed medium is dead, the global elite, through their control of media corporations, will have total control over what everyone reads or hears or sees across all spectrums. Imagine how hard, if not impossible, it would be to reach the public with a message that runs counter to what the elite media corporations want. The media can be called the "misinformation industry," seeing as all media outlets have become nothing but propaganda machines for different global elite interests.

Another aspect worth noting in the global scheme of enslavement is the vicious cycle of feeding the masses unhealthful food (salted, sweetened with sugar, or genetically modified) and then overmedicating people when they get older and ill as a result of having consumed only unhealthful food during their lifetime. The combination of unhealthful lifestyle due to long working hours and stress on the job, along with an inactive lifestyle and an unhealthful diet has created an inescapable situation. Only few people can financially afford healthful and organic or non-processed food. Even fewer have the time in their schedule to actually be in the kitchen cooking from scratch and then cleaning up. Few people in any working population have working schedules that leave them enough time and energy to work out or live an active lifestyle that protects them from the onset of global epidemic diseases such as obesity and diabetes and heart problems associated with long working hours, unhealthful food, and stressful lifestyles. All this also leads us to think about the mental health issues facing people and the lack of response to it—other than prescribing more pills, the sales of which significantly benefit the pharmaceutical industry.

PRIVATE MONEY, PUBLIC POWER

As we noted earlier, the American and French revolutions were endeavors intended to create a new structure of power that gave people the illusion that power was now in their hands while in reality it remained in the hands of the global elites. There was a realization from early on that over time the elites were going to need a focused and concentrated effort to maintain their hold on the true levers of power. These efforts have been proceeding in earnest and today we see the fruits of that labor in the influence of money and big donors on elections and elected officials. The influence of lobbies and special interests has also grown to unprecedented levels. Even the judiciary system faces questions on the issues of private prisons and judges receiving campaign contributions from the companies that own and operate these prisons. Law enforcement in many areas is also part of different arrangements with private security and private intelligence organizations. The shadow of private interests and private money casts itself on all levels of the political and judicial system.

FROM NATION-STATE TO ONE WORLD GOVERNMENT

The creation of the idea of nationalism and the movement in international relations to the nation-state as a unit of analysis is questionable. Who came up with this idea and why? Why has it persisted? Is it because the powers that be saw that it saves their interests to keep the focus on the nation-state (and by extension governments) and move attention away from the real players and the real centers of power? (Such as the global elite and private power.) Until when will the nation-state remain the main actor and unit of analysis? As technology and artificial intelligence move forward, will we see the emergence of new global power centers? When will we see the end of the nation-state? Is the nation-state even currently relevant? Is it even the issue? The issue is that we need to be able to look past the nation-state and recognize where real power lies.

The key conversation seems to hinge on two ideas and their relevance and consequence: the nation-state and democracy. We understand world politics in the context of the interaction between nation-states and we see democracy as the true measure of political development. But if at the end of the day, democracy is not all that it is cracked up to be, then where does all of this leave us? What can we say about the future of world politics if we are seeing democracy morph into a global system controlled by a global complex that includes the media, military, industry, corporations, private intelligence, pharmaceuticals, agriculture, banking, and finance? Connect all of these on one global network and add artificial intelligence to it and what do we have? We have a global system that has a complete grip not only over our physical and political freedom but also over our taste, interests, products we buy, and so on. Does this not sound like a one global controlling-governing entity? (Call it One World Government or what you want.)

Some have speculated that this move toward One World Government is some form of a communist or U.N. or even fascist attempt to take over the United States and do away with people's freedoms. As we have noted in our earlier discussion, the global elite in the United States are part and parcel of the global elite that is running the whole world.

It is important here to note that the reason we are heading toward a One World Government is not some secret group meeting in some dark room somewhere deciding this, but rather the meeting of many interests and forces and technological innovations that has since the dawn of history been moving humanity in this direction (we should note that there are some global venues where these elites meet and discuss things and do some coordination). It is called greed and wanting more wealth, power, resources, land, and trade. From the earliest empires to this day, the path of globalization has been moving forward. What we have now is the most advanced stages of this globalization aided by technology and soon artificial intelligence. This means we are moving closer to the "one world everything" that may possibly bring world tyranny and the end of freedom. Why tyranny? Because power corrupts, and absolute power corrupts absolutely. Imagine a world where a few people with a few clicks of a mouse decide what happens in the world. Doesn't someone like Zuckerberg of Facebook control so many of the settings on Facebook that he therefore has control over what millions of people all over the world can and cannot do on their social media? Soon enough we will have a Zuckerberg for media, banks, shopping, education, and more. How hard will it be for 20 or 30 Zuckerbergs to control the world? And once the structural and systemic entities are put in place, how easy will it be for the people at the helm of these entities to run all global affairs? Imagine if a tyrannical leader somewhere declared martial law and, in addition to his control over the government, managed to get control over entities like Google, Apple, Facebook, Twitter, and the stock market (which are all controlled electronically). With a simple decision he can assert control over domains of human life that no one has ever been able to do. This level of control can very easily ensure that any opposition to the system will be detected in its infancy and will be dealt with accordingly. Go ahead, stretch your imagination and try this mental exercise!

Potential tyranny, the end of freedom, and the total subjugation of the global population of this planet brought to you courtesy of rogue capitalism, greed, technological innovation, convenience, and trying to stay cool by adopting the newest tech gadgets and being on social media and the Internet. That is the other part of enslavement: they create a world where in order to be hip and cool and connected, and even to be able to get into college or get a job after college, you have to go online and have an email account and be part of the existing system. That is how people get trapped in the system. People are willingly and happily entering the cage of global enslavement. In the past, you had to force people into the cage, you had to fight them and win to get them to do that. The second you could not maintain your forceful control over them, they were out of the cage. Today, people are racing each other to go deeper and deeper into the cage. Now if that isn't the epitome of conspiracy I don't know what is. Having the public so duped and hypnotized that they enslave themselves voluntarily and happily without requiring the global elite to use any kind of force—now that is genius.

ANSWERING THE "SO WHAT" QUESTIONS AND HOPE FOR THE FUTURE

People are able to see tyranny and loss of freedom when it is perpetrated by clear, tangible, and identifiable entities or individuals. We often see the references to Stalin and communism, or Hitler and fascism, as the types of dangers people need to be cautious about in terms of protecting their freedom and liberty. What is harder for people to grasp, or even become aware of, is when their life is controlled and their freedom stolen by more invisible, subtle, and inconspicuous systemic forces such as some that we have tried to shed some light on in this book.

In answer to the important so-what question about the significance of this work: if this book and these thoughts instigate students to start looking critically at this world and not only question the false consciousness imposed upon them, but also ask more questions in search of deeper truths, then this would be significant. If students start seeking more light and knowledge in their attempt to remove the blindfolds and peek through the misinformation industry draped over them to discover the true matter of things, then that is significant.

As the evidence shows, we the common people in this world are certainly in a bind, but all hope is not lost. Over the centuries of human experience we have made significant advances in evolving our modes of government, even though as we noted earlier, each iteration was nothing but a new structure for the elite to assert their global control. It is evident, however—particularly with the defeat of fascism and the collapse of communism—that people in this world yearn for freedom (both political and economic) and equality. They also seek systems of governance that give people equal opportunity, equal protection under the law, and respect for human rights. Democracy and capitalism as they stand now need some serious adjustment to correct their deviations from these ideals, adjustment to make them truly what they should be: government by the people and for the people. We can certainly sit and wait for a global disaster of some sort to bring about some wave of creative destruction that would correct this deviation in our democratic and capitalist systems of government. The better alternative is to start taking baby steps at grass-root levels that would bring about the changes we want. Below are some thoughts to ponder on how to fix some of the global problems that we have explored.

Fixing the educational system and ensuring quality education for everyone is certainly the first step in any reform process. We cannot have an enlightened population if this population is not properly educated. We need some academic reform for some disciplines. The disciplines of political science/international relations, economics, history, sociology, and others need to reexamine how they approach their choice of topics for inquiry and their teaching methods in their fields. Are we going to continue teaching only the abstract theories and quantitative methods of research, or are we going to also start teaching and researching the true locus of power in this world? Will our research agenda continue to be tied to what journals will publish and corporate printing presses print? In order to have a world population capable of addressing its challenges, we need these populations to be aware of the true nature of these challenges, and this can be done only by expanding the scope of inquiry in academia. We also need better media outlets that offer better coverage of world events and this can be done only by public viewership that will tune in only to the media outlets that offer true, substantial, and in-depth coverage of the events that matter. No offense to the Kardashians, but their daily lives are not world news and should not be subject matter for major news media networks. We should give serious consideration to going back to the low-tech world and low-tech gadgets. It may sound like a retro fashion statement, but the ability to control the world and its people during the low-tech days was much lower. Low-tech or even no-tech ensures privacy, freedom, individual control, and maybe even some sense of individuality and character. If enough people break away from the global technology empire, the chances of winning reform goes up considerably.

It is time we all wake up from the hypnosis we are under, time to see the truth and to do something to make the world a better place. Only with proper information and knowledge and by getting involved and active can we change things to ensure that the global elite do not continue dragging us into things that serve only their financial interests and their hidden agendas. Freedom and the truth are precious and worth every effort to achieve and maintain.

☐ CONCLUSION

by Aref N. Hassan

T his book is by no means intended to be a comprehensive source for the introductory study of world politics, but it is our belief that it certainly adds a perspective that is thoroughly lacking, not only in introductory courses, but also in the wider disciplines of international relations and political science as a whole. While there are many in-depth books and articles on the various issues we have covered in this book, there aren't any that try to integrate, summarize, or even present a glimpse into all these perspectives and present them in an introductory book. The hope here is that students start looking at world politics with a new lens, one that puts the focus not so much on the appearance of what is happening but rather on the deeper and more sinister motivations and forces behind what is happening.

We hope students will now take everything they read, everything they study, and everything they get exposed to by the media with a grain of salt and with a penetrating eye that seeks to identify the puppeteers behind the puppets and the financial and monetary interests behind the political powers and actors. This book does not even begin to scratch the surface of an area of knowledge that is very deep.

Students who are interested in more light and more knowledge can now move forward with their own readings and research, knowing that such sources of knowledge exist and all they need to do is seek them. You only need to knock on the door and you will hear the response.